Irish governance in crisis

MANCHEStER
1824

Manchester University Press

Irish governance in crisis

Edited by
NIAMH HARDIMAN

Manchester University Press
Manchester and New York

distributed in the United States exclusively
by PALGRAVE MACMILLAN

Published by Manchester University Press
Oxford Road, Manchester M13 9NR, UK
and Room 400, 175 Fifth Avenue, New York, NY 10010, USA
www.manchesteruniversitypress.co.uk

Distributed in the United States exclusively by
Palgrave Macmillan, 175 Fifth Avenue, New York,
NY 10010, USA

Distributed in Canada exclusively by
UBC Press, University of British Columbia, 2029 West Mall,
Vancouver, BC, Canada V6T 1Z2

British Library Cataloguing-in-Publication Data
A catalogue record for this book is available from the British Library

Library of Congress Cataloging-in-Publication Data applied for

ISBN 978 07190 8222 1   hardback

ISBN 978 07190 8223 8   paperback

First published 2012

Typeset by Servis Filmsetting Ltd, Stockport, Cheshire
Printed in Great Britain
by Bell & Bain Ltd, Glasgow

Contents

Tables, boxes and figures

Tables

Boxes

Figures

Contributors

Sebastian Dellepiane is currently a Research Fellow at the Institute of Development Policy and Management, University of Antwerp, prior to which he was a Research Fellow in the School of Politics and International Relations at University College Dublin. He has worked as a policy analyst at the Ministry of Economics in Argentina. His PhD is from the University of Essex, and he teaches at the Essex Summer School in Research Methods.

Claire Finn is a Policy Analyst with the National Economic and Social Council. She completed her PhD while based at the UCD Geary institute. She has conducted postdoctoral research on health economics at the UCD Geary Institute and Dublin City University, and in Australia, where she held an Endeavour Scholarship.

Niamh Hardiman teaches in the School of Politics and International Relations at UCD, where she is also a Research Fellow in the Centre for Regulation and Governance and at the UCD Geary Institute. She studied at Nuffield College, Oxford and was Fellow and Tutor in Politics at Somerville College, Oxford.

Lee Komito teaches in the School of Information and Library Studies at UCD. He received his PhD in anthropology from the University of Pennsylvania, and has previously worked in the Information Technology in Society programme at Manchester Metropolitan University.

Brigid Laffan is Jean Monnet Professor of European Politics at the UCD School of Politics and International Relations She was principal of the UCD college of Human Sciences from 2004 to 2011. She led a six-country cross-national research project on EU enlargement funded by the EU Framework Programme grant. She is a member of the Royal Irish Academy and of the Research Council of the European University Institute (EUI) in Florence.

Muiris MacCarthaigh is Research Officer at the Institute of Public Administration, having completed his PhD at the UCD School of Politics and International Relations. His continuing publications on modes of accountability develop the themes of his doctoral research. His ongoing work on public sector organization is linked to a research network based at the University of Leuven.

Seán McGraw teaches at the University of Notre Dame. He completed his PhD at Harvard University and his Masters degree at the LSE. His interests in comparative party mobilization, party competition and comparative political culture result in an ongoing engagement with analysing Irish politics.

Aogán Mulcahy teaches at the UCD School of Sociology. His interest in social order and social control originated in his work on the interdisciplinary doctoral programme in Law and the Social Sciences at the School of Justice Studies at Arizona State University. He has conducted research on criminology at the University of Leeds and at Keele University.

Jane O'Mahony teaches in the School of Politics and International Relations at the University of Kent in Canterbury. She completed her PhD at Trinity College Dublin, and was a Post Doctoral Research Fellow on the EU-funded Fifth Framework Research Project 'Organising for European Union Enlargement' under the directorship of Professor Brigid Laffan of University College Dublin.

Diane Payne teaches at the UCD School of Sociology and is a research fellow at the UCD Geary Institute and UCD Complex and Adaptive Systems Laboratory. She has held research positions at the ICS Groningen and at Cambridge University, and has taught at Trinity College Dublin. She is the Irish representative for the Steering Committee of the European Science Foundation (ESF) Programme Quantitative Methods in the Social Sciences (QMSS).

Peter Stafford is an economic and business research analyst in Dublin. He holds a PhD in Politics from the University of Manchester. He was formerly Head of Research and Policy Development with the Construction Industry Federation in Dublin. He was a Research Fellow at the UCD Geary Institute where he worked on the politics of urban regeneration and city governance with Diane Payne.

Jonathan Westrup teaches on professional development and corporate strategy programmes at the Irish Management Institute. Jonathan has an MPA from Harvard's Kennedy School and a PhD in comparative political economy from Boston University. He was a Research Fellow at the Institute for International Integration Studies and has taught at Trinity College Dublin and at Boston University. He has previously worked in the financial services sector with NCB Stockbrokers.

Preface

During the phase of steady international economic growth in the 1990s and 2000s, Ireland seemed to represent a successful model of domestic adaptation to changing international conditions, and was often seen as an exemplar to other societies engaging in economic catch-up. The plan for this book developed from the insight that any model of development, not just the Irish one, is embedded in a complex of institutional structures, networks of interests, and patterns of decision-making, which belie easy summary. We sought to understand the politics of how Ireland's particular distribution of power and advantage has been shaped. We wanted to understand how democratic deliberation and political accountability works, and what the implications may be for the kind of lives ordinary people live.

Each chapter in this volume draws on a common concern with the exercise of state authority and investigates in detail how this works out in a specific empirical policy context. The book was originally conceived as an analysis of shortcomings in Irish governance practices and capabilities which seemed too often to be overlooked during the good times. We cannot be happy that our book now proves timely in providing insights into what went so spectacularly wrong. But we will be content if our work contributes in some measure to clarifying hard choices for hard times.

The book originated in the interdisciplinary Governance Research Programme based at the UCD Geary Institute. We are grateful to the Director of the Geary Institute, Professor Colm Harmon, for giving us project space. We owe a particular debt of gratitude to the public research funding from which the work in this volume has benefited. Our collaborative work grows directly from the Higher Education Authority's Programme of Research in Third-Level Institutions (PRTLI) funding initiative. Work on the individual chapters could not have been undertaken without funding from the Irish Research Council for Humanities and Social Sciences (IRCHSS) and other funding sources. We hope it will be clear from our work that research funding for the social sciences continues to be vitally important even during phases of cutbacks in public spending. The editor would like to acknowledge the National University of Ireland for its grant toward the final publication of this volume.

1

Introduction: profiling Irish governance

Niamh Hardiman

Introduction

No discussion of Irish government and governance can proceed without acknowledging from the outset the sudden and devastating collapse in economic performance at the end of the 2000s. Much of the analysis of Irish politics and of economic and social policy during the preceding decade had focused on the factors explaining Ireland's unexpected spell of steady growth, rising living standards, and steady job creation, and the implications for domestic politics of deepening European integration. The international economic crisis had a severe effect on the growth and employment performance of all the advanced societies, but its impact was very much more severe in some than in others. Ireland, along with the Mediterranean rim countries and the Baltic states, was particularly badly affected.

The longer-term effects of crisis cannot readily be discerned as the process is unfolding. But the proximate effect is to stimulate fresh reflection on features of Irish politics and government in order to understand underlying patterns of governance. From this we may be able to discern what might have been different, and what reform initiatives might now be required.

Comparative studies in economics, sociology and public policy have made significant advances in analysing Irish policy outcomes against the spectrum of comparative policy performance (Barry 1999; Fahey, Russell and Whelan 2007; McGuinness, McGinnity and O'Connell 2009; Whelan 2000; Whelan and Layte 2006; Whelan, Layte and Maitre 2002). Studies in Irish political science have made excellent contributions to illuminating the competition for power, the impact of the electoral system, its effects on the party system, and the profile of what parties stand for (Benoit and Laver 2006; Carter and Farrell 2010; Marsh and Gallagher 2008; Marsh, Sinnott, Garry and Kennedy 2008).

What has also begun to emerge is a growing interdisciplinary literature analysing the institutional and organizational underpinnings of policy choices, that is, analysing the state as a structure of power, with a set of policy capacities that are amenable to comparison with those of other advanced industrial societies (Adshead, Kirby and Millar 2008; Hayward and MacCarthaigh 2007;

Kirby 2010). The complexity of the policy mix in place at any one time can make it particularly challenging to characterize the Irish state with reference to a single underlying dynamic. 'Competition state' may be relevant if what we have in mind is the emphasis on a low-tax regime and reliance on attracting inward investment as the principal source of generating high-skilled employment (Smith 2007). But this designation must sit alongside the conception of the state power as having been shaped in important ways by partnership processes and a strong reliance on consent given through negotiation in exchange for other kinds of benefits (O'Donnell 2008). The Irish state has some 'developmental' features through which growth policies have been actively managed within the context of a liberal market economy (Hardiman 2009; Ó Riain 2004). But the uneven features of the Irish growth model, in which growth in the domestic sector has lagged behind the foreign-owned sector, and significant inequalities in life chances persist in the face of economic growth, makes this appellation problematic for some commentators (Kirby 2002, 2004). After all, an earlier phase of sustained state-led 'developmental' growth in the Asian Tiger economies had been accompanied by more systematic equality-enhancing policy measures (Haggard 1990). A profile of domestic politics that seems to prioritize growth in individual earnings over improvements in collective benefits is surely no surprise: this was the prevailing trend in the US from the 1980s onwards. But how this is managed politically remains relatively unexplored in the Irish context.

One way to do justice to the multi-faceted aspect of state policy is to conceive of the state as a multitude of power centres, in each of which different interests are in contention to establish a dominant project or set of priorities (Ó Riain 2008). But the cost of doing this may be that we weaken our capacity to form an integrating theoretical conception of the manner in which these assorted power centres might cohere. In addition, the velocity of change in policy performance over time can mean that the characterization of the state at one point becomes inappropriate when the economic situation changes. Commentary on Irish politics has been good at analysing each phase just as it comes to a close. But the volatility of economic performance has meant that analysts have sought to account in turn for the role of the state in economic sclerosis (Guiomard 1995), economic boom (Barry 2005; Hardiman 2005) and economic crisis (Allen 2010; Kirby 2010). The next challenge is to understand how and why we may discern such variation, and what the underlying political and social factors might be that explain these outcomes.

The present volume assembles a set of studies of the governance of Irish society, and specifically of the changing role of the state in governance. 'Governance' is a term that has a variety of meanings, sometimes implying ways of organizing public life without direct state involvement. This is not the conception at work in this volume. The authors have taken the role of the state to be inescapable in any reflection on governance practices (Goetz 2008). Governance as used here starts with the ways in which people interact through the formal structures of political life, and investigates how political practices work out dynamically through the involvements between political actors and social and economic interests (Treib, Bähr and Falkner 2005).

The State And Political Life

In some respects Ireland might be conceptualized as a 'stateless' society, or perhaps as a 'weak state' as the US has also sometimes been termed (Dyson 1980; Migdal 1988). Ireland commits a relatively small proportion of aggregate wealth to support income transfers and social services. It offers tax incentives as a form of state subsidization to avail of market provision in areas such as housing, healthcare and pensions, much as happens in the US. The dominant political discourse has tended to be favourable to globalization, economic openness, competitiveness, and, on balance, European integration (Antoniades 2010; Schmidt 2006; Smith 2005; Smith and Hay 2008).

The low degree of ideological differentiation among political parties, compared with many other European states, may contribute to the relative invisibility of the state. The absence of a left–right political cleavage, and the clustering of electoral support to the centre-right, has tended to depoliticize the way political choices are framed, so that distributive issues are not seriously contested (Kennedy and Sinnott 2006; Marsh 2008). Policy decisions are more easily cast as matters of technical evaluation than as matters that are appropriate for interest-based contestation (Kennedy and Sinnott 2006; Marsh 2008; TASC 2010). All the major parties have long agreed on the basic framework of industrial policy, and the main features of the low-tax model and support for foreign direct investment (FDI) have been in place since the 1960s (Bradley 2000; FitzGerald 2000). This meant that when external circumstances shifted to create conditions favourable for this model to generate rapid growth, Ireland was well placed to take advantage; the 'luck' of international economic conditions complemented a policy to which Ireland had 'stuck' consistently.

The politics of growth has thus sometimes been depicted as whatever measures best suit the needs of 'Ireland Inc.', a national economy dedicated to maximizing corporate interests understood as the interests of corporations. This conception of the state would also render its political character all but invisible. It is perhaps further supported by the fact that since the 1980s, the Irish state withdrew from areas of economic activity in which it had previously been engaged, such as food production for example. The plausibility of a competitiveness-based discourse increased with the growing interdependencies associated with the completion of the Single European Market in 1992 and especially with adoption of the Euro. Agreement on the principal aims of economic policy solidified the performance of social partnership despite occasional flare-ups of distributive conflict (Hardiman 2002).

But as in the USA, where the role of the state in providing core services is often invisible to its citizens precisely because it is so embedded in everyday life, so also in Ireland we can find underlying assumptions about what the state is expected to do that belie the image of minimalist politics and robust reliance on the market. Ireland can be understood as indeed being a 'statist' society in the sense that the state plays an active role in setting the terms of economic growth and distribution, just as is now widely recognized in the case of the US (Block 2008; Sheingate 2009).

It may therefore be less helpful to think in terms of state strength and weakness as if the state were entirely separate from the society, than to think about how states as institutional clusters are able to exercise a capacity for policy choice and implementation through the relationships they have with different parts of the economic and social structure. Thus what is at issue is really 'state capacity', the ability to achieve particular objectives through the projection of public power (Weiss 1998). It will matter therefore what kinds of alliances political actors are able to build with organized social and economic interests. And the institutional framework through which these alliances are worked out may make the crucial difference to both process and outcome. The design of consultative, policy-making and policy-implementing structures needs to be responsive to the variety of interests in society, for in a democracy plurality and diversity are inevitable. But the capacity to aggregate diversity and formulate policy that is both effective and acceptable requires something else, that is, a certain distance from the ferment of public opinion and the often very selective lobbying inputs from organized interests. States need to possess the capacity to formulate policy choices as reflecting some conception of public interest considerations. They need to create some coherence across policy commitments, and to be capable of combining a strategy for economic growth with the means of distributing the results of growth that will be socially acceptable. What is implied here may be termed 'infrastructural power' (King and Lieberman 2009), that is, the capacity of state institutions to work with different economic and social interests to achieve political objectives; or what Linda Weiss has termed 'governed interdependence' (Weiss 1998). And what best supports this kind of power is a state administration that is sufficiently responsive to economic and social needs to be flexible and capable of change, but sufficiently distant to be able to withstand selective pressures that would seek to capture the use of state power for narrow or sectional interests. The most effective states, it is argued, are those that are both 'embedded' in the society, and 'autonomous' of particularistic interests (Evans 1995). In a related sense, much of the contemporary literature on 'good governance' has come to focus on the importance of a well-functioning classic system of bureaucratic administration – good governance as responsive yet 'impartial' state institutions (Rothstein and Teorell 2008).

The Irish state possesses a number of these attributes. The responsiveness of the Irish state to social concerns is not much in doubt; the expectation that effective state action will flow in response to social needs is well established. However, what is less certain is whether the political system is capable of performing aggregating processes at a sufficient distance from selective social and economic pressures, or implementing policy decisions that will be effective as well as legitimate. 'Policy capacity' and 'impartial government institutions' are among the most problematic issues in Irish public life.

Public expectation that politics will be responsive to social concerns runs deep. But confidence that the political process will deliver solutions that are both effective and efficient is perhaps less widespread. The very commitment of political parties to appear responsive can itself compromise their capacity to make effective choices. The two principal political parties (Fianna Fáil and Fine Gael) may both be characterized as centre-right, but the party platforms span a broad range of internal commitments on the right–left continuum (Hardiman, McCashin and Payne 2006). Single-issue local concerns can gain a good deal of traction in national politics as politicians strive to avoid losing sections of the coalitions of support on which they rely. Ministers tend to wish to preside over good news such as job creation announcements; similarly, strong expectations emerge that geographically concentrated job losses will attract remedial government attention to benefit local communities. The politics of the 'pork-barrel' is also apparent in Ireland (as in the Unites States). Occupancy of ministerial office has a proven effect on the regional concentration of public spending, with benefits disproportionately channelled into projects in the minister's own constituency (Suiter 2009).

But it is not only voters or local communities that expect state-led delivery of benefits. Political scandals in recent decades have involved private business interests that have sought and obtained preferential advantage from politicians in the allocation of public benefits. There have also been cases where business interests made substantial payments to politicians, yet where the benefits they may have obtained remain obscure. Examples of the former include disbursement of grants, rezoning of land for development purposes and property deals (Byrne 2010; Kerrigan and Brennan 1999; O'Toole 2010). All these scandals have originated in the relationships between domestic business interests and government in industries such as beef production, domestic broadcasting, and construction, and in the process of land valuation and rezoning for development purposes. The foreign-owned manufacturing and services sectors in Ireland have not been the subject of corruption investigations.

There has therefore been a tendency among politicians and business interests alike to consider some public resources and assets as being available for allocation in the form of privately disbursed benefits. This is also apparent in the way a number of public officials came to treat the benefits of office. Slack oversight of organizational budgets, a relaxed attitude to expenses, and a weak culture of enforcing personal accountability resulted in public scandals about personal expenses, waste and even corruption in the public sector. One striking example was the state training agency FÁS, whose budget rose sharply during the 2000s when the economy was experiencing full employment, and whose training contracts were distributed in ways that escaped any serious scrutiny or value-for-money assessments (Ross and Webb 2010). Unsurprisingly, revelations of this sort create disillusionment among voters, cynicism about the motivations of politicians, and suspicion of the allocative fairness and efficiency of the public sector itself.

It may be that growing evidence of poor standards in public ethics is merely the counterpart of comparable trends in the private sector during the years of economic boom. Performance-related pay gained in credibility in the business sector, and income inequality at the top pulled away from the median (Nolan and Maitre 2007). Even in sectors where increased profitability had little to do with productivity, particularly banking and finance during the era of cheap credit and light regulation, people in senior positions paid themselves ever greater sums in both basic pay and bonus packages. The trend toward boosting top-level pay spread to the public sector. Little else may have changed in recruitment patterns, performance levels or productivity, but the rationale of using the private sector as the benchmark for public sector pay resulted in a sharp upward turn in pay scales across the upper reaches of public sector employment (Hardiman and MacCarthaigh 2011).

The spectrum of public power

How then can we best capture these diverse features of the Irish state? The papers collected in this volume take a historical-institutionalist approach: they analyse governance with reference to the structures through which public power is exercised, and the actors who engage with one another within these frameworks (Hall and Taylor 1996; March and Olsen 1984; Steinmo 2007).

But the criteria for establishing the public or private location of the exercise of public power may not be entirely obvious (Börzel and Risse 2010; Hardiman 2012; Hardiman and Scott 2009; Roberts 2010; Scott 2008b). Public governance embraces 'all institutions designed for the deliberate solving of collective problems, irrespective of the private or public character of the actors involved and the hierarchical or horizontal mode of their (purposive) intervention' (Mayntz 2007: 6).

Most familiarly perhaps, public power can be exercised directly through governmental institutions, principally through the core governmental and administrative systems of the state. This is sometimes characterized as the 'hierarchical' way of establishing governance, as it functions primarily through bureaucratic practices that are for the most part bounded by rules and precedents, within a statutory framework (Olsen 2006: 1).

Public power may also be indirectly exercised through the delegation of authority to other state bodies, such as regulatory agencies or grant-giving bodies, or bodies dedicated to service delivery, or specialist agencies such as the Industrial Development Authority (IDA). The delegation of public power to state bodies may be justified in a number of ways. One of the most common reasons for setting up new agencies is to create distance from political direction so as to gain credibility for the impartiality of decision-making – particularly important for bodies such as regulatory agencies. Other reasons include, for example, the need to recruit specialist expertise, or to give organizational focus to a policy area, or to devolve policy delivery out from core departments in the interests of securing greater efficiency (Flinders 2009; Gilardi 2008; Thatcher and Stone Sweet 2004).

But public power may be devolved even further, in the case of the authority accorded to rule-making by non-state organizations. An example here might include the wide discretionary sphere of action permitted to religious interests in education and health care delivery, not only in Ireland but also in other European countries, especially those with well-established Catholic churches (Inglis 1998; van Kersbergen and Manow 2009). We might also include here the public recognition of privately organized professional standard-setting in areas such as recruitment to the legal profession, press regulation, advertising standards, and accounting standards in pensions policy (Rudder 2008; Scott 2008a).

This can be seen as part of a wider phenomenon of 'networked' state power or 'governed interdependence', in which civil society interests are extensively consulted about issues within the range of their interest. The issue as to how 'networks' are defined, and how autonomous they can really be of overarching state power, is contested (Dowding 1995; Kassim 1994; Rhodes 1992). Inevitably, it will assume a different form in continental European and Scandinavian countries in which the legal system is highly codified and public powers are formally delegated to organized interests, especially economic interests, than in common-law countries in which industrial relations are more voluntarist in character (Crouch 1993; Offe 1981). Some form of structured engagement with civil society interests – not only consultatively but also to ensure policy delivery – is a routine element of governance across most democratic societies. In the Irish case, the social partnership institutions that developed between 1987 and 2010 can be seen as a 'networked' form of routinized consultation and pre-commitment on a growing range of policy issues (Hardiman 2006). As Scharpf has noted:

> much effective policy is produced not in the standard constitutional mode of hierarchical state power, legitimated by majoritarian accountability, but rather in associations and through collective negotiations with or among organizations that are formally part of the self-organization of civil society rather than of the policy-making system of the state. (Scharpf 1997: 204)

A further question arises over where the boundary of state power begins and ends relative to the market, and especially the question as to which goods are allocated or services provided through market mechanisms, how employment rights are configured, and the terms on which welfare payments are paid as well as the levels at which they are set. Variations in how these entitlements are configured underpins the distinctions between 'worlds of welfare capitalism' (Esping-Andersen 1999). There is nothing automatic or merely technical about decisions to extend or limit social protection in any particular policy area. Market economies feature a wide range of ways in which welfare states are made compatible with good economic performance. We can discern varying kinds of trade-offs in different cases. No single model can simultaneously optimize economic growth, job creation, poverty reduction and fiscal controls. The policy choices that emerge in any particular society are the result of distributive choices. They will benefit different groups unequally and so may be the subject of contestation and even conflict. Debates over current decisions are made within the path-dependent legacy of past choices, and within the constraints of other policy commitments about domestic economic organization and the scope of involvement in the international economy.

Although there is a limit to the scope of the exercise of both direct and indirect state power, the state is often held responsible for the meta-governance of many issues that are formally outside political arbitration (Bell and Hindmoor 2009). Putting some issues beyond direct political control is itself a political choice. Capitalism and democracy imply principles of organization that are amenable to a wide range of differently institutionalized accommodations. There are many potential points at which political contestation may raise new questions about what precisely is to be allocated through the market and what through political or social organization. The boundaries of state, market, and society can never be assumed to be fixed (Polanyi 1944/2002). Ultimately, political decision-making can itself change the rules of the game. Indeed the very possibility of political intervention can shape and condition the terms of engagement between actors – in Fritz Scharpf's terms, many areas of non-state negotiation or coordination are undertaken 'under the shadow of hierarchy', that is, in the context of an awareness that an authoritative statutory intervention is also possible (Scharpf 1997: 204).

The state in Irish governance

Following from this discussion of what the features of effective state capability require, and recognizing that public power can be exercised in different ways, we now turn to consider some of the distinctive features of the role of the Irish state in governance. In this volume, we focus on the institutions through which power is exercised, the implications for the interactions between public and private actors, and the consequences for the quality of decision-making. Three features may be identified: the dominance of executive powers in which party interests can spill over into the public sphere; the weaknesses apparent in connecting decision-making with effective outcomes; and the difficulties associated with building a democratic social order that might generate higher levels of responsiveness from the political system.

The spillover of parties

One of the striking features of the Irish state is the degree to which executive power can be exercised relatively unconstrained by effective formal legislative challenge. In comparison with other west European democracies, Ireland and Britain occupy an extreme place on the spectrum of executive dominance. This is facilitated by the fact that government ministers normally continue to hold their legislative seats, and governments can exercise strong party discipline. Most other European legislatures possess greater constitutional and procedural capacity both to scrutinize and amend legislation, and to exercise oversight of government and hold it to account through parliamentary mechanisms (Döring 2001, 2004; Strøm 2000). Freedom of executive manoeuvre is convenient for incumbent governments, but it comes at a price. Opposition politicians have found it all but impossible to investigate allegations of political corruption, or of administrative malpractice, through the channels available to them. Oireachtas (that is, parliamentary) committees do not normally have specialized expertise available to them to advise on complex policy issues. Their powers of investigation were curtailed by a Supreme Court ruling in 2002, reversal of which would require a constitutional amendment (Houses of the Oireachtas Joint Committee on the Constitution 2010). Patterns of recruitment to public life tend to create a bias against basing a parliamentary career on national-level policy deliberation. When major political scandals break, there is no obvious means of undertaking an investigation. Hence the increasing recourse since the 1980s to Tribunals of Inquiry and investigative commissions, which are extra-parliamentary and quasi-judicial proceedings. However, tribunals have proven very cumbersome – lengthy and extremely expensive, with little to show in the form of attribution of responsibility (Office of the Comptroller and Auditor General 2009).

Political scandals typically raise questions about the appropriate reforms that need to be put in place to prevent any recurrence. Muiris MacCarthaigh shows in this volume that many different mechanisms have been introduced in Irish politics to try to enforce greater levels of political accountability. Major scandals in areas such as payments to politicians and conflicts of interest, especially over land-rezoning issues, have resulted in specific pieces of legislation or codes of conduct to try to ensure that such things do not happen again. But grafting on new layers of compliance requirements does not address the fundamental issue, which is the core weaknesses in parliamentary practices, and risks making the system more complex and with yet more gaps.

The relatively unconstrained uses of executive power are especially advantageous to a party that can either create single-party government or exercise dominant power in a coalition. Because of its long experience of incumbency, Fianna Fáil has had better opportunities than the other parties to build durable coalitions of support among powerful organized interests (Dunphy 1995; Leahy 2009). During the 2000s, the party's long-established ties with construction and property development interests were again prominent, as the property boom got under way. The permeability of the government system to powerful external interests, and the poor boundary lines between public interest, party interest and the private interests of political figures, were all facilitated by the fact that the constitutional means of holding executive power within limited borders were so weak.

Irish political parties, and especially Fianna Fáil, can avail of opportunities to use state power and resources that spill beyond the strict confines of office. But this should not be taken to imply that parties are thereby disconnected from civil society or dependent on state resources to maintain their organizational capability, in the manner of 'cartel' parties (Wolinetz 2002). Irish political parties, as Seán McGraw shows, are deeply connected to civil society, and throughout the extensive changes in economic organization, social structure and value systems, political parties have retained their organizational coherence and vote-catching capacity through a remarkable process of ongoing adaptation.

But the way the parties have adapted brings its own problems. The remarkable success of parties as mobilizers of votes comes at the expense of an aggregating capacity on difficult policy choices. There are two reasons for this. The first is that the leaders of parties have found it convenient to avoid or defuse conflict over issues that are likely to lose them vote-share. Government office makes it possible to deflect contentious issues into conflict-diffusing channels such as commissions of inquiry or social partnership consultative structures, or if necessary, non-governmental decision mechanisms such as referendums. Governments also show an ability to try to dissipate conflict before it gets to this point, and one means of doing this is for the leading party or parties simply to absorb the challenges coming from smaller parties. The Irish political landscape bears witness to a number of instances of challenger parties being swallowed by the embrace of a larger party that has managed to move into its preferred policy space and make this its own.

The result is that the larger parties, and again especially Fianna Fáil, are themselves coalitions of opinion with relatively wide internal spreads of preferences. Each constituency contest is in one sense a separate election campaign, varying with the personality of the candidate and their organizational resource base. But unlike the similarly ideologically amorphous parties in the United States,

Irish political parties functioning within a parliamentary system also have every incentive to keep control over who stands for election and on what terms. This is because parties need to maintain overall party discipline in parliament to secure control over numbers in legislative votes and, when in government, to maintain their majority support. Although there is no reference to political parties in the Irish constitution, party control over voting in the Dáil, the lower house of the Oireachtas, is central to the functioning of executive and legislature alike, and breaches in bloc voting in parliament are rare.

Parties in Ireland therefore have a paradoxical role. They have an excellent capacity to mobilize local support, but they do this through demobilizing the potential for conflict and diffusing emergent grievances. This means that once in power, there is relatively little incentive for developing coherent and consistent policy choices, and greater payoff for trying to keep a variety of interests on board. The trend is further reinforced by the pattern of recruitment to activist politics. It is difficult to be elected through developing a specialized concern with policy issues, because a greater premium attaches to maximizing constituency service. And since appointment to cabinet office is completely drawn from membership of the Dáil (the provision to appoint two members of the Seanad or upper house of parliament to ministerial office has rarely been exercised), the same trends are repeated inside government.

State coordinating capacity

State power, as noted earlier, is exercised not only through hierarchical departmental channels through which much of the standard business of government is conducted, but through 'governed interdependence'. Many aspects of public policy require the engagement of a wider range of institutions and interests that are not directly managed by government or ministerial departments. The capacity of the state to negotiate with other social and economic interests, and to coordinate them in the production of collective goods, can be seen to be quite uneven in Ireland. Industrial development is often seen as a particularly successful area in which government policies, discharged through state agencies, have worked well in achieving their declared objectives (Barry 2007; Hardiman and MacCarthaigh 2010; Ó Riain 2000). Yet even here, questions have been raised about the unevenness of economic development policy, particularly with respect to the balance struck between attracting inward investment and supporting indigenous enterprise, the systematic investment in skills upgrading, and the quality of the transport, energy, communications, and other infrastructural investments necessary to sustain new phases of growth (Forfás 2008; Hardiman 2009; National Competitiveness Council 2009; Ó Riain 2009; Science Foundation Ireland 2009). But in other areas in which public power is exercised, where some coordinating capacity is required with actors in the wider society, policy is less sure-footed and the shortcoming in the outcomes may be easier to identify.

The expansion of the state's capacity for regulatory governance is one of the striking features of western societies since the mid-1980s. Very often, the growth of new regulatory functions followed directly from the withdrawal of the state from direct provision or production. For example, where the state divests itself of ownership of a natural utility in which effective market-based competition is unrealistic, the creation of a regulator's office to determine the conditions of supply of the goods or services has tended to be the response of choice. Equally, the standardization of practices in areas such as food safety, environmental quality and licensing of new medical treatments, has been delegated to regulatory agencies. In European countries, as Jonathan Westrup notes in this volume, the EU itself has played an important role in extending regulatory practices (Levi-Faur 2005; Radaelli 2009). But as Westrup also notes, the financial regulatory system in Ireland failed spectacularly during the 2000s and was a principal cause of the collapse of the banking system after 2008. The regulatory function is devolved from core government management precisely to ensure its political independence. But one of the great risks of regulatory activity is that of regulatory capture, the danger that the office of the regulator will become too closely aligned with the interests of those whose activities are to be regulated. The adoption of a light-touch or principles-based regulatory regime in financial services in Ireland was consistent with successive governments' support for the International Financial Services Centre (IFSC), which attracted investment in internationally traded services through a combination of tax incentives and assurances of minimal government interference. The delegation of functions to 'non-majoritarian' agencies that are outside the direct line of government authority can be a powerful means of gaining credibility in the independence of that agency's activity. But the disastrous experience of Irish financial regulation demonstrates that delegated governance is, by itself, no guarantee of effectiveness.

The financial crisis exposed in very sudden and stark way the accumulation of other problems in the Irish economy, as the chapter by Dellepiane and Hardiman shows. Governments have no direct power to 'govern' the economy through hierarchical or directive means. But the nature and quality of economic governance is a classic case of how the linkages between state and economy, between organized interests on the one hand, and the policy-makers on the other, may make all the difference for economic performance. Some of the problems of economic coordination in the Irish case follow directly from the porousness of the party system itself. An overly close alignment between Fianna Fáil-led governments and the construction industry meant that too little political attention was paid to the growing reliance of the tax system on cyclical sources of revenue. Tax-based incentives for investment in property, by homeowners as well as property developers, continued to fuel construction activity long after its bubble properties should have become apparent (Kelly 2009). In addition though, Dellepiane and Hardiman outline the consequences of a recurring tendency on the part of Irish governments to adopt pro-cyclical fiscal policy, fuelling economic upturns with boosts to spending, resulting in the need for correction which further worsens the inevitable downturns. Within the constraints of European Monetary Union, active fiscal controls are among the few policy instruments available to government, as part of the broader requirement to maintain cost-based competitiveness.

The underlying laxity of the government macroeconomic stance made other policy activities more difficult to manage. In particular, it made it more difficult to manage 'governed interdependence' through social partnership. The national-level approach to coordinating pay bargaining, which had arguably functioned effectively in managing the adjustment from the crisis of the 1980s to the growth conditions of the 1990s, came under increasing strain during the 2000s in the context of domestic inflationary pressures and runaway housing costs (Barry 2009; Culpepper 2008; Hastings, Sheehan and Yeates 2007; McGuinness, Kelly and O'Connell 2010; Roche 2009). The failures of economic governance and the government's incapacity to get a grip on the boom eventually meant that Ireland was obliged to abandon political control over the terms on which economic policy is set, as it entered a three-year EU–IMF loan programme in November 2010.

The capacity of the state to pursue policy goals depends crucially on cooperation with wider social interests when it comes to delivering services, especially those in which a range of professional or organizational interests are involved and management of which requires a complex coordinating capacity. This volume surveys the projection of public power in two areas of service delivery, one of them in social services – that is, healthcare – and the other in infrastructural services – that is, environmental regulation and especially waste management. In both cases, though for different reasons, we can see that the policy outcomes are problematic because the institutional framework is defective.

Finn and Hardiman focus on one of the central determinants of poor acute healthcare in Ireland: that is, the mix of public and private funding that underlies a two-tier structure of access to healthcare, based on ability to pay rather than medical need. Although about half the Irish population holds private health insurance, it is clear that the system is viewed as both inefficient and inequitable. The Health Services Executive (HSE) is a major employer and channels large sums of money into health and other social services. But the coordination of policy is problematic. The separation of responsibilities between the Department of Health and Children, charged with shaping overall policy direction, and the principal health agencies – the HSE with responsibility for service delivery and the Health Information and Quality Authority (HIQA) with responsibility for regulating quality and safety standards – remains contentious. Within the HSE, hierarchical organizational management was known to be suboptimal, since the creation of this new agency through the amalgamation of ten regional boards and a variety of other agencies had not resulted in the anticipated rationalization of the functions that had previously existed in regional health structures. But the problems associated with improving equity of access and quality of healthcare have other sources too. Healthcare reform in Ireland remains constrained by the pre-existing commitment to tax-incentivized private inputs. Hospitals' current funding models depend on their being able to treat private patients. Yet when total costs are considered, the cross-subsidization of health care runs from the public to the private sector.

In the case of waste management, the problems of policy coordination are different. Laffan and O'Mahony show that governments have made efforts to expand the statutory and regulatory framework for waste management, since economic growth and rising living standards made the older dependence on landfill increasingly unsustainable. Among the new policy options put into play are a greater emphasis on recycling and a capacity for incineration. Implementing a coherent policy runs into problems because of the openness of the political system to the actions of veto players. 'NIMBY' interests, once mobilized, make it difficult for local government to create coherent policy, as elected councillors are set at odds with their own managers and officials. Indeed, very similar issues arise over the rationalization of hospitals, and defence of local hospitals has provided a successful electoral platform for several independent politicians. Local area-based issues are all too quickly translated into national politics. Candidates for national election have every incentive to embrace local electoral concerns, bringing policy stasis into the heart of government. The conflicts may well divide ministers responsible for local government and environmental policies from their own party base. The EU has acted as a powerful force to break national policy deadlock on many issues of environmental regulation. But its remit is limited, and the limitations of Irish state coordinating capacity remain starkly evident.

Democratic participation and social order

The Irish state is highly centralized, as the example of waste management illustrates. This raises a third set of problems, to do with the democratic accountability of the political system to citizens. The governance capacity of the state depends ultimately on the consent it can generate among those who are to be ruled. Democratic legitimation comes primarily through the ballot-box. It comes too from the sense of citizen efficacy, of being capable of exercising influence, of having some input into the decisions through which social order is maintained.

The weakness of local government in Ireland has given rise to new kinds of citizen demand for political inclusion, as the chapter by Payne and Stafford shows. Urban regeneration in other European systems is typically a project of local government. In Ireland, the development of Temple Bar in Dublin's city centre, which became a model for other urban regeneration schemes, was initiated and led by central government, under the direct control of the Taoiseach or prime minister. A new state body, Temple Bar Properties, was created for the purpose, bypassing Dublin City Council entirely. While this might seem to infringe the prerogatives of local democracy, the move was welcomed by local residents' organizations, who believed their voices were more effective and authoritative in this arena than they would have been if channelled through local government. The autonomy of the political executive, noted earlier, is here welcomed as the only vehicle for achieving policy targets effectively. But the corollary is that direct intervention by the Taoiseach's office is seen as the only way to overcome the malfunctioning of the political system itself.

A similar tendency toward a high degree of ministerial centralization is considered in Aogán Mulcahy's chapter on the governance of crime and security. Maintaining social order in Ireland was long seen as fairly unproblematic, notwithstanding the challenges associated with political subversion and the implications of the Troubles in Northern Ireland for politics in the Republic. Maintaining social order was therefore dealt with through conventional hierarchical chains of command within the core civil service. But in the absence of any means of keeping the law-enforcers accountable, problems arose over the democratic legitimation of security policy. Mulcahy documents the tensions between a tendency to maintain strong centralized political control and the need to be seen to devolve effective powers to new accountability procedures. The Irish police force, the Garda Síochána, traditionally generates higher levels of public trust than most other public bodies. But criminal justice policy remains strongly informed by principles of control and enforcement. A commitment to engage in networked forms of governance is apparent in initiatives to do with community policing and consultation with liaison groups. But the need to cultivate and guarantee popular legitimacy through good accountability mechanisms does not seem to have played as prominent a role in the design of police and security policy as might have been expected.

A paradox of the Irish political system is that Irish citizens believe themselves to possess quite high levels of personal political effectiveness. That is, they believe they can personally make a difference, yet they have relatively low levels of confidence in 'system effectiveness', of the responsiveness of the political system to their inputs (Garry 2006, Table 5.1). One of the respects in which the democratic character of Irish governance might be improved is through the use of new technologies. Komito's chapter assesses these possibilities in the light of e-governance initiatives, and an experiment in highly networked communications in a small Irish town. His conclusions are mixed. The innovations were very promising. But they fell short where they met the established structures of government, both local and national. An increase in the potential and capacity for participatory democracy is clearly something that Irish citizens welcome. But in the absence of wider institutional changes, new kinds of mobilizing capacity will run into old kinds of unresponsive bureaucratic structures.

Conclusion: revisiting state capacity

The exercise of state power has many dimensions. It is projected through the institutions of the state itself, both directly (hierarchically) and indirectly (through the delegation of functions to state agencies). It is exercised through its capacity to engage with organized interests in the society, aggregate preferences, and come to coherent and effective policy decisions (governed interdependence). It is exercised through the delegation of powers to non-state bodies to discharge particular kinds of activities. It is exercised through the framework of legislation and institutional design that facilitates market functioning, and it manages the policy areas that are to be subject to the discipline of market forces. There is no single or even optimal way of organizing these institutional configurations. The statutory and institutional arrangements that underpin the capacity of the state to function vary across societies; so too does the pattern of engagement between state officials and organized interests.

State power is used in many different ways in contemporary Irish governance. But the theoretical framework outlined here can help us analyse the diversity of forms in which state power is expressed. Three main features emerge from this discussion. Firstly, the Irish state is highly centralized, with an unusually strong concentration of powers in the hands of the political executive, that is, the government of the day. Secondly, the Irish state engages in networked governance, but lacks the capacity to aggregate inputs and to distance itself from particularistic interests. The diffuse nature of parties is part of the story here; so also is the lack of coordinating capacity in the core public administration itself. Thirdly, while the political system is responsive to pressure groups and veto players, what is lacking is a wider set of values promoting formal and institutionalized democratic accountability. In its absence, citizens are all too likely to fall back upon clientelist and personalized networks of influence to get things done.

Bibliography

Adshead, Maura, Peadar Kirby and Michelle Millar, eds. 2008. *Contesting the State: Lessons from the Irish State*. Manchester: Manchester University Press.

Allen, Kieran. 2010. *Ireland's Economic Crash: A Radical Agenda for Change*. Dublin: The Liffey Press.

Antoniades, Andreas. 2010. *Producing Globalisation: Politics of Discourse and Institutions in Greece and Ireland*. Manchester: Manchester University Press.

Barry, Frank, ed. 1999. *Understanding Ireland's Economic Growth*. Basingstoke: Macmillan.

Barry, Frank. 2005. Future Irish Growth: Opportunities, Catalysts, Constraints. *ESRI Quarterly Economic Commentary* (Winter 2005): 1–25.

Barry, Frank. 2007. Foreign Direct Investment and Institutional Co-Evolution in Ireland. *Scandinavian Economic History Review* 55 (3): 262–88.

Barry, Frank. 2009. Social Partnership, Competitiveness and Exit from Fiscal Crisis. *Economic and Social Review* 40 (1): 1–14.

Bell, Stephen and Andrew Hindmoor. 2009. *Rethinking Governance: the Centrality of the State in Modern Society*. Cambridge: Cambridge University Press.

Benoit, Kenneth and Michael Laver. 2006. *Party Policy in Modern Democracies*. London: Routledge.

Block, Fred. 2008. Swimming Against the Current: The Rise of a Hidden Developmental State in the United States. *Politics and Society* 36 (2): 169–206.

Börzel, Tanja A. and Thomas Risse. 2010. Governance Without a State: Can it Work? *Regulation & Governance* 4 (2): 113–34.

Bradley, John. 2000. The Irish Economy in Comparative Perspective. In *Bust to Boom? The Irish Experience of Growth and Inequality*, edited by Brian Nolan, Philip J. O'Connell and Christopher T. Whelan, 4-26. Dublin: IPA.

Byrne, Elaine. 2010. *Political Corruption in Ireland*. Manchester: Manchester University Press.

Carter, Elisabeth and David Farrell. 2010. Electoral Systems and Election Management. In *Comparing Democracies 3*, edited by Larry LeDuc, Richard Niemi and Pippa Norris, 25–44. Oxford: Oxford University Press.

Crouch, Colin. 1993. *Industrial Relations and European State Traditions*. Oxford: Oxford University Press.

Culpepper, Pepper. 2008. The Politics of Common Knowledge: Ideas and Institutional Change in Wage Bargaining. *International Organization* 62 (1): 1–33.

Döring, Herbert. 2001. Parliamentary Agenda Control and Legislative Outcomes in Western Europe. *Legislative Studies Quarterly* XXVI (1): 145–65.

Döring, Herbert. 2004. *Patterns of Parliamentary Behaviour: Passage of Legislation Across Western Europe*. London: Ashgate.

Dowding, Keith. 1995. Model or Metaphor? A Critical Review of the Policy Network Approach. *Political Studies* 43: 136–58.

Dunphy, Richard. 1995. *The Making of Fianna Fáil Power in Ireland, 1923-1948*. Oxford: Oxford University Press.

Dyson, Kenneth H.F. 1980. *The State Tradition in Western Europe: A Study of an Idea and Institution*. Oxford: Oxford University Press.

Esping-Andersen, Gosta. 1999. *Social Foundations of Postindustrial Economies*. Oxford: Oxford University Press.

Evans, Peter. 1995. *Embedded Autonomy: States and Industrial Transformation*. Princeton, NJ: Princeton University Press.

Fahey, Tony, Helen Russell and Christopher T. Whelan, eds. 2007. *Best of Times? The Social Impact of the Celtic Tiger*. Dublin: IPA.

FitzGerald, John. 2000. The Story of Ireland's Failure – and Belated Success. In *Bust to Boom? The Irish Experience of Growth and Inequality*, edited by Brian Nolan, Philip J. O'Connell, and Christopher T. Whelan, 27-57. Dublin: IPA.

Flinders, Matthew. 2009. *Delegated Governance and the British State: Walking Without Order*. Oxford: Oxford University Press.

Forfás. 2008. *Monitoring Ireland's Skills Supply: Trends in Education/ Training Outputs 2008*. Dublin: Forfás.

Garry, John. 2006. Political Alienation. In *Irish Social and Political Attitudes*, edited by John Garry, Niamh Hardiman and Diane Payne, 60–77. Liverpool: Liverpool University Press.

Gilardi, Fabrizio. 2008. *Delegation in the Regulatory State: Independent Regulatory Agencies in Western Europe*. Cheltenham: Edward Elgar.

Goetz, Klaus H. 2008. Governance as a Path to Government. *West European Politics* 31 (1-2): 258–79.

Guiomard, Cathal. 1995. *The Irish Disease and How to Cure it: Common-Sense Economics for a Competitive World*. Dublin: Oak Tree Press.

Haggard, Stephen. 1990. *Pathways from the Periphery: The Politics of Growth in the Newly Industializing Countries*. Ithaca, NY: Cornell University Press.

Hall, Peter A. and Rosemary Taylor. 1996. Political Science and the Three New Institutionalisms. *Political Studies* 44 (4): 936–57.

Hardiman, Niamh. 2002. From Conflict to Coordination: Economic Governance and Political Innovation in Ireland. *West European Politics* 25 (4): 1–24.

Hardiman, Niamh. 2005. Politics and Markets in the Irish 'Celtic Tiger'. *The Political Quarterly* 76 (1): 37–47.

Hardiman, Niamh. 2006. Politics and Social Partnership: Flexible Network Governance. *Economic and Social Review* 37 (3): 347–74.

Hardiman, Niamh. 2009. Bringing Politics Back Into Varieties of Capitalism: Shaping Ireland's Productive Capacity Working Paper 2009/13. Dublin: UCD Geary Institute. Available at http://ideas.repec.org/p/ucd/wpaper/200913.html.

Hardiman, Niamh. 2012. Governance and State Structures. In *Oxford Handbook of Governance*, edited by David Levi-Faur. Oxford: Oxford University Press.

Hardiman, Niamh and Muiris MacCarthaigh. 2010. Organizing for Growth: Irish State Administration 1958-2008. *Economic and Social Review* 43 (3): 367–93.

Hardiman, Niamh and Muiris MacCarthaigh. 2011. The Un-Politics of New Public Management in Ireland. In *Administrative Reforms and Democratic Governance*, edited by Jean-Michel Eymeri-Douzans and Jon Pierre, 55–67. London: Routledge.

Hardiman, Niamh, Anthony McCashin and Diane Payne. 2006. Understanding Attitudes to Poverty and Wealth. In *Irish Social and Political Attitudes*, edited by John Garry, Niamh Hardiman and Diane Payne, 43-59. Liverpool: Liverpool University Press.

Hardiman, Niamh and Colin Scott. 2009. Ordering Things: Classifying State Agencies. Working Paper 2009/07. Dublin: UCD Geary Institute. Available at http://ideas.repec.org/p/ucd/wpaper/200907.html.

Hastings, Tim, Brian Sheehan and Padraig Yeates. 2007. *Saving the Future: How Social Partnership Shaped Ireland's Economic Success*. Dublin: Blackhall Publishing Ltd.

Hayward, Katy and Muiris MacCarthaigh, eds. 2007. *Recycling the State: The Politics of Adaptation in Ireland*. Dublin: Irish Academic Press.

Houses of the Oireachtas Joint Committee on the Constitution. 2010. *Call for Written Submissions: Review of the Parliamentary Power of Inquiry, Article 15 of the Constitution*. Dublin: Stationery Office.

Inglis, Tom. 1998. *Moral Monopoly: the Rise and Fall of the Catholic Church in Ireland.* Dublin: UCD Press.

Kassim, Hussein. 1994. Policy Networks, Networks and European Policy-Making: A Sceptical View. *West European Politics* 17: 15-27.

Kelly, Morgan. 2009. The Irish Credit Bubble. UCD Centre for Economic Research Working Paper. Dublin: University College Dublin. Available at WWW.UCD.ie/t4cms/wp09.32.pdf.

Kennedy, Fiachra and Richard Sinnott. 2006. Irish Social and Political Cleavages. In *Irish Social and Political Attitudes*, edited by John Garry, Niamh Hardiman and Diane Payne, 78-93. Liverpool: Liverpool University Press.

Kerrigan, Gene and Pat Brennan. 1999. *This Great Little Nation: The A-Z of Irish Scandals and Controversies.* Dublin: Gill and Macmillan.

King, Desmond and Robert C. Lieberman. 2009. Ironies of State Building: A Comparative Perspective on the American State. Review Article. *World Politics* 61 (3): 547–88.

Kirby, Peadar. 2002. *The Celtic Tiger in Distress: the Growth of Inequality in Ireland.* Basingstoke: Palgrave.

Kirby, Peadar. 2004. Development Theory and the Celtic Tiger. *The European Journal of Development Research* 16 (2): 301–28.

Kirby, Peadar. 2010. *Celtic Tiger in Collapse: Explaining the Weaknesses of the Irish Model.* Dublin: Palgrave Macmillan.

Leahy, Pat. 2009. *Showtime: The Inside Story of Fianna Fail in Power.* Dublin: Penguin Ireland.

Levi-Faur, David. 2005. The Global Diffusion of Regulatory Capitalism. *The Annals of the American Academy of Political and Social Science* 598: 12–32.

March, James G. and Johan P. Olsen. 1984. The New Institutionalism: Organizational Factors in Political Life. *The American Political Science Review* 78: 734–49.

Marsh, Michael. 2008. Explanations for Party Choice. In *How Ireland Voted 2007: The Full Story of Ireland's General Election*, edited by Michael Gallagher and Michael Marsh, 105–31. Basingstoke: Palgrave Macmillan.

Marsh, Michael and Michael Gallagher, eds. 2008. *How Ireland Voted 2007: The Full Story of Ireland's General Election.* Basingstoke: Palgrave Macmillan.

Marsh, Michael, Richard Sinnott, John Garry and Fiachra Kennedy, eds. 2008. *The Irish Voter: The Nature of Electoral Competition in the Republic of Ireland.* Manchester: Manchester University Press.

Mayntz, Renate. 2007. *The Architecture of Multi-Level Governance of Economic Sectors.* Cologne: Max Planck Institute for the Study of Societies. Available at www.mpifg.de/pu/mpifg_dp/dp07-13.pdf.

McGuinness, Seamus, Elish Kelly and Philip J. O'Connell. 2010. The Impact of Wage Bargaining Regime on Firm-level Competitiveness and Wage Inequality: The Case of Ireland. *Industrial Relations* 49 (4): 593–615.

McGuinness, Seamus, Frances McGinnity and Philip J. O'Connell. 2009. Changing Returns to Education During a Boom? The Case of Ireland. *Labour: Review of Labour Economics and Industrial Relations* 23: 197–221.

Migdal, Joel. 1988. *Strong Societies and Weak States: State-Society Relations and State Capabilities in the Third World.* Princeton, NJ: Princeton University Press.

National Competitiveness Council. 2009. Dublin. Available at www.competitiveness.ie/media/ncc090818_acr_2009.pdf.

Nolan, Brian and Bertrand Maitre. 2007. Economic Growth and Income Inequality: Setting the Context. In *Best of Times? The Social Impact of the Celtic Tiger*, edited by Tony Fahey, Helen Russell and Christopher T. Whelan, 27-42. Dublin: Institute of Public Administration.

O'Donnell, Rory. 2008. The Partnership State. In *Contesting the State: Lessons from the Irish Case*, edited by Maura Adshead, Peadar Kirby and Michelle Millar, 73–99. Manchester: Manchester University Press.

O'Toole, Fintan. 2010. *Ship of Fools: How Stupidity and Corruption Sank the Celtic Tiger*. London: Faber and Faber.

Ó Riain, Seán. 2000. The Flexible Developmental State : Globalization, Information Technology and the 'Celtic Tiger'. *Politics and Society* 28 (3): 3–37.

Ó Riain, Seán. 2004. *The Politics of High Tech Growth: Developmental Network States in the Global Economy*. Cambridge: Cambridge University Press.

Ó Riain, Seán. 2008. Competing State Projects in the Contemporary Irish Political Economy. In *Contesting the State*, edited by Maura Adshead, Peadar Kirby and Michelle Miller, 165–85. Manchester: Manchester University Press.

O Riain, Sean.2009. Addicted to Growth: State, Market and the Difficult Politics of Development in Ireland. In *The Nation-State In Transformation: The Governance, Growth and Cohesion of Small States under Globalisation*, edited by M. Böss, 163–90. Aarhus: Aarhus University Press.

Offe, Claus. 1981. Organized Interests and Public Policy in Germany. In *Organizing Interests in Western Europe: Pluralism, Corporatism and the Transformation of Politics*, edited by Suzanne Berger, 123–58. Cambridge: Cambridge University Press.

Office of the Comptroller and Auditor General. 2009. *Special Report 63: Tribunals of Inquiry*. Dublin: Government Publications Office. Available at www.audgen.gov.ie/viewdoc.asp?DocID=1134&&CatID=5&StartDate=1+January+2009.

Olsen, Johan P. 2006. Maybe It Is Time to Rediscover Bureaucracy. *Journal of Public Administration Research and Theory* 16 (1): 1–24.

Polanyi, Karl. 1944/2002. *The Great Transformation*. New York: Beacon Press.

Radaelli, Claudio M. 2009. Measuring Policy Learning: Regulatory Impact Assessment in Europe. *Journal of European Public Policy* 16 (8): 1145–64.

Rhodes, R.A.W. 1992. Policy Networks in British Politics. In *Policy Networks in British Government*, edited by David Marsh and R.A.W. Rhodes, 1–26. Oxford: Oxford University Press.

Roberts, Alasdair. 2010. *The Logic of Discipline: Global Capitalism and the Architecture of Government*. Oxford: Oxford University Press.

Roche, William K. 2009. Social Partnership: From Lemass to Cowen. *Economic and Social Review* 40 (2): 183–205.

Ross, Shane and Nick Webb. 2010. *Wasters*. Dublin: Penguin.

Rothstein, Bo and Jan Teorell. 2008. What is Quality of Government? A Theory of Impartial Government Institutions. *Governance* 21 (2): 165–90.

Rudder, Catherine E. 2008. Private Governance as Public Policy: A Paradigmatic Shift. *The Journal of Politics* 70 (04): 899–913.

Scharpf, Fritz W. 1997. *Games Real Actors Play: Actor-Centred Institutionalism in Policy Research*. Boulder, CO: Westview Press.

Schmidt, Vivien A. 2006. Adapting to Europe: Is it Harder for Britain? *British Journal of Politics and International Relations* 8: 15–33.

Science Foundation Ireland. 2009. *Powering the Smart Economy 2009-13*. Dublin: SFI. Available at www.sfi.ie/uploads/documents/upload/SFI_Smart_Economy.pdf.

Scott, Colin. 2008a. Regulating Everything. Working Paper 2008/24. Dublin: UCD Geary Institute. Available at http://geary.ucd.ie/images/Publications/WorkingPapers/gearywp200824.pdf.

Scott, Colin. 2008b. Understanding Variety in Public Agencies.Working paper 2008/04 Dublin: UCD Geary Institute. Available at http://geary.ucd.ie/images/Publications/WorkingPapers/gearywp200804.pdf.

Sheingate, Adam. 2009. Why Can't Americans See the State? *The Forum* 7 (4): Article 1.

Smith, Nicola. 2005. *Showcasing Globalisation: The Political Economy of the Irish Republic*. Manchester: Manchester University Press.

Smith, Nicola and Colin Hay. 2008. Mapping the Discourse of Globalisation and European Integration in the United Kingdom and Ireland Empirically. *European Journal of Political Research* 47 (3): 359–82.

Smith, Nicola J. 2007. Mapping Processes of Policy Change in Contemporary European Political Economies: The Irish Case. *British Journal of Politics and International Relations* 8 (4): 519–38.

Steinmo, Sven. 2007. Historical Institutionalism. In *Approaches in the Social Sciences*, edited by Donatella Della Porta and Michael Keating, 113–38. Cambridge: Cambridge University Press.

Strøm, Kaare. 2000. Delegation and Accountability in Parliamentary Democracies. *European Journal of Political Research* 37: 261–89.

Suiter, Jane. 2009. Pork-Barrel Spending in Ireland – Fact or Fiction?, PhD thesis, Department of Political Science, Trinity College Dublin.

TASC. 2010. *The Solidarity Factor: Public Responses to Social Inequality in Ireland*. Dublin: TASC. Available at www.tascnet.ie/upload/file/Solidarity%20Factor_upload.pdf.

Thatcher, Mark and Alec Stone Sweet, eds. 2004. *The Politics of Delegation*. London: Frank Cass.

Treib, Oliver, Holger Bähr and Gerda Falkner. 2005. Modes of Governance: A Note Towards Conceptual Clarification. In *EUROGOV No. N-05-02*. Available at www.connex-network.org/eurogov/pdf/egp-newgov-N-05-02.pdf.

van Kersbergen, Kees and Philip Manow, eds. 2009. *Religion, Class Coalitions, and Welfare States*. Cambridge: Cambridge University Press.

Weiss, Linda. 1998. *The Myth of the Powerless State: Governing the Economy in a Global Era*. Cambridge: Polity Press.

Whelan, Christopher T. 2000. Urban Housing and the Role of 'Underclass' Processes: the Case of Ireland. *Journal of European Social Policy* 10 (1): 5–21.

Whelan, Christopher T. and Richard Layte. 2006. Economic Boom and Social Mobility: The Irish Experience. *Research in Social Stratification and Mobility* 24 (2): 193–208.

Whelan, Christopher T., Richard Layte and Bertrand Maitre. 2002. Multiple Deprivation and Persistent Poverty in the European Union. *Journal of European Social Policy* 12 (2): 91–105.

Wolinetz, Steven. 2002. Beyond the Catch-All Party: Approaches to the Study of Parties and Party Organization in Contemporary Democracies. In *Political Parties: Old Concepts and New Challenges*, edited by Richard Gunther, Jose Ramon Montero and Juan J. Linz, 136-65. Oxford: Oxford University Press.

2

Governance and accountability: the limits of new institutional remedies

Muiris MacCarthaigh

Introduction

Contemporary ideas of good governance commonly accord a prominent role to the means whereby political and administrative actors at the heart of the state can be held accountable for their actions. The global financial crisis creates a new urgency over the means whereby oversight and scrutiny of executive authority are assured. But conventional parliamentary forms of enforcing accountability were already held to be deeply flawed prior to this, and in Ireland as elsewhere, new institutional solutions have been introduced to remedy some of the gaps that had become apparent in the capacity of democratic politics to hold executive power to account (Bovens 2007, 2010). Yet the creation of new institutional mechanisms for assuring accountability can sit uneasily with established practices. This can give rise to a paradoxical outcome whereby more institutional structures may even worsen the chances of achieving the desired outcomes. This chapter reconsiders the role of parliamentary accountability in the context of the new layers of accountability-enhancing institutions. It was precisely the perceived limitations of what parliamentary methods could achieve that gave rise to the demand for the creation of new bodies. But bypassing parliament is problematic for both the effectiveness and the democratic legitimation of the Irish accountability regime in general. There is no escape from the need to strengthen the quality of the work of the legislature.

The modern evolution of accountability

Accountability has *de jure* always been a feature of democratic government, but the concept has gained currency in recent decades, augmenting or even replacing terms such as responsibility and oversight (Dubnick 2005). Political failures, policy implementation deficits and general deviations from normative conceptions of good governance are now routinely attributed to problems of accountability. Public accountability is expected not only of core state institutions but of ever broader ranges of institutional performance, giving rise to new mechanisms for ensuring it. But new monitoring and regulatory frameworks such as independent regulatory agencies and Ombudsman's offices can pose challenges to traditional democratic governing and accountability relationships (Christensen, Lie and Laegreid 2007; Gilardi 2008).

From its roots in administrative law, accountability now encompasses issues of control, responsiveness, responsibility, audit, liability and blameworthiness (Mulgan 2000, 2003). The structure of accountability regimes, particularly reporting mechanisms, forms a large part of contemporary literature on corporate governance (Bovens 1998: 50–51; Procter and Miles 2003; Sternberg 2004). There is also a growing literature on the role of private actors in public accountability regimes (Dowdle 2006).

Traditionally understood, accountability implied a set of agreed rules between actors, in which an external principal reserves the power to sanction an agent for failing to act in the principal's interest. The principal–agent model has been extensively used to capture the linear nature of accountability in democratic government, with citizens as the ultimate principals (Strøm 2000). This distinguishes it from the concept of responsibility which referred to internal controls inspired by professional or personal ethics (DeLeon 2003). Accountability chains are normally conceptualized as hierarchical; they can only be as strong as the weakest link. However, accountability relationships have increasingly come to be envisaged in terms of more diffuse relationships, as networks rather than hierarchies, in which contrasting dichotomies are nested, such as political versus administrative accountability, internal versus external accountability and centralised versus devolved accountability (Thomas 2003).

To speak of 'multiple accountabilities' may therefore throw the meaning of accountability itself into some question (Philp 2009). Accountability is sometimes presented as a zero-sum phenomenon such that a decline in one form of accountability results in an increase in another, and only one mode can prevail (Hodge and Coghill 2007). The intuition is that an accountability relationship exists when an actor can be called to give an account of their actions or inactions to a person or group who, if their conditions are not met, may exercise the right to seek remedial action or impose a sanction. The potential ability held by a forum to call an actor to account may be as important an influence on the behaviour of that actor as the actual process of account-giving itself.

Accountability has therefore both direct and indirect importance (Bovens 2007). Directly, it fulfils a key element of democratic government, that of popular control. It helps to guard against corruption and the abuse of power, and provides a means of learning for bureaucrats and politicians. Indirectly, accountability provides the basis for the legitimacy of public governance.

Some classic accountability mechanisms are well established for ensuring that governments as agents act in the interests of their ultimate principals, the public. From the mid-nineteenth century, oversight of government in common law countries centred on both financial accountability, such that audit of the accounts of public administration became a central duty of government, and political accountability, which institutionalized parliamentary scrutiny of the executive and ideas about collective government responsibility. In many jurisdictions, financial accountability required Courts of Auditors and Auditors-General to report independently to parliament rather than government.

During the early twentieth century, the judicial accountability of the state emerged as a core characteristic of democratic government in response to Diceyan concerns about the growing state bureaucracies. Tensions between executive and judicial pillars of state became more common as supreme courts became final arbiters on issues of responsibility, and even perhaps agenda-setters on issues of policy. Governments also established innovative methods of redress and grievance-handling in response to a growing citizen propensity to vindicate their rights through the courts. The duty of the state to its citizens was increasingly ensured in democratic states by the development of robust mechanisms of financial, political and judicial accountability.

Parliamentary accountability

The role of the legislature in parliamentary systems of government varies considerably depending on the role played by constitutional and historical influences and norms of parliamentary conduct (Döring 1995b; Strøm, Müller and Bergman 2006). But parliament is in all cases central to ensuring political and financial accountability. It may even be argued that what matters most is not so much the role played by parliament in the selection of the cabinet of ministers as the toleration by a parliamentary majority of that cabinet (Strøm et al. 2006: 12). Within parliamentary democracies, the central accountability relationship is that of the executive to the legislature. In practice, use of sanctions by parliaments is rare, and in many countries party discipline radically diminishes the possibility of using the ultimate sanction of unseating a government from power. Rather, executives are encouraged to function in a manner that stands up to scrutiny by the capacity of parliamentarians to insist upon disclosure of information, and the potential embarrassment and indeed damage to government authority that would follow from discovery of malpractice.

For parliaments – or more precisely parliamentary oppositions – to hold government to account, they require information. The reality of political partisanship means that governments are not inclined to provide too much information while non-government members will routinely complain of limitations in their access to information. The rules and norms governing parliamentary proceedings vary widely (Döring 1995a, 2004). Westminster-style parliaments are most prone to encounter difficulties in the constitutional duty to hold the executive to account (Flinders 2001; MacCarthaigh 2005; Mulgan 2003).

The expanding role of state and rising citizen expectations contribute to the growth in supplementary or alternative forms of executive oversight;

most countries have adopted innovative accountability mechanisms such as Ombudsman's offices, freedom of information entitlements, and data protection legislation (Bennett 1997). Within the EU, the proliferation of regulatory bodies has been driven by policy learning as well as by the terms of directives: the delegation of decision-making to independent regulatory agencies serves many functions, from improving the technical inputs to the policy process, to distancing governments from politically difficult decisions (Thatcher and Stone Sweet 2004). Indeed, a common justification for establishing new agencies is that their independence demonstrates credible commitment on the part of government, and thereby underwrites high standards of accountability for effective policy performance (Gilardi 2008).

The limitation of parliamentary accountability is that it depends so heavily on a degree of institutionalized independence from executive control. In Ireland, as in Britain, this is not well developed. The rule system grants considerable veto power to the executive, and the conduct of parliamentary politics is strongly adversarial. A key development in Irish and other Westminster-style parliamentary politics in recent years has been the attempt to move away from the traditional means of accountability exemplified by the doctrine of ministerial responsibility to more direct forms of scrutiny (MacCarthaigh 2005: 52–93, 2007). An example of this in Ireland is the power granted to parliamentary committees to question public servants or the CEOs of state agencies directly, made possible by the Committees of the Houses of the Oireachtas (Compellability, Privileges and Immunities) Act, 1997.

The Irish legislature, like parliaments elsewhere, has acquired more resources to support its oversight function,[1] and a functioning parliamentary committee system has developed. Yet even as the powers of the legislature have been cautiously augmented, the scope and complexity of the public bureaucracy has expanded, making effective oversight somewhat inconsistent and occasional (MacCarthaigh 2010). The explosion of non-departmental bodies or agencies[2] at national and local levels over the last two decades, and the varying degrees of autonomy which accompany the performance of their functions, presents new kinds of accountability challenges for parliament (Clancy and Murphy 2006; McGauran, Verhoest and Humphreys 2005; OECD 2008: 294–313). The wide variety in legal form, organizational structure and size has resulted in wide variation in the pattern of management of these agencies by their parent departments.

Against this backdrop, an independent review concluded that regulatory bodies were only poorly subject to parliamentary oversight: 'the ability of Oireachtas committees effectively to hold regulators to account [appeared] to be limited because they lack the specialist knowledge to do so' (Economist Intelligence Unit 2009: 54). The poor performance of the Irish Financial Services Regulatory Authority has been blamed for the development of the crisis in the banking sector (Regling and Watson 2010). But the role of various Oireachtas committees in overseeing the regulator's performance – and more than one had potential jurisdiction – has largely been ignored.

Accountability and complexity

A simple and linear superior–subordinate accountability framework has never existed in the Irish state, and recent developments have created quite a complex accountability environment. There are multiple account *holders* and account *holdees* (Behn 2001). Traditional political, financial and judicial audit has been supplemented by an extended reach for public sector audit, and the subjection of public bodies to a new range of non-judicial oversight, grievance handling mechanisms and oversight by ethics bodies. There are also many new applications of the term accountability, in the sense of what individual politicians or civil servants are expected to be accountable for. For example, new codes of conduct for civil servants and public office holders lay emphasis on peer or professional accountability in addition to normal legal requirements.

New and complex modes of governance invariably produce demands for new accountability systems, and this can make the accountability framework more complex without necessarily making it either more effective or more democratically legitimate. We may argue that with ever-greater accountability requirements comes the potential for redundancy, incoherence and lacunae in accountability rules (Peters 1998: 296): redundancy because rules may overlap; incoherence because they are poorly connected together; lacunae because some gaps in coverage remain unaddressed.

More accountability will not necessarily ensure better accountability. Dubnick argues that the greater the use of administrative accountability mechanisms in a bureaucracy, the less likely it is that bureaucrats will behave responsibly, ethically and professionally (Dubnick 2005). Behn also notes this 'accountability dilemma' faced by those involved in devising and implementing policy (Behn 2001).

Of course, the concern with accountability is not confined to actions of the administrative apparatus of state. As a result of corruption scandals in Ireland, demand increased for greater transparency in public life, and the conduct of political parties and politicians is subject to more intense scrutiny that ever before. Among the innovations, in Ireland as elsewhere, have been new rules to regulate the conduct of parties during elections, and public declarations on interests and income.

Table 2.1 (adapted from MacCarthaigh 2005: 23) describes the development of both parliamentary and non-parliamentary or 'public' means of enforcing accountability, and each form as both an old and a new variant.

Under consideration here are innovations in non-parliamentary modes of enforcing accountability. The Standards in Public Office Commission (SIPO)

Table 2.1 Parliamentary and public mechanisms of accountability

		Mechanism	Used to hold whom to account	Accountable to what institution
Parliamentary accountability	Old	PQs, debate, motions and resolutions	Executive (including the public administration), individual ministers and parliamentarians	Dáil Éireann
	New	Parliamentary Committees (including committees on members' interests)	Executive (including the public administration), individual ministers and parliamentarians	Houses of the Oireachtas
Public accountability	Old	Ombudsman	Public Administration	Independent office*
		Comptroller and Auditor-General	Public administration	Independent office by virtue of constitutional guarantee
	New	Freedom of Information	Executive (including the public administration)	Independent office*
		Standards in Public Office Commission	Political parties, public representatives	Houses of the Oireachtas

* While the Ombudsman and Freedom of Information Commissioner are appointed by the Houses of the Oireachtas and present reports to both Houses, they are in fact independent of those Houses and not accountable to them.

has been in existence since 2001, and is responsible for the conduct of political parties and public representatives, reporting to the Houses of the Oireachtas. The Office of the Freedom of Information Commissioner, established in 1997, oversees the executive and is an independent non-parliamentary office. These case studies demonstrate the challenges posed by introducing new accountability arrangements into an existing accountability framework. The creation of both offices followed considerable criticism levelled at the decision-making process in light of sustained revelations of political corruption and administrative mal-practice in Ireland during the 1990s. But the threefold problems of grafting new arrangements onto old structures are all in evidence here: we find redundancy, incoherence and lacunae in the patterns of accountability arrangements that ensue. Multiple accountability requirements may not achieve better or more democratically legitimate forms of governance.

The Standards in Public Office Commission (SIPO)

The Standards in Public Office Commission owes its origins to the 1995 Ethics in Public Office Act, which updated the law on the prevention of corruption and provided for the annual registration of interests by people in key public positions. These include parliamentarians and members of the Cabinet, senior civil and public servants, state agency board members and senior executives of commercial state enterprises, as well as special advisers to ministers. The parliamentary com-mittee system was not fully embedded by this stage, so no role for committee chairs was specified under the Act. It obliged members of the Oireachtas, when speaking or voting on an issue, to make a formal declaration if the issue involved a potential conflict of interest, and to provide a written account of their interests to the Clerk of either House. But the accuracy of these statements of interest was not checked by any of the staff of the Houses and the only incentive for members to declare their assets was the potential negative publicity for not doing so.

The Act also provided for the establishment of a Public Offices Commission, whose role was to monitor compliance with the provisions of the Act by the public office holders mentioned above. Its members were the Ceann Comhairle (Speaker) of Dáil Éireann, the Comptroller and Auditor-General, the Ombudsman and the Clerks of Dáil and Seanad Éireann. Following recommen-dations made by the final report of the 1997 Dunnes Payments Tribunal (better known as the McCracken Tribunal after its chairman, Brian McCracken), the Ethics in Public Offices Act was amended by the Standards in Public Office Act, 2001. The most notable feature of the new Act was the creation of the Standards in Public Office Commission, which replaced the Public Offices Commission. The Standards in Public Office Commission did not include in its membership the Ceann Comhairle. Instead, he or she was to be replaced by a member of the judiciary appointed by the President on the advice of the government, and who would fulfil the role of Chairperson. The new legislation also allows the Commission to appoint another member of its choosing, and it appointed a former minister to that position.

The Commission is principally concerned with regulating and monitoring the financial activities of the political parties. As well as its founding legislation, the remit of the Commission extends from the Electoral Acts 1997 to 2005, and the Oireachtas (Ministerial and Parliamentary Offices) (Amendment) Act, 2001. Amongst other functions, these Acts give the Commission the power to ensure that election expenditure limits are adhered to, and to monitor the disclosure of political donations, public funding of qualified political parties, and reimbursement of expenses incurred by election candidates. Since its creation, the focus of the Standards in Public Office legislation has broadened. It has advanced from a position where disclosure of interests and reporting of possible conflicts of interest were the principal features, to a more prescriptive mode which includes certification of tax clearance for public service appointees, performing inquiries or recommending areas for further legislative development.

The Commission's work in disclosing the levels of expenditure by the political parties during elections and the identification of those private interests who donate money to the party has been of considerable media and public interest. Its work has undoubtedly contributed to the development of a culture of financial probity which was previously absent from the political process and arguably from political parties themselves. Members of the Oireachtas who are not office holders as defined under the Acts are responsible to the Committees on Members' Interests of the Dáil or Seanad. The Ethics in Public Office Act (and later Standards in Public Office Act) established these committees to monitor the implementation of their recommendations, as well as to sanction members who broke the guidelines established by the legislation. This was a significant development as it introduced a new mechanism of oversight within the Oireachtas itself, by empowering elected members to hold their peers to account. However, as will be detailed below, the committees have encountered several difficulties in fulfilling their remit.

Members of the Oireachtas must now provide a statement of registerable interests each year. The completed Register of Interests is then laid before the Houses. Oireachtas members who are members of the government must also provide an annual statement of additional interests (i.e. relevant family interests).

The Commission also has a function in respect of the bureaucracy, insofar as elected members may make complaints against public servants to it. In doing so it allows parliamentarians to circumvent a key element of ministerial responsibility which designated the appropriate minister to be 'responsible' for the activities of civil servants. Thus the Commission offers another alternative to Dáil Éireann in terms of administrative oversight.

Freedom of Information (FOI) and the Office of the Information Commissioner
The Standards in Public Office Commission has shed new and very public light on the activities of politicians and political parties. It has been matched by enhanced access for the public to the activities of the state administration: the Freedom of Information Act was introduced in 1997. It initially applied only to central government and related departments, but even though some way from

total coverage, the range of public bodies under its remit has grown substantially since then. The Act provided for extensive powers of disclosure to the public of documentation which previously would not have been released until a period of thirty years had elapsed under the 1986 National Archives Act. This new legislation drew on best practice from other Westminster-style democracies including Canada, Australia and New Zealand, and was created to allow citizens to have rights of access to information held by public bodies as of April 1998. At the same time, Ireland's Freedom of Information legislation had to ensure citizens' rights of privacy and to ensure that fair procedures were followed. The legislation provided for the establishment of an Information Commissioner and this role was subsequently conjoined with that of the Ombudsman.

The Information Commissioner was presented with substantial powers under the Act, such as the ability to authorize the release of information that might previously have been withheld in response to a citizen's request. In brief, the legislation created three new statutory rights:

- A legal right for each person to access information held by public bodies.
- A legal right for each person to have official information relating to him/herself amended where it is incomplete, incorrect or misleading.
- A legal right to obtain reasons for decisions affecting oneself.

The Information Commissioner derives legitimacy from the fact that his or her appointment is made by the President on the advice of the government following a resolution of both Houses of the Oireachtas. The decision to make the Ombudsman the Information Commissioner was made on the basis that the Ombudsman's office had considerable expertise in the area of disclosure of public records.[3] Indeed, the Ombudsman/Information Commissioner's offices share their premises with the Standards in Public Office Commission. However, internal work and systems processes, as well as staffing arrangements, are distinctive for each office.

The Act's provisions for disclosure were initially used extensively by journalists (and students) and led to a number of issues being widely publicized in the media. These included, for example, overspends on information technology projects in government departments or reports on elder abuse in state-funded nursing homes. The Freedom of Information Act was regarded as among the most progressive of its type (and informed similar legislation elsewhere, including Britain), and as representing a substantial step in the development of public accountability in Ireland. It also improved the quality of record-keeping in public offices. A consultancy report on Irish public service reform found that the Freedom of Information Act 'has generated additional workloads across Departments/Offices, but it has undoubtedly improved the accountability of the civil service to the wider public' (PA Consulting 2002: 88).

The Standards in Public Office Commission and Office of the Information Commissioner are manifestations of the institutional response to concerns with ethics and accountability in public life. Combined, they have significantly increased the volume of publicly accessible material on administrative and political processes in Ireland. They also offer an alternative to the traditional source of information on the work of the bureaucracy i.e. through ministerial response to parliamentary questions, which in effect allowed ministers to veto the release of such information. However, whether or not the new institutions achieve their goal of introducing more accountability in public life cannot be fully evaluated with reference to their interaction with existing accountability structures.

Difficulties with the new institutions

The Standards in Public Office Commission and Office of the Information Commissioner seek to tackle low standards of governance manifest in issues such as corrupt political payments and poor administrative practice. The difficulties experienced by the two offices in fulfilling their remit may be viewed as teething difficulties of a sort than any relatively new bodies might encounter. However, as with much of institutional reform, there have been unintended consequences which have served to undermine the intentions of the institutions themselves. We may identify all three of the problems referred to above when new accountability practices are overlaid on the old, without comprehensively addressing their interactions: in each case, we may identify problems of redundancy, coherence and lacunae. More fundamentally, the new accountability mechanisms tackle the symptoms of poor governance, but they do not and cannot address their root cause, which is the failure of existing democratic mechanisms of oversight. Yet there is little sign of substantive parliamentary reform (MacCarthaigh 2005).

Standards in Public Office: redundancy

By 2010, the Standards in Public Office Commission had dealt with two general elections (2002 and 2007). In relation to the first, in 2003 the Commission released details of spending by candidates during the election and found that 56 of the incoming 166 TDs (members of parliament) had overspent their quota as established under the Electoral (Amendment) Act, 2001, amongst them the Taoiseach and indeed most of the Cabinet. Some of this overspending was the result of a court decision on the eve of the election, which held that Oireachtas members must count in their spending estimation services such as mail and secretarial services. Unlike 2002, the 2007 election saw no candidate or parties overspending their statutory limits.

The money spent by candidates in parliamentary elections is only counted from the time that such an election is called. There is nothing to prohibit parties from spending money on canvassing in advance of this date and what money is spent need not be included in the final figures submitted to the SIPO. This practice of frontloading spending also occurred in 2007 (of approximately €10 million spent during the final three weeks of that campaign, only €1.3 million could be publicly accounted for) and has resulted in the SIPO calling for the creation of an Electoral Commission and a review of the ethics legislation. Any attempt to regulate the activities of political actors more closely is problematic, since non-cash assets and human resources cannot be easily quantified. This is particularly relevant since Irish electoral competition attaches considerable importance to candidates' local profile and features intense intra-party competition. The Commission has no practical method of taking into account the activities of party activists and the value of their efforts. Thus while political actors are technically adhering to the requirement of the legislation, the practice would appear to be to find ways to work around its stipulations, including soliciting donations that are fractionally lower than the disclosure thresholds. Figures released in 2009 recorded the lowest figures on record for donations to political parties since 1997.

Other cases have arisen whereby the powers of the Commission have not been deemed sufficient to inquire into cases that appeared to fall within its remit. In 2004 a conflict of interest was alleged in the case of a minister awarding a public relations contract to a consultant with whom he had a close political relationship. While the allegations were later proved to be unfounded, the matter was deemed serious enough at the time for the Taoiseach to remove from ministers the power to directly employ public relations consultants. Despite the fact that the issue appeared to be one for which the Commission was created to investigate, its annual report brushed over the matter, arguing that:

> The evidence before the Standards Commission did not establish a *prima facie* case which would have warranted an investigation within the terms of the legislation in question. In that regard, the grounds for possible investigation by the Standards Commission could not extend beyond the scope of the relevant legislation. (Standards in Public Office Commission 2005: 16)

In 2007, the Commission stated that complaints received by it from members of the public in relation to 'loans/gifts' received by the then Taoiseach from groups of businessmen would not be investigated by it as it had 'decided that there is no basis on which to initiate an investigation under the Ethics in Public Office Acts 1995 and 2001' (Press release of 19 September 2007).

SIPO: incoherence
In order to support the work of the Commission within the Oireachtas, the 1995 and 2001 Acts both provided for the creation of Committees on Members' Interests in both Houses. In fact, the Dáil Committee on Members' Interests is one of few committees with a non-government majority membership. The

position of Chair is held by a member of the government parties. Neither committee has the power to alter, revise or otherwise change the findings of the Standards in Public Office Commission. The principal role of the committees is to implement the Standards in Public Office legislation in respect of those members of either House who are not office-holders. In practice, however, there appears to be uncertainty concerning the relationship between the SIPO and the committees, particularly in relation to censuring parliamentarians.

The 2003 annual report of the SIPO noted the inability of the Commission to censure a deputy who had returned a false tax clearance certificate. The Commission stated that the legislation governing its work required that for it to take action, a complaint must be made against a TD. As none had been made, it had been left with no option but to refer the matter on to the Dáil Committee on Members' Interests. Yet it did not take any action and referred the matter back to the Commission. By this stage the time limit within which the Commission could take action had been reached and it could not therefore pursue the matter further itself. In the event, the issue was investigated by police authorities and the member received a fine and suspended jail sentence.

The role of the committees is to provide support within the legislature for the provisions of the Ethics Act. But there have been difficulties recruiting members to these committees: it appears that politicians are reluctant to be seen to be monitoring their peers' behaviour. During the latter stages of the 1997–2002 government, the Dáil Committee on Members' Interests was asked to investigate the actions of two members, Ned O'Keeffe and Denis Foley. In both cases, the issue before the Committee was that the TD did not declare an interest during a debate. The Committee recommended suspensions in both cases, but not before committee members voiced their displeasure at the nature of their work. In 2010, the equivalent Seanad Committee was asked following a complaint to inquire into expenses claimed by Senator Ivor Callely but the Senator decided to challenge the Committee's procedures in the courts, a significant development in terms of constitutional separation of powers.

SIPO: lacunae

One of the most conspicuous gaps in the remit of the SIPO is that it does not extend to political lobbyists. Several of the quasi-judicial tribunals have featured lobbyists quite prominently, particularly the Flood Tribunal where former Fianna Fáil press officer, Frank Dunlop, admitted bribing local councillors on behalf of property developers. Yet this sector remains largely unregulated. Neither does the SIPO have any role in relation to regulating local election spending, even though limits were introduced by statute for the first time in 2009 and it has the ability to investigate breaches of relevant legislation by local politicians.

Questions have also been raised over the accuracy of the Register of Members' Interests. Allegations emerged during 2006 that some members of the government had not declared substantial property portfolios in which they had an interest. One of the members, a Minister of State, eventually resigned from his position as a consequence, but the SIPO Commission had no role in this.

One of the most difficult areas for the Commission is that its role as regulator of political competition places it in constant proximity to the jurisdiction of Dáil Éireann in censuring members' misconduct, and the demarcation of their respective jurisdiction is unlikely to become any easier. The Commission tried to expand its powers by asking in its 2004 annual report for the government to allow it to appoint an 'inquiry officer' to investigate issues initiated by the Commission itself. This request was rejected by the Minister for Finance in July 2006. Another opportunity arose for such an office to be created the following year when the Ethics in Public Office (Amendment) Bill, 2007 was introduced, but again the opportunity was not taken. (Despite being passed by the Seanad, this Bill, which sought to provide new limits on the value of gifts which parliamentarians could accept, was never debated in the Dáil and therefore its provisions could not enter into law). Labour Party front bench member Joan Burton TD sought to introduce a new Bill in 2008 to legislate for an inquiry officer, but this Private Member's Bill was never debated. The Commission thus still relies on parties external to it to request an inquiry before it initiates action.

Freedom of Information: redundancy

Just as in the case of Standards in Public Office measures, new provisions to ensure more open availability of official information, and hence improve accountability of decision-making, have had unintended consequences that complicate the Irish accountability regime.

The Freedom of Information Act was due for review after five years in operation. Following re-election in 2002, the Fianna Fáil/Progressive Democrat government decided to amend it and established an ad hoc committee of five senior civil servants to consider revising certain clauses in the original Act. The government asserted that it was amending the Act in light of experience gained since its introduction to reduce the considerable financial and human resource cost to the civil service involved in meeting the large numbers of requests. But many suspected more defensive and politically motivated reasons for change, particularly when the Government introduced new legislative proposals without consultation with the Information Commissioner or public-interest users of the legislation such as journalists and academics. The amending legislation moved quickly through both Houses of the Oireachtas, causing great consternation in the media and on the opposition benches.

The principal amendments to the Act included:

- Extension of the period after which public could access government records from 5 to 10 years.

- Extension of the type and number of official documents to which the original Act could not apply.
- Protection from the scope of FOI Act for parliamentary briefing records, including documents relating to parliamentary questions.
- Introduction of fees for all FOI requests.

The amendments substantially extended the scope of records that fell under the title of 'government papers', and included sub-committees or other advisory bodies which government reserved the right to specify. The amending Act significantly curtailed the effectiveness of the original Act, and it provoked criticism by the Council of Europe. The Office of the Information Commissioner initiated an investigation into the operation of the Act in light of these changes and found that:

- Overall usage of the Act has fallen by over 50% while requests for non-personal information have declined by 75%.
- The media are now less likely to use the Act and usage by journalists declined steadily throughout 2003.
- Between the first quarter of 2003 and the first quarter of 2004 the number of requests fell by 83% and still continues to decline.
- Other users of the Act, individuals and representative bodies, use the Act far less than before to access information on decisions that affect them directly or indirectly. (Office of the Information Commissioner 2004b)

The Office of the Information Commissioner's annual report for 2003 noted that 'some in the public administration continue to view FOI with suspicion, and hold genuine beliefs that that it can act as an impediment to good government' (Office of the Information Commissioner 2004a: 6). The report also noted that statistics provided to the Office by public bodies regarding FOI usage 'were not always reliable' and that this was related to the fact that there was no statutory obligation on these bodies to compile the relevant information. In 2006, the Information Commissioner told a conference on freedom of information and data protection that there was 'a very urgent question as to whether Freedom of Information legislation is still achieving its purpose' (Hogan 2006: 14).

There is much evidence that FOI has had the opposite effect to that intended and that its original goals, particularly in relation to government decision-making, are now redundant. In his memoir, former Government Press Officer Frank Dunlop noted the tendency of civil servants to write their comments on 'post-it' notes which can be removed from files if necessary (Dunlop 2004: 141). In a similar vein, a former government adviser turned Senator informed an Oireachtas Committee early in 2006 that because of FOI, he had 'come across a situation where a top-level committee which previously had minuted discussions and views of particular departments changed its recording arrangement to simply setting out agreed conclusions' (Wall 2006). The Freedom of Information Commissioner also pointed out at the same meeting that a recent report on clinical malpractice had recommended that the Department of Health protect clinical governance records and risk-management clinical incident reports from the application of the FOI Act. It was argued that unless these documents were outside the scope of the Act, they were unlikely to be created at all, and opportunities for learning from mistakes would be lost (Wall 2006).

Freedom of Information: incoherence

Traditionally, one of the main routes for the parliamentary opposition to inquire into the activities of government was through the use of parliamentary questions (PQs) to members of the government. The relationship between PQs and FOI requests has not received much scholarly attention in spite of their common purpose of providing access to information on the administrative apparatus of state. As Zimmerman points out, the legislation breaches the 'corporation sole' doctrine which places each minister as solely responsible for his or her department (Zimmerman 2001: 79). Multiple routes for accessing information on the activities of the state bureaucracy can present resource challenges for public servants, and risks duplication of effort in retrieving some kinds of information. Many TDs, from both government and opposition parties, now use FOI requests instead of PQs to find out information on behalf of constituents. Though not originally designed to play any role in party political discourse, opposition parties also use the legislation to investigate aspects of policy process and to challenge government, in a manner similar to the use made of PQs. This practice is unlikely to encourage governments to extend the range and scope of FOI provisions in future legislation.

Freedom of Information: lacunae

Perhaps one of the most glaring inadequacies of the FOI legislation is its incomplete coverage of the public service. As MacCarthaigh and Scott identify, a significant number of public bodies engaged in public services or exercising public authority are not subject to FOI legislation (MacCarthaigh and Scott 2009). Gaps in coverage show little consistency, and the appearance of arbitrariness brings the credibility of the legislation into question. Annual reports of the Office of the Information Commissioner regularly call for its remit to be extended. In July 2006, the Joint Oireachtas Committee on Finance and the Public Service was asked to consider recommendations from the Information Commissioner that almost 50 non-disclosure provisions should be made subject to the Freedom of Information Act. However, the government majority voted against the proposals. It remains the case that many areas of the public service, including the police service, remain outside the remit of the Information Commissioner.

Conclusion

A defining feature of governance in Ireland over the last two decades has been the fragmentation of the public service due to outsourcing, privatization and functional delegation; this is consistent with international trends (Verhoest, Bouckaert and Peters 2007). Functional and structural disaggregation creates new problems of policy coordination in its turn, prompting governments to initiate joined-up or 'whole of government' approaches to reconnecting organizationally disparate but functionally related parts of the public service (Christensen et al. 2007). This implies that an ever-greater degree of shared accountability will be required. Accountability for the newly complex political and administrative system has expanded beyond the parliamentary arena, and a variety of new oversight and scrutiny mechanisms have been created to try to match the range of activities undertaken in the name of public authority. But the complex overlay of responsibilities brings new problems in its turn, the extent of which is only beginning to be understood.

In many European countries, these issues do not become problematic, because the legislature exercise a strong role, and new accountability mechanisms are subordinate to the democratically elected deliberate forum through which overlapping oversight jurisdictions are reconciled. But the Irish system of parliamentary accountability has traditionally been weak, and the legislature has few formal constraining powers in relation to the executive (Lane and Ersson 1999: 236). Adding new layers of accountability monitoring generates new problems without addressing the fundamental institutional weaknesses that make them necessary in the first place. Many of the new accountability institutions are designed to tackle the immediate symptoms rather than the cause of malpractice in both political and administrative practice. The cases analysed here, the Standards of Public Office Commission and Office of the Freedom of Information Commissioner, undoubtedly play an important role in providing more public information on the activities of political and administrative actors and institutions. But these functions cannot be divorced from the ultimate accountability of those same actors and institutions to the authority of democratically elected institutions.

This is no simple matter to remedy though. The wider social and political environment changes rapidly, and democracy functions in new ways accordingly. Distrust of government and disaffection from politics more generally is widespread, and parties' capacity to engage with their electorate is coming into question across the developed world (Mair 2009). The demand for intensified accountability can be understood as part of a rising trend toward a politics of 'surveillance' (Rosanvallon 2008). Where the institutionalization of accountability-seeking stems from deep mistrust of those in authority, it seeks to minimize the scope for discretion, personal or professional ethics, and value-based approaches to responsibility, and to replace these with formal compliance, audit and reporting requirements. Quality of outcome risks being replaced by a preoccupation with measurable processes.

Parliamentary accountability remains fundamental to the institutional protections available in democracies. But we may need to reformulate our understanding of parliamentary accountability to recognise the polycentric nature of public accountability and the negative externalities that can arise with overlapping jurisdictions. Clarifying accountability requirements requires a stronger sense of the hierarchy of practices in which parliamentary accountability must provide a focal point. Ultimate responsibility for managing networks of accountability effectively rests with democratic legislatures. Unless the oversight of policy choices and administrative practices is strongly linked back to a democratic deliberative capacity, problems of redundancy, incoherence and lacunae are bound to proliferate. The cost of permitting this is the further erosion of trust in government impartiality, and a loss of legitimacy for public authority (Peters and Pierre 2006: 216; Rothstein and Teorell 2008).

Despite its many failings and persistent criticism, the system of parliamentary accountability in Ireland must remain key to the legitimate functioning of the political and administrative systems. New conceptions of accountable governance should not view the legislature as peripheral to the decision-making process, but rather as an integral part of it. As demonstrated in the case studies used here, new institutional configurations raise difficulties if not adequately coordinated with existing systems. Democracy is impoverished if new networks of governance come to supplant democratic channels for effective decision-making (Papadopoulos 2003: 493). The role of core accountability structures must be rethought to improve the quality of democratic governance.

Notes

1 In 2004, the Houses of the Oireachtas assumed control of their own budget for the Department of Finance. Monies are now paid over in three-year envelopes and it is largely at the discretion of the Houses as to how that money is to be spent. The funding allowed for considerable augmentation of the parliamentary research and assistance services available to members.

2 Defined neatly by Pollitt et al., 2001 as 'an organisation that stands at arm's length from its parent ministry or ministries and carries out public functions'.

3 Since 2007, the Office of the Information Commissioner has also been assigned the role of Commissioner for Environmental Information, a forum for appeals by members of the public concerning environmental information held by public bodies.

Bibliography

Behn, Robert. 2001. *Rethinking Democratic Accountability*. Washington DC: Brookings Institution Press.

Bovens, Mark. 1998. *The Quest for Responsibility: Accountability and Citizenship in Complex Organisations*. Cambridge: Cambridge University Press.

Bovens, Mark. 2007. Analysing and Assessing Accountability: A Conceptual Framework. *European Law Journal* 13 (4): 447–68.

Bovens, Mark. 2010. Two Concepts of Accountability: Accountability as a Virtue and as a Mechanism. *West European Politics* 33 (5): 946–67.

Christensen, Tom, Amund Lie, and Per Laegreid. 2007. Still Fragmented Government or Reassertion of the Centre? In *Transcending New Public Management: The Transformation of Public Sector Reform*, edited by Tom Christensen and Per Laegreid, 17-42. Aldershot: Ashgate.

Clancy, Paula, and Gráinne Murphy. 2006. *Outsourcing Government: Public Bodies and Accountability*. Dublin: TASC at New Ireland.

DeLeon, Linda. 2003. On Acting Responsibly in a Disorderly World: Individual Ethics and Administrative Responsibility. In *Handbook of Public Administration*, edited by B. Guy Peters and Jon Pierre, 569–80 London: Sage.

Döring, Herbert, ed. 1995a. *Parliaments and Majority Rule in Western Europe*. London: Palgrave Macmillan.

Döring, Herbert. 1995b. Time as a Scarce Resource: Government Control of the Agenda. In *Parliaments and Majority Rule in Western Europe*, edited by Herbert Döring 223–46. New York: St. Martin's Press.

Döring, Herbert. 2004. Controversy, Time Constraint, and Restrictive Rules. In *Patterns of Parliamentary Behaviour*, edited by Herbert Döring and Mark Hallerberg, 141-68. Aldershot: Ashgate.

Dowdle, Michael W., ed. 2006. *Public Accountability: Design, Dilemmas and Experiences*. Cambridge: Cambridge University Press.

Dubnick, Melvin. 2005. Accountability and the Promise of Performance: In Search of the Mechanisms. *Public Performance and Management Review* 28 (3): 376–417.

Dunlop, Frank. 2004. *Yes, Taoiseach*. Dublin: Penguin.

Economist Intelligence Unit. 2009. *Review of the Regulatory Environment in Ireland*. Dublin: Department of the Taoiseach. Available at www.betterregulation.ie/eng/EIU_Independent_Report_on_Review_of_the_Economic_Regulatory_Environment.pdf.

Flinders, Matthew. 2001. *The Politics of Accountability in the Modern State*. Aldershot: Ashgate.

Gilardi, Fabrizio. 2008. *Delegation in the Regulatory State: Independent Regulatory Agencies in Western Europe*. Cheltenham: Edward Elgar.

Hodge, Graeme A. and Ken Coghill. 2007. Accountability and the Private State. *Governance* 20 (4): 675–702.

Hogan, Siobhán. 2006. FOI – Still Achieving its Purpose? *Public Affairs Ireland* December: 14-15.

Lane, Jan-Erik and Svante Ersson. 1999. *Politics and Society in Western Europe*. London: Sage.

MacCarthaigh, Muiris. 2005. *Accountability in Irish Parliamentary Politics*. Dublin: Institute of Public Administration.

MacCarthaigh, Muiris. 2007. The Recycling of Political Accountability. In *Recycling the State: The Politics of Adaptation in Ireland*, edited by Katy Hayward and Muiris MacCarthaigh, 201-22. Dublin: Irish Academic Press.

MacCarthaigh, Muiris. 2010. Parliamentary Scrutiny of Departments and Agencies. In *The Houses of the Oireachtas: Parliament in Ireland*, edited by Muiris MacCarthaigh and Maurice Manning, 358-76. Dublin: Institute of Public Administration.

MacCarthaigh, Muiris and Colin Scott. 2009. 'A Thing of Shreds and Patches': Fragmenting Accountability in a Fragmented State. *Working Paper 2009/15*. Dublin: UCD Geary Institute. Available at www.ucd.ie/geary/static/publications/workingpapers/gearywp200915.pdf.

Mair, Peter. 2009. *Representative Versus Responsible Government*. Cologne: Max Planck Institute for the Study of Societies. Available at www.mpifg.de/pu/workpap/wp09-8.pdf.

McGauran, Anne-Marie, Koen Verhoest and Peter C. Humphreys. 2005. *The Corporate Governance of Agencies in Ireland: Non-Commercial National Agencies*. Dublin: Institute of Public Administration.

Mulgan, Richard. 2000. Accountability: An Ever-Expanding Concept? *Public Administration* 78 (3): 555–73.

Mulgan, Richard. 2003. *Holding Power to Account: Accountability in Modern Democracies*. London: Palgrave Macmillan.

OECD. 2008. *Review of the Irish Public Service*. Paris: OECD.

Office of the Information Commissioner. 2004a. *Annual Report for 2003*. Dublin: Office of the Information Commissioner.

Office of the Information Commissioner. 2004b. *Review of the Operation of the Freedom of Information (Amendment) Act, 2003*. Dublin: Office of the Information Commissioner.

PA Consulting. 2002. *Evaluation of the Progress of the Strategic Management Initiative / Delivering Better Government Modernisation Programme*. Dublin: PA Consulting.

Papadopoulos, Yannis. 2003. Cooperative Forms of Governance: Problems of Democratic Accountability in Complex Environments. *European Journal of Political Research* 42 (4): 473–501.

Peters, B. Guy. 1998. Managing Horizontal Government: The Politics of Coordination. *Public Administration* 76 (2): 295–311.

Peters, B. Guy and Jon Pierre. 2006. Governance, Government and the State. In *The State: Theories and Issues*, edited by Colin Hay, Michael Lister and David Marsh, 209–22. Basingstoke: Palgrave Macmillan.

Philp, Mark. 2009. Delimiting Democratic Accountability. *Political Studies* 57 (1): 28–53.

Pollitt, Christopher, K. Bathgate, Janice Caulfield and Amanda Smullen. 2001. Agency Fever? Analysis of an International Policy Fashion. *Journal of Comparative Policy Analysis: Research and Practice* 3: 271–90.

Procter, Giles and Lillian Miles. 2003. *Corporate Governance*. London: Cavendish.

Regling, Klaus and Max Watson. 2010. *A Preliminary Report on the Sources of Ireland's*

Banking Crisis. Dublin: Government Publications Office. Available at www.bank inginquiry.gov.ie/Preliminary%20Report%20into%20Ireland's%20Banking%20Cri sis%2031%20May%202010.pdf.

Rosanvallon, Pierre. 2008. *Counter-Democracy: Politics in an Age of Distrust*. Cambridge: Cambridge University Press.

Rothstein, Bo and Jan Teorell. 2008. What is Quality of Government? A Theory of Impartial Government Institutions. *Governance* 21 (2): 165–90.

Standards in Public Office Commission. 2005. *Standards in Public Office Commission: Annual Report 2004*. Dublin: Standards in Public Office Commission.

Sternberg, E. 2004. *Corporate Governance: Accountability in the Marketplace*. London: Institute of Economic Affairs.

Strøm, Kaare. 2000. Delegation and Accountability in Parliamentary Democracies. *European Journal of Political Research* 37: 261–89.

Strøm, Kaare, Wolfgang C. Müller and Torbjörn Bergman, eds. 2006. *Delegation and Accountability in Parliamentary Democracies*. Oxford: Oxford University Press.

Thatcher, Mark and Alec Stone Sweet, eds. 2004. *The Politics of Delegation*. London: Frank Cass.

Thomas, P.G. 2003. Introduction. In *Handbook of Public Administration*, edited by B. Guy Peters and Jon Pierre, 549–56. London: Sage.

Verhoest, Koen, Geert Bouckaert and B. Guy Peters. 2007. Janus-Faced Reorganisation: Specialisation and Coordination in Four OECD Countries in the Period 1980-2005. *International Review of Administrative Sciences* 73 (3): 327.

Wall, Martin. 2006. FoI needs more scope – O'Reilly. In *The Irish Times*, 17 March. Dublin.

Zimmerman, J.F, 2001. The Irish Ombudsman–Information Commissioner. *Administration* 49 (1): 78–102.

3

Adaptive governance: the art of party politics in contemporary Ireland

Seán McGraw

Introduction

Amidst unprecedented social and economic change, Ireland's political parties have demonstrated an unusual aptitude for generating successful strategies to manage the electoral arena. Few developed countries have experienced the depth of social and economic transformation experienced by Ireland from the late 1980s onwards, when it was catapulted within a span of less than a generation from one of the poorest to one of the wealthiest countries in Europe. In less than two decades, Ireland witnessed intense modernization, a re-structuring of its economy, the marginalization of the once dominant Catholic Church, a reversal of its historic out-migration patterns, and increased urbanization, to name only some of the more salient changes.

These rapid transformations have posed profound challenges to Irish society, relating to changes in family structure, women in the workforce, childcare and education costs, the legalization of divorce, and social benefits for non-traditional families. Furthermore, these large-scale shifts have placed new demands on the state in terms of infrastructure, social welfare and the inclusion of new groups and non-nationals into Irish society.

Ireland represents a case where the social realities that defined its social and political cleavage structure from the very beginning of electoral politics have virtually disappeared. The collective identities of key social groups and political parties have mutated, shared interests have dissipated, and the strategic social actors organizing and reproducing these social divisions have experienced significant erosion. The founding nationalist cleavage has waned as broad consensus among voters and parties toward Northern Ireland has muted and re-shuffled the intractable differences between the original warring parties. Increasingly distant and vague civil war identities have little purchase on the younger generations of voters. The galvanizing collective experience that once united Ireland against its colonial occupier, and then split the main Irish political party, Sinn Féin, into opposing sides of a bitter civil war, has also sundered, ushering in a post-nationalist phase. Furthermore, in an earlier era, an all-pervasive cultural Catholicism and its attendant beliefs and practices provided strong cultural bonding that undergirded Irish identity. The travails experienced by the Church in recent decades have eroded yet another key ingredient of national identity. Ireland's previously insulated and largely sedate agrarian society has metamorphosed within one generation into a highly developed, post-industrial European society.

The salience of Ireland's historic civil war cleavage long ago dwindled into merely symbolic significance. But it left its residue in the form of a binary divide between Fianna Fáil and Fine Gael, otherwise close to one another in policy terms, as potentially leading parties within any conceivable coalition government. The absence of other competing social and cultural cleavages presents Irish parties with a potentially fluid and contentious political arena, as they seek to channel and represent society's interests.

We might well have expected that far-reaching social change would provide a rich context for the emergence of new political issues, cleavages and successful challenger parties to alter the party system.[1] But this has not been the case. It is true that elections have become more sharply contested in an era of declining party attachment, increasing numbers of floating voters and a more heterogeneous set of values among citizens. Yet the three traditional political parties in Ireland have successfully maintained their overall electoral predominance (Mair 1987; Marsh, Sinnott, Garry and Kennedy 2008; Sinnott 1995).

This chapter seeks to examine the question of how Irish parties have adapted to these new challenges, and to explore the implications for governance of strong continuities in the profile of the party system. The pace and scope of change affecting virtually every aspect of Irish life raises critical questions about the capacity of parties to play an effective mediating role between the state and society, and just how they articulate these relationships. The set of institutional responses by parties to these challenges, in turn, holds important consequences for the quality and character of governance in Ireland.

The representative and institutional functions of political parties

Philippe Schmitter has made a useful distinction between the 'representative' and 'institutional' functions of parties. The representative function of parties includes aggregating interests and values within society, providing symbolic identities and a stable set of political goals, and structuring electoral competition. The institutional function of parties involves gaining office and filling various roles within legislative and executive offices (Schmitter 2001: 67–89). In this latter capacity, parties are critical actors for ensuring the state's ability to provide the elements of effective democratic governance, which include high quality democratic practice, the protection of citizen rights, economic growth and effective remedy of serious social problems (Mainwaring and Scully 2009).

Ireland's established parties successfully provide symbolic identities and structure electoral competition – essential elements of their representative function – but they have been less successful in articulating long-term political goals. Nor have they been particularly successful in aggregating effectively a cohesive set of longer-term interests and policies. Instead, Irish parties have continued to rely heavily on carrying out their representation function by depending on long-standing practices of local constituency service, paying less attention to longer-term national policy goals.

However, as we shall see, Ireland's established parties have succeeded electorally not only because of the myriad ways they have developed to carry out their representative function, especially at the local level, but also as a result of how they perform their institutional functions. This chapter will underscore the novel ways in which Irish parties have combined representational and institutional functions. In addition to their well-oiled attention to local constituency service, Irish parties have employed, and even in some cases invented, state institutions and have brought to the table a broad set of actors in civil society to enhance governance. How Irish parties have managed critically important policy domains such as economic growth and serious social problems has surely influenced their electoral fortunes, but the practices of governance they have adopted, because of the balance of representational and institutional functions they have employed, have not always resulted in the most effective or coherent longer-term policy outcomes.

Recent scholarship on political parties suggests that a rift is developing between the representative and institutional (or governing) functions of parties, a rift, it is argued, that has had deleterious consequences for the quality of democracy in some advanced industrial democracies (Mair 2005, 2009). Parties, it is argued, have become less effective in their representative role and have come to rely increasingly on the state for their survival. Therefore, it is further argued, parties have become less adept at forging strong linkages to networks within civil society (Krouwel 2006: 251–2, 258–61). In the lexicon of Katz and Mair, they have become 'cartel parties' (Katz and Mair 1995). These scholars argue that increasing reliance upon institutional rather than representative functions can lead to a diminished capacity to mobilize support among the electorate and ultimately can undermine the quality and legitimacy of democracy itself over the medium and longer term (Mair 2005; Schmitter 2001).

Political parties across advanced industrial democracies face challenges very similar to those faced by Irish parties as they seek to deal with underlying structural changes in society, dealignment, declining party identities and changes in value orientation (Dalton and Wattenberg 2000; Gunther, Montero and Linz 2002; Mair, Muller and Plasser 2004: 1–7, 264–74). Like many other European parties, Irish parties have attempted to deal with these challenges by adapting strategically in three different arenas: the organizational arena, the ideological arena and the institutional arena (Mair et al. 2004: 10–14). The most common organizational adaptations include increased professionalization and centralization, more stringent candidate selection criteria, outreach to targeted social groups and greater reliance on market research and financial support to attract voters. Ideologically, successful parties have become proficient at shifting programmatic positions and policies in order to respond opportunistically to changes in society and to offset the appeals of challenger parties and independents (McGraw 2009). Other successful ideological strategies employed by parties have included deflecting unwanted issues that emerge through party competition and, when unwanted issues are inescapable, adopting positions similar to competing parties, thereby creating the appearance of cross-party consensus (Mair 1997). Finally, parties across Europe have also relied on institutional measures such as increasing state financing and altering electoral rules in order to enhance their electoral prospects within an increasingly combative electoral context.

While Irish parties have also sought to adapt along these three dimensions, the specific ways in which they have done so illustrates an unusual blend of representative and institutional functions. Irish parties appear to part company in significant ways from the general tendencies that predominate in other European countries. Specifically, Irish parties are unusual in the degree to which they emphasize local constituency service. This trend persists even at the expense of the parties' own policy-aggregating capabilities, and can seriously undermine aspirations to carry out their representational function, especially as it pertains to a stable set of long-term policy goals. At the same time, however, the institutional strategies Irish parties have adopted have brought a wide variety of social actors into the policy-making process, especially when addressing controversial and complex issues.

The ways in which Irish parties have responded by resorting to measures within the institutional arena are particularly striking. In addition to turning to the state for increased funding, Ireland's main parties have benefited from a series of 'institutionalized issue displacements' that have had the result of insulating them from some of the most pressing challenges confronting the nation during a period of unprecedented change (McGraw 2008). When faced with potentially divisive issues, governments have frequently responded by managing the issue in an alternative political arena, or creating a new body to which the issue can be delegated. For example, referenda have arguably served this purpose. So too have Tribunals of Inquiry, new state agencies, and even perhaps social partnership institutions. All the major parties have mastered the art of deploying these institutions as instruments through which they can re-shape the terms of electoral competition and thus ensure their own longer-term electoral interests. Irish parties have become quite adept at removing themselves from a series of contentious issues, thereby greatly reducing the range of issues that parties – especially challenger parties – can use to mobilize electoral support.

At the very moment when new issues threaten to reshuffle the electoral market, the established parties deploy state institutions to constrain them. The result has been to narrow the electoral market, and to deliberately prevent new and potentially polarizing issues from reshaping existing electoral alignments. Critical issues concerning the economy, the EU, Northern Ireland, religion and morality, corruption and immigration have been displaced, side-stepped or relegated to these other institutional fora. The Irish National Election Study found four critical dimensions in Irish electoral competition: religious/conservative versus secular/liberal, strong versus moderate nationalism, pro- versus anti-environmentalism, and pro- versus anti-European integration. These do not fit into a neat left–right pattern of party competition on socio-economic issues.

> Instead what emerge are two principal dimensions, one relating to the role of government and markets and the other to attitudes regarding economic equality and the distribution of economic resources. Left–right self-placement is unrelated to either of these dimensions, being instead (weakly) related to the conservative versus liberal dimension. (Marsh et al. 2008: 42)

Highly contentious issues are like Sherlock Holmes's 'dogs that did not bark' – they do not become the stuff of electoral competition. Instead, institutional arrangements have generally kept contentious issues outside of the electoral arena. This makes it easier for the parties to reinforce long-established patterns of partisan politics. Electoral stability is prioritized over giving voice to newly contentious issues.

Why have these strategies worked in Ireland?

To understand why strategies employed by Ireland's traditional parties have successfully contributed to preserving their electoral predominance, and why it matters for governance, I examine three crucial factors in this section: 1) the partisan legacies of the Irish Civil War; 2) the role of the PR-STV electoral system; 3) the underlying logic of collusion guiding the actions of the established parties. I conclude in the final section of the chapter with an analysis of the somewhat unique combination of representational and institutional functions of Irish parties and how their confluence might shape patterns of governance in Ireland.

The party legacy of the civil war

Bitter divisions resulting from the civil war crystallized into two large catch-all parties, Fianna Fáil and Fine Gael, whose origins in nationalist rather than primarily socio-economic conflict endowed them with high levels of ideological flexibility. This enhanced their capacity over the longer term to adapt opportunistically to thorny issues confronting an evolving Irish society. Taking specific stands on controversial issues risked igniting troublesome internal party divisions. The cross-class character of the social bases of Ireland's parties permitted them to eschew electoral appeals that could expose them to unwanted electoral risk (McGraw 2009; Whyte 1974: 619–51). Instead of mobilizing voters on the basis of the politics of contention, the established parties have relied on extensive networks of personal, family and organizational ties to secure their vote. Thus parties represent the interests of society in ways that focus more on the tangible interests of individuals and specific geographic areas than they do on the interests of identifiable social groups or national issues. And what is more, the established parties have persistently found effective ways to satisfy party loyalists. By serving localist and partisan interests, the established parties have been responsive to evolving social needs, but not always in ways that were concerned about the longer-term impact of policy decisions.

The PR-STV electoral system

Ireland's Proportional Representation-Single Transferable Vote (PR-STV) electoral system creates a distinctive mixture of highly competitive, locally driven elections that encourage clientelist relationships, alongside relatively strong and stable party competition at the national level (Farrell 2001; Gallagher and Mitchell 2005; Sinnott 2005). The PR-STV system invites voters to weigh separately the relative merits of candidates and their parties, as well as to weigh independently the appropriate balance between the local and national issues in electoral campaigns. The PR-STV electoral formula tends to mute strong differences in the stance taken by political parties and to reinforce the catch-all character of the major parties. In order to be successful, candidates must appeal not only to core supporters and the undecided, but they must also position themselves to attract vital lower preference votes from supporters of all parties (Gallagher and Mitchell 2005: 523).

Irish voters usually favour one party more than the others, but a majority of voters cast their votes for candidates from more than one party. In the 1989 election, for example, 65 per cent of voters voted for more than one party. In 2002, most individuals voted for candidates from two (34 per cent) or three (28 per cent) parties (Marsh et al. 2008: 20). As a result, only a minority of candidates in each general election is elected on first preference votes alone, highlighting the importance of broadening one's appeal sufficiently to attract these critical lower preference votes. In fact, only 19 per cent (32 out of 166) of elected TDs in the 2007 election were elected on the first counting iteration (the 'first count') and did not need to rely on transfers from other candidates. The overwhelming majority of candidates, 81 per cent, required transfers to get elected (Collins 2007).

The PR-STV system also encourages intra-party competition. Given that the first candidate from a party to get eliminated generally transfers their lower preference votes to their party colleague, there is fierce competition within political parties to remain ahead of one's party colleagues throughout the early counts.

This dynamic, combined with a political culture that privileges a high level of constituency service, as Irish parliamentarians are expected by voters to garner distributive benefits for their constituency, contributes further towards reinforcing the pre-eminence of individual candidates and local interests over and above more ideologically driven politics.[2]

In proportional representation systems, smaller niche parties can often take advantage of contentious issues to enhance their electoral appeal. However, Ireland's idiosyncratic electoral system, and the ways in which the major parties have managed competition within it, has undermined the ability of challenger parties to elbow their way into the electoral market. This is not to say that it is uncommon for independents and candidates from small parties to get elected (Weeks 2009). Challenger parties and independents have consistently surfaced at key moments when growing disquiet emerges that the established parties are no longer adequately addressing the pivotal issues. Yet, perhaps curiously, challenger parties have not been able to capitalize electorally over the longer term.

Whereas many PR-list systems allow niche parties that gain a certain percentage of votes nationally to win seats, the PR-STV system in Ireland requires candidates to secure sufficient support within a given local constituency to be elected. Given that most successful candidates in the 2007 election relied on lower preference votes, and a majority of candidates were elected by the fourth count, there exists a strong incentive for challenger parties to moderate their ideological appeals in order to attract lower preference votes from competing parties' supporters. Evidence from manifesto data analysis and a study of the 2007 election campaign confirms these moderating trends (McGraw 2009). In this sense, the mobilizing capacity of potentially controversial issues is muted by the incentives of the electoral system, except in rare instances where high concentrations of supporters for such causes exist within specific local constituencies.

Furthermore, because Ireland's established parties enjoy flexibility to shift their ideological positions to co-opt more popular stances, major parties often cannibalize the positions of challenger parties, leaving them orphaned. And since the PR-STV system further reinforces local politics, its effects redouble the advantage of the traditional parties, whose highly elaborate networks and access to patronage dwarfs that of the challenger parties. Time after time, the established parties, Fianna Fáil in particular, have been successful in thwarting challenger parties from 'owning' issues that are most salient among the broader electorate. And as Fianna Fáil successfully co-opts these issues, they induce the other established parties to do the same, and to adopt copycat positions on these issues. Parties in general will seek to avoid contentious issues where possible as a means of lowering their salience, but taking a position is sometimes necessary given the demands of the electorate (Meguid 2005). Once a challenger party adopts a position on a particular issue, a larger or governing party can choose either to adopt a similar position, preventing a niche party from owning the issue, or it can assume an adversarial position that directly confronts the smaller party. If the incumbent or established party is able to undermine the perceived relevance of an issue connected to niche parties, or to raise questions about the distinctiveness and credibility of the niche party on that dimension, the challenger is likely to lose votes, but if the larger party or parties adopt an adversarial position, the niche party tends to gain in both credibility and vote share. The capacity of the established parties to shift programmatic positions in order to absorb the more successful policies of the challenger parties has, over the longer term, undermined even the most promising of initial challengers.

The combination of shifting party appeals on the one hand, and the workings of the electoral system on the other, can pre-empt contentious issues becoming a threat to the electoral hegemony of the established parties. Ireland's established parties have customarily returned the focus of electoral competition to the delivery of local goods where they have proven organizational and institutional advantages. The fateful Irish electoral dilemma in which challenger parties find themselves, which has been described as the 'cycle of ideological competition', relentlessly squeezes challenger parties out over the longer term (McGraw 2009).

Two of the most successful recent challenger parties, the Workers' Party and the Progressive Democrats, emerged and then disappeared since the 1980s. Both sought to shift party competition away from traditional nationalist politics toward more class-based politics – one from the left, the other from the right. Ironically, these parties may have won the day in that left-leaning policies were incorporated by party platforms in the 1980s and right-leaning policies were adopted by all the parties by the 2000s. However, theirs was a pyrrhic victory: their initial successes only invited the established parties to co-opt their policies and once again to preserve their overall hold on the electoral market. Indeed, the Workers' Party, having changed to Democratic Left as a result of a split in the party in 1992, joined the Labour Party in 1999. The Progressive Democrats, in contrast, dwindled at the polls and wound up their party in 2008.

A final way in which the electoral system constrains party competition concerns the dynamics of coalition formation. All parties are now eligible coalition partners with one or other of the two major parties, effectively lowering the incentives for all parties to adopt more extreme positions. As we have already seen, advancing more radical positions can alienate potential voters (and their crucial lower preference votes), but it can also undermine a party's ability to form a governing coalition with other parties after the election. While challenger parties have performed a pivotal role in joining governing coalitions, ultimately it is the established parties which have benefited more significantly from these coalitional dynamics. Smaller parties risk losing their identity in the larger coalition, exposing themselves to co-optation by the established parties which are always the senior partners within the coalition.

The narrowing of the electoral arena: tacit collusion among the established parties

Irish elections do not lack strong, often vicious, inter- and intra-party competition. However, the narrowing of the electoral arena resulting from parties' ability to remove, avoid, and park controversial and complex issues implies a tacit collusion on the part of established parties to constrain ideological debate during elections as a means of preserving their predominance within the party system. 'Collusion' is defined here as an agreement between two or more individuals or groups, especially ostensible opponents, to act to the prejudice of a third party (*Shorter Oxford English Dictionary* 2002). This does not mean that the leaders of Ireland's main parties have privately met to discuss their electoral strategies, but rather that their cumulative actions have served to constrain ideological debate at a time when Ireland's rapidly changing society has altered Ireland's once homogeneous society in ways that could have kindled more diverse ideological debates. Therefore the vicious competition that does occur eventually revolves around a more constrained set of issues, leaving national parties fighting over arcane coalitional possibilities, and local candidates distinguishing themselves by how well they represent the local constituency. In effect, the multiple goals that each individual candidate has, including re-election, influence within parliament and good public policy, get subordinated to the proximate goal of getting elected (Mayhew 2004: 16). The following examples reveal how competition at the national and local levels is shaped by this tacit collusion among the established parties.

Consider the national level. Institutionally, Ireland is similar to the Westminster system whereby the combination of a strong executive and a weak parliament ensures that government control of the decision-making process is virtually uncontested (MacCarthaigh 2005: 292). Ireland's executive dominance and weak opposition in parliament holds several implications for Irish party competition, and the ability of candidates to fulfil the aforementioned three primary goals (re-election, parliamentary influence and good policy). First, the weakness of challenger parties means that, if they wish to shape policy, they must cosy up to the larger parties. The only realistic option available to policy-driven challenger candidates and parties is to join a governing coalition. As we have repeatedly seen in the Irish case – in the 1940s and 1950s, as well as in the period since 1989 – challenger parties have played a pivotal role in several coalitions. However, coalitional politics are a double-edged sword. The unintended consequence for participating in a governing coalition for challenger parties is the co-option of their policies with little or no credit among the electorate – and even electoral death over the medium term in several cases. In fact, smaller parties have generally suffered disproportionately from dissatisfaction with the government in subsequent elections.

This underlying coalitional dynamic can shape the behaviour of the larger parties as well. For example, their inability to affect policy when in opposition has been one of the primary motivations driving Fine Gael and Labour into regular coalitions with one another as they have chosen to form coalitions more out of a desire to oppose Fianna Fáil than from any shared vision for Irish society. In fact, despite sharing similar programmatic positions during the late 1960s and 1970s, each of these parties has actually exhibited more programmatic similarities with Fianna Fáil than they have with each other for much of their existence (McGraw 2009). Nevertheless, prior to each general election both Fine Gael and Labour must make a decision as to whether they should compete as part of an electoral coalition with one another or campaign independently so as to keep post-election options open; and in the case of Labour, to serve as the kingmaker in a potential alternative coalition. A tension exists between these parties' policy-seeking and office-seeking aspirations. Only once, in 1973, did they agree to a pre-election pact, and explicitly asked voters to transfer preferences across each other's candidates. Without any significant increase in vote share, this resulted in a significant boost in seat share. Both parties are more typically careful to guard their distinctive identities in campaigns. This tendency is strengthened by the openness of Fianna Fáil to coalition membership since 1989, because Labour's coalition options are correspondingly broadened, in principle at least.

The effects of coalitional dynamics within the Irish party system are extremely important. Despite a seemingly compressed ideological spectrum along which voters identify Irish parties, there are nonetheless differences among the parties in principle (Mair 1987). Therefore, a decision to enter a coalition implies that both Fine Gael and Labour could have to moderate certain policy positions. The incentive to coalesce also encourages parties to think about what will be necessary in order to implement their policy initiatives once in government and this too can have a moderating impact. So the decision to enter a coalition can come at considerable cost. On the other hand, Labour's go-it-alone strategy has proven only marginally successful in terms of eclipsing Fine Gael as the second largest party or in terms of implementing its top policy priorities. Labour's reluctance to enter into a governing coalition with Fianna Fáil, despite sharing more in common with Fianna Fáil on a number of issues, is due to an inherited distrust accumulated as a result of long-standing patterns of oppositional politics, and this has constrained Labour coalition choices.[3]

These coalition dynamics ultimately favour the continued predominance of Fianna Fáil and Fine Gael. Historically, given the levels of electoral support enjoyed by the parties, one of these two main parties must form part of any viable governing coalition. It is squarely in the interests of Fianna Fáil and Fine Gael to maintain this coalitional logic despite the declining salience of the civil war cleavage and its attendant identities, especially given the fact that they are appealing to very similar demographics.

The 'unbridgeable' chasm between Fianna Fáil and Fine Gael affects virtually every aspect of party competition in Ireland. It allows Fianna Fáil and Fine Gael to mobilize their core support base by appealing to cultural differences between these otherwise very similar centrist, catch-all parties. In adopting often very similar policy programs, these two parties force the smaller parties to gravitate towards the centre in order to gain lower preference votes. By removing contentious policy issues from the electoral arena, these parties prevent challenger parties from gaining ownership over new issues in ways that might destabilize competitive dynamics. In rejecting a grand coalition, they preserve their role in the system and ensure that electoral competition will be more about the 'horse race' and various coalition possibilities rather than around substantive policy differences. Finally, maintaining this division ultimately reinforces the focus on the local delivery of goods to constituents. Once again, the established parties possess the advantage.

Consider how the parties have addressed allegations of inappropriate relations between politicians and the private sector. Incontrovertible and widely publicized evidence of improper relationships exists in Ireland, and Irish citizens are increasingly concerned about it. It is not surprising that the traditional parties would try to defuse the issue through extra-parliamentary means, in this case tribunals. But why did their strategy work? Presumably opposition parties have more to gain from pointing out official corruption, even though as a valence issue all parties would be anti-corruption. Unsurprisingly, Fine Gael emphasized the issue of corruption most when they were lowest in the polls and after suffering their worst electoral defeats (e.g. in the late 1950s and after the 2002 general election), and least when they were experiencing higher levels of popular support in public opinion polls and elections (Byrne 2012). The issue has proven an effective tool in mobilizing core support against Fianna Fáil, the primary target of several corruption investigations. At the same time, however, there is a fine line between corruption and patronage, and Fine Gael and other parties are cautious about undermining a central tenet of the Irish political system: once in government, they too will be expected to deliver the goods to their local constituencies and support bases. Irish public opinion punishes politicians lining their own pockets, but there is latent public support for politicians who turn favours as a means of creating opportunities for the local constituency. Indeed, several TDs with the highest first preference vote totals in 2007 were precisely those who were under scrutiny for benefits they allegedly gained as a result of their official roles in parliament and government, including the then Fianna Fáil Taoiseach Bertie Ahern, fellow Fianna Fáiler Beverly Cooper-Flynn, and the former Fine Gael front-bencher Michael Lowry.

Consider competition at the local constituency level where the effect of the confined ideological debate within the electoral arena results in the persistent focus on delivery of local goods. Again, what matters in Irish politics is activating

local networks and establishing name recognition as the candidate who best
serves local needs. Each candidate must develop a core support base with a
sufficiently broad geographic outreach within the constituency (Carty 1981).

The evidence from Irish electoral constituencies suggests that there is very
little fluctuation within constituencies with respect to votes and the allocation
of seats for the various parties. For example, in Dublin South-East, there tends
to be one successful candidate elected from each of the three largest parties,
with an additional seat open to a candidate from one of the challenger parties
(i.e. Greens, Progressive Democrats (PDs) or Sinn Féin) or potentially a second
Fianna Fáil candidate. In this scenario, the fiercest competition takes place
around gaining the party nomination. This is less about internal policy differences than it is about proving one can build an organization and mobilize support (Interviews with Áine Brady, TD, and Jim O'Callaghan, FF general election
candidate, 2007). Once the nomination is secured, the election itself is also
about mobilizing the candidate's base rather than about differentiating oneself
programmatically from competing party candidates.

When salient policy issues do emerge, candidates within any given constituency generally adopt similar positions, especially when particularistic benefits are
at stake.[4] No candidate can risk allowing another candidate to claim sole credit
for local benefits. This is consistent with the policy convergence observed among
candidates from different parties and suggests why candidates at local level frequently espouse positions at variance with their party at the national level. The
autonomy and flexibility of individual candidates to do whatever is necessary to
preserve their seats – even distancing themselves from their own party's stated
policy positions – can only be partially explained by the incentives of the PR-
STV system. The way parties have been able to remove contentious issues and
include non-party actors in the policy-making process has weakened the salience
of ideological differences, thereby freeing candidates from concerns of experiencing ideological backlash during elections because of their policy positions.

Consider some examples from the 2007 General Election. In Dublin South-
East, the primary 'NIMBY' (not in my back yard) issue in 2007 was the proposed
incinerator in Dublin Bay. Every candidate opposed the incinerator, including
those from the government parties (Fianna Fáil and PDs), which had supported
this project at cabinet level. Chris Andrews (FF) proclaimed that he had written
a letter to the European Parliament urging an end to incineration in Dublin Bay,
while Minister for Justice Michael McDowell (PD) trumpeted his Dáil remarks
in opposition to the project. This is a classic case of politicians prioritizing local
interest and distancing themselves from party policy at the national level – or
of being in government and opposition at the same time, a charge often made
against Fianna Fáil. Given that every candidate opposed the incinerator, the
degree to which each candidate was perceived to oppose the project became decisive. Ironically (as the chapter by Laffan and O'Mahony sets out in greater detail)

John Gormley, Green Party Leader and TD for Dublin South-East, who became Minister for the Environment after the 2007 election, benefited from his vehement opposition to the incinerator during the election campaign, but he had to defend the government position to implement it as a Government Minister. Office-seeking motivations trumped policy-seeking ones in the end.

Kildare North provides another example of how candidates can leverage their local situation to support the party when it suits them, but also to distance themselves when necessary. Michael Fitzpatrick, TD, a self-described 'Fianna Fáil man', is an example of how individual candidates vary their stance on local or party policy, depending on whether that policy will offer specific versus general benefits. Although the Fianna Fáil government had recently announced that there would be only one national children's hospital located in Dublin, Fitzpatrick decried that decision on local radio, arguing that Naas hospital's children's services desperately needed to be enhanced. He defended his position against that of the party:

> I had a personal view on that, not the party view. I believe that we have made great strides in Kildare in updating our county hospital, Naas Hospital, and we are continuing to develop it and need to improve it. The government policy is that we would have one major hospital based in Dublin. My sticking up for Naas is good because someone in the party may see that I have a point here. (Fitzpatrick, Interview, July 2007)[5]

Yet when asked about his policy stance on other policy positions, such as the nurses' strike, he evinced incredulity that one might take a position in opposition to that of the party:

> We are the government party. We will always be supportive of the government line . . . So, I would not think that I should start driving another road for the rest of us to go down rather than the one which the government had. (Fitzpatrick, Interview, July 2007)

These types of comments are commonplace given that candidates seek to maximize both party and individual candidate support. Candidates go with the party only if the expected electoral penalty will not significantly increase their chances of losing the seat. In a highly competitive electoral arena, candidates can ill-afford to lose out on local appeals (Mayhew 2004: xix). The imperative to secure one's own turf in service to the local constituency guides the actions of candidates in Irish elections. This simultaneously reinforces the incentive to avoid contentious and/or extreme positions. Again, what seems natural for candidates to do in order to beat their opponents would not be as feasible without the other politically constraining measures that parties have been able to take. The next section will explore the significance of these practices for how parties exercise their representational and institutional functions.

The Irish blend of representative and institutional functions

The Irish case offers a modified version of the cartel party thesis that highlights the increased reliance of parties on the state. The Irish system also exhibits several characteristics essential for the emergence of cartel parties, including substantial reliance on patronage, for example in the profile of appointments to the boards of state agencies (Clancy, O'Connor and Dillon 2010) and a climate of inter-party cooperation (Krouwel 2006). Parties can use state institutions to displace controversial and potentially electorally de-stabilizing issues. To this must be added the access that governing parties enjoy to the coffers of the state to deliver goods at the local level.

However, in contrast to the model of cartel parties, Irish parties have not abandoned their representative role. Rather, they have employed alternative mechanisms to represent the interests of society in the policy-making process and have continued to be intimately connected to individuals at the local level. And though Irish parties have gained some increased state financing, they do not receive significant state subsidies, one of the most emphasized components of the cartel party thesis.[6]

The capacity to deliver goods and services, so vital for enhancing candidates' electoral appeal at the constituency level, is of upmost importance for voters (Marsh et al. 2008). While an opposition TD can provide indirect access to government officials and the broader state apparatus, only TDs from governing parties benefit from the direct distribution of government largesse to constituencies, groups and individuals. Government grants are highly contingent upon the Taoiseach, Minister of Finance and the minister or junior minister from the relevant department distributing programmes and services (Suiter 2009). Placing party officials in these key government positions helps maintain strong party discipline and, if they deliver, can go a long way to ensuring electoral success.

Ireland's established parties have employed agencies and mechanisms of the state to systematically displace contentious issues, constrain electoral competition, and thereby preserve their own electoral stability. Employing this tactic allows parties to side-step contentious issues without closing off popular debate or denying new parties or actors within civil society a voice within the political system. Challenger parties have been seduced into a particular way of 'doing politics' by focusing on seeking office and on the delivery of goods at the local level to accomplish their goals, revealing subtle but powerful means by which Ireland's established parties shape the political arena. As a result, challenger parties generally find themselves competing on what is primarily Fianna Fáil's chosen ground, where the incumbent party enjoys an advantage. Significant normative concerns regarding the quality of democracy over the longer term emerge as a consequence.

As E.E. Schattschneider argued in his classic work on American politics, the failure of parties to adequately represent the interests of society over time can lead to changes in the party system as political conflict is addressed and resolved in ways that may take shape outside the scope of party articulation (Schattschneider 1960). The experience of other countries suggests that inattention to critical issues latent in civil society can result in an erosion of the democratic regime itself. For example, the eruption of Pim Fortuyn onto the Dutch political scene during the 2000s revealed weaknesses in the mainstream parties' capacity to deal with issues of immigration and social and cultural integration (Kriesi, Grande, Lachat, Dolezal, Bornschier and Frey 2008). The landslide defeat of the Liberal Democratic Party in the 2009 Japanese elections after fifty-five years of nearly uninterrupted single-party governance suggests the rapidity with which dominant parties can decline if they are perceived to be disconnected from burning issues in civil society, and if they come to be explicitly and widely blamed for financial woes and corruption.

It would be an exaggeration to suggest that the Irish political system faces anything like these threats to its stability. At the same time, tough challenges await Ireland's established parties in the wake of the global economic crisis at the end of the first decade of the twentieth century. Fianna Fáil's support plummeted in local elections in 2009 and in opinion polls in 2010 to all-time lows in its 80-year history, due to widespread anger over the party's mismanagement of the Celtic Tiger economy and what was perceived to be its excessively close links to the construction and financial sectors. In both the Irish and the Japanese cases, there is a fine line between attention to selective interests within the policy-making process and maintenance of effective governance. If the gap between localized service delivery and national policy competence grows too great, the dominant party may be in real trouble.

While the established Irish parties have been criticized for their lack of ideological differentiation, several dimensions of Irish politics ensure that society's interests are represented – just not always by parties. This dispersal of roles and functions should not automatically be interpreted as a sign of weakness on the part of political parties. Instead, the decision to relinquish some of their autonomy in both their representational and institutional functions may have actually served to enhance the capacity of the major Irish parties to survive electorally. Consider a few examples.

First, the Irish electoral system incentivizes candidates and parties to create strong local ties and personal networks. Successful candidates are acutely aware of the interests of their constituents. If anything, Irish parliamentarians may be too dependent on their representative function: serving local constituency needs generally trumps programmatic appeals. Yet this in turn holds its own dangers, as it can make it difficult to aggregate interests into coherent policy choices, especially when hard choices have to be made. Politicians appear so focused on local constituency service that they appear unwilling to risk electoral unpopularity to propose longer-term solutions, which can undermine the longer-term policy-making process and effective governance.

Second, the regular use of the referendum privileges the representation of society's interests but does so by constraining the role that parties might play in aggregating and representing interests. The requirement that any amendment be ratified by referendum has meant that Irish voters have had their voices directly heard on a wide array of issues, including contentious moral issues, Northern Ireland, European integration, the electoral system, citizenship and the relationship of the state with the Catholic Church. However, the fact that governments are prevented from using state money to influence the outcome of a referendum, and the established parties' reluctance to use limited resources they desperately need to conduct election campaigns, has meant that the established political parties have consistently sidelined themselves or adopted minimalist positions during referenda. It is striking that no matter how contentious the issue, nor how sharp the polarization within the Irish electorate, the two major Irish parties, Fianna Fáil and Fine Gael, have rarely adopted opposing positions during referenda. Of the three dozen referenda that have taken place in Ireland since 1937, the two major parties have directly opposed each other only three times in four decades (Gallagher 1996; Shu 2003; Sinnott 2002).[7]

On the one hand, this can be seen as a failure by the parties to aggregate interests and to structure electoral competition in ways that offer ideological choices to the electorate. On the other hand, the lack of active leadership from the established parties during referendum campaigns has paved the way for groups within civil society to perform a key mobilizing role, which was especially relevant during the abortion and divorce referenda in the 1980s and 1990s. While opening up of debate to non-party actors may have reduced the autonomy of parties in shaping certain policy outcomes, it also allowed the major parties to avoid damaging internal party divisions on controversial issues, thereby ultimately enhancing their electoral fortunes. The use of referenda in Irish politics also shields the established parties against the danger that challenger parties might mobilize around a potentially winning issue in general election campaigns. It is also an effective way of mitigating the impact that contentious issues can have on society as a whole. In the Netherlands, the use of Royal Commissions serves something of the same function of taking difficult issues off the immediate agenda. This can be an especially valuable recourse when contentious issues are likely to cause tensions between coalition partners (Andeweg and Irwin 2005).

A third aspect of how interests are represented in the Irish context relates to social partnership. There is considerable debate over whether social partnership is making Irish politics more, or less, representative (Baccaro and Simoni 2007; Ó Cinnéide 1999). While more groups have become involved in the process, there is less transparency in parliament as government parties negotiate behind closed doors with business, unions and civil society groups (Dukes, Interview,

February 2007). On the other hand, the inclusion of additional actors within the policy arena provides effective and efficient mechanisms whereby emergent issues for key social groups can be articulated and brought to political attention (O'Donnell and Thomas 2006). The broader agenda and the inclusion of more social actors suggest both a flexible and adaptive governance structure that complements the means by which interests are represented within the political arena (Hardiman 2006). And while the pay deal at the heart of tripartite processes collapsed in late 2009 in the context of employer resistance to cost increases and government implementation of severe budgetary measures in response to crisis, the bias toward consultative and partnership-based processes remained very much in evidence. Overall, this system continues to evolve as parties seek to balance their representational role with effective policy outcomes (Hardiman 2010).

In sum, Ireland represents an unusual mixture of parties maintaining their representational role within the electorate, while at the same time sharing this role with other groups within civil society, ranging from unions and business leaders to single-issue groups. Such inclusiveness within key domains of policy-making has thus far mollified frustration with parties. In the end, the Irish case offers a challenge to normative arguments about how the representational and institutional functions of political parties may be combined. What seems essential is the degree to which citizens have their voices heard and meaningfully included in the governing process (Hirschman 1970). Parties need not be the sole representatives of these interests. The long-term success of Ireland's established parties has been closely linked with their ability to foster consensus via these extra-parliamentary bodies. This ongoing inclusiveness has provided voters with an effective means to express themselves and a vehicle for parties to copper-fasten their role as the principal arbiters of Irish politics.

Conclusion

The Irish case presents a compelling example of how both the representational and institutional functions have been employed by parties to ensure relative political stability in the face of dramatic social and economic change. On the one hand, Irish parties continue to be deeply embedded in civil society, unlike many contemporary European parties. On the other hand, they have adapted to a rapidly evolving society by employing extra-parliamentary bodies to strengthen their institutional function. The use of referenda and the inclusion of a wide array of social groups in social partnership enabled parties to eliminate contentious issues from the electoral arena and to seek to build common ground on difficult issues across all aspects of Irish society.

These developments have helped to preserve Ireland's established parties' predominance in the electoral system. Their contribution to effective governance presents a more mixed picture. Inclusiveness and an ability to generate broad consensus have been critical to ensuring Ireland's political stability. At the same time, however, almost obsessive attention to particularistic issues on the part of parties, and the salience of personality as opposed to policy in electoral choice, has hindered more effective medium- and longer-term policy-making outcomes at the national level. While the established parties have succeeded in preserving their electoral predominance over the long term, they have perhaps done so at the cost of constraining programmatic alternatives that parties might offer on any given policy. In the end, this could have adverse policy-making effects. The challenge for Ireland's parties as they look to the future, especially in the context of the global economic crisis that finally brought the Celtic Tiger era to an end, will be to find ways to build sufficient consent to strong and effective national policies to respond to the critical challenges the country faces in the coming years. They must do so while at the same time re-balancing, and in some cases reinventing, the representational and governance roles parties have played, and which have provided the context of political stability that has served Ireland so well.

Irish parties have been flexible in adapting and combining their representative and institutional functions in novel ways. The increased reliance on state institutions has not closed off public debate or discourse, but rather redirected contention into extra-parliamentary arenas. Strong networks at the local level have ensured that the linkages between politicians and voters continue to be vibrant, and that the representation function of parties at the local level remains robust. Yet the corresponding weaknesses in both representative and institutional functions of parties point toward problems in the quality of governance that are not easily remedied within the contours of the current system.

Notes

1 The Irish party system has fluctuated between periods of two-and-a-half party competition and multi-party competition, with the established parties of Fianna Fáil, Fine Gael and Labour persisting in each period. Therefore, the other, smaller parties are defined as 'challenger parties' in this chapter.

2 Some scholars argue that while STV does ensure intra-party competition, this does not mean that this electoral system requires more constituency work than is expected of members of parliament in other electoral systems: see Gallagher and Komito. 2010. The emphasis on constituency service existed among nineteenth-century Irish MPs in the British parliament and therefore is not necessarily a result of the electoral system. Generally, the most common characteristics of elected TDs are having had a family member who was previously a TD, having served as a local councillor (80 per cent), or being a local personality due to business, sports or entertainment-related activities.

3 The fact that the last two Labour Leaders (Pat Rabbitte and Eamon Gilmore) are part of the Democratic Left wing of Labour has significantly influenced the antipathy toward

Fianna Fáil. Many Labour TDs would not have a problem forming a governing coalition with Fianna Fáil.

4 McGraw includes a detailed case study of the 2007 election and highlights this dynamic within three constituencies: Dublin South-East, Kerry South and Kildare North. See McGraw 2009.

5 For a sense of how things do not change much, see 'What to ask your candidate about health and medical services', *Irish Times*, 19 February 1973. The article suggests that during the 1973 election the 'real question' that needed to be addressed was the status of local hospitals: 'Paradoxically, the answers [candidates] give which are most likely to please many of the local pressure groups, would not always result in an improvement in health care since it is true to say that the preservation of small hospitals, trying to provide modern surgical care, will generally result in a marginally higher morbidity and mortality than would the transfer of patients to larger, although more distant, surgical units.'

6 The emphasis on controlling media requirements is relevant in the Irish case because parties are allotted proportional time on RTÉ, the national television station, based on the percentage of votes received in the previous election. Exceptions have been made in recent years to provide smaller parties with slightly more disproportionate air time in a way that reflects the growing importance of smaller parties in forming governments. The guidelines for proportional attention do not apply to radio and print media.

7 Fianna Fáil and Fine Gael took opposing sides in the 1986 divorce referendum and the 1992 and 2002 abortion referenda.

Bibliography

Andeweg, Rudy B. and Galen A. Irwin. 2005. *Governance and Politics of the Netherlands.* London: Palgrave.

Baccaro, Lucio and Marco Simoni. 2007. Centralized Wage Bargaining and the 'Celtic Tiger' Phenomenon. *Industrial Relations* 46 (3): 426–55.

Byrne, Elaine. 2012. *Political Corruption in Ireland.* Manchester: Manchester University Press.

Carty, R. Kenneth. 1981. *Party and Parish Pump: Electoral Politics in Ireland.* Waterloo, Ont.: Wilfrid Laurier University Press.

Clancy, Paula, Nat O'Connor and Kevin Dillon. 2010. *Mapping the Golden Circle.* Dublin: TASC. Available at www.tascnet.ie/upload/file/MtGC%20ISSU.pdf.

Collins, Stephen, ed. 2007. *The Irish Times Nealon's Guide to the 30th Dail and 23rd Seanad.* Dublin: Gill and Macmillan.

Dalton, Russell J. and Martin P. Wattenberg, eds. 2000. *Parties Without Partisans: Political Change in Advanced Industrial Democracies.* Oxford: Oxford University Press.

Farrell, David. 2001. *Electoral Systems: A Comparative Introduction.* Basingstoke: Palgrave.

Gallagher, Michael. 1996. Ireland: The Referendum as a Conservative Device? In *The Referendum Experience in Europe*, edited by Michael Gallagher and P.V. Uleri, 86–105. New York: St. Martin's Press.

Gallagher, Michael and Lee Komito. 2010. The Constituency Role of Dáil Deputies.

In *Politics in the Republic of Ireland*, edited by John Coakley and Michael Gallagher, 230–62. London: Routledge/PSAI Press.

Gallagher, Michael and Paul Mitchell, eds. 2005. *The Politics of Electoral Systems*. Oxford: Oxford University Press.

Gunther, Richard, Jose Ramon Montero and Juan Linz, eds. 2002. *Political Parties: Old Concepts and New Challenges*. Oxford University Press: Oxford.

Hardiman, Niamh. 2006. Politics and Social Partnership: Flexible Network Governance. *Economic and Social Review* 37 (3): 347–74.

Hardiman, Niamh. 2010. Economic Crisis and Public Sector Reform: Lessons from Ireland Working Paper 2010/13. Dublin: UCD Geary Institute. Available at www.ucd.ie/geary/static/publications/workingpapers/gearywp201013.pdf.

Hirschman, Albert O. 1970. *Exit, Voice, and Loyalty: Responses to Decline in Firms, Organizations and States*. Cambridge, MA: Harvard University Press.

Katz, Richard S. and Peter Mair. 1995. Changing Models of Party Organization and Party Democracy: The Emergence of the Cartel Party. *Party Politics* 1 (1): 5–28.

Kriesi, Hanspeter, Edgar Grande, Romain Lachat, Martin Dolezal, Simon Bornschier and Timotheos Frey. 2008. *West European Politics in the Age of Globalization*. Cambridge: Cambridge University Press.

Krouwel, André. 2006. Party Models. In *The Handbook of Party Politics*, edited by Richard Katz and William Crotty, 349–69. London: Sage.

MacCarthaigh, Muiris. 2005. *Accountability in Irish Parliamentary Politics*. Dublin: Institute of Public Administration.

Mainwaring, Scott and Timothy Scully, eds. 2009. *Democratic Governance in Latin America*. Stanford: Stanford University Press.

Mair, Peter. 1987. *The Changing Irish Party System: Organisation, Ideology and Electoral Competition*. London: Pinter.

Mair, Peter. 1997. Nominations and Reflections: The Periphery-Dominated Centre. *European Journal of Political Research* 31: 63–71.

Mair, Peter. 2005. *Democracy Beyond Parties*. London: Centre for the Study of Democracy.

Mair, Peter. 2009. *Representative Versus Responsible Government*. Cologne: Max Planck Institute for the Study of Societies. Available at www.mpifg.de/pu/workpap/wp09-8.pdf.

Mair, Peter, Wolfgang C. Muller and Fritz Plasser, eds. 2004. *Political Parties and Electoral Change: Party Responses to Electoral Markets*. London: Sage.

Marsh, Michael, Richard Sinnott, John Garry and Fiachra Kennedy, eds. 2008. *The Irish Voter: The Nature of Electoral Competition in the Republic of Ireland*. Manchester: Manchester University Press.

Mayhew, David R. 2004. *Congress: The Electoral Connection*. New Haven: Yale University Press.

McGraw, Seán. 2008. Managing Change: Party Competition in the New Ireland. *Irish Political Studies* 23 (4): 627–48.

McGraw, Seán. 2009. Managing Change: Party Competition in the New Ireland. PhD Thesis, Government Department, Harvard University, Cambridge, MA.

Meguid, Bonnie. 2005. Competition Between Unequals: The Role of Mainstream

Party Strategy in Niche Party Success. *American Political Science Review* 99 (3): 347–59.

O'Donnell, Rory and Damien Thomas. 2006. Social Partnership and the Policy Process. In *Social Policy in Ireland: Principles, Practice and Problems*, edited by Sean Healy and Brigid Reynolds, 117–46. Dublin: The Liffey Press.

Ó Cinnéide, Séamus. 1999. Democracy and the Constitution. *Administration* 46 (4): 41–58.

Schmitter, Philippe. 2001. Parties Are Not What They Once Were. In *Political Parties and Democracy*, edited by Larry Diamond and R. Gunther, 67–89. Baltimore, MD: The Johns Hopkins University Press.

Schattschneider, E.E. 1960. *The Semi-Sovereign People: A Realist's View of Democracy in America*. New York: Reinhart and Winston.

Shu, Min. 2003. Cope with Two-Dimensional Cleavage Structure: Party Politics in Referendums on European Integration. ECPR Workshop Paper. Edinburgh.

Sinnott, Richard. 1995. *Irish Voters Decide: Voting Behaviour in Elections and Referendums Since 1918*. Manchester: Manchester University Press.

Sinnott, Richard. 2002. Cleavages, Parties, and Referendums: Relationships Between Representative and Direct Democracy in the Republic of Ireland. *European Journal of Political Research* 41: 811–26.

Sinnott, Richard. 2005. The Rules of the Electoral Game. In *Politics in the Republic of Ireland*, edited by John Coakley and Michael Gallagher, 105–34. London: Routledge.

Suiter, Jane. 2009. Pork-Barrel Spending in Ireland – Fact or Fiction?, PhD Thesis, Department of Political Science, Trinity College Dublin.

Weeks, Liam. 2009. We Don't Like (to) Party: A Typology of Independents in Irish Political Life, 1922-2007. *Irish Political Studies* 24 (1): 1–27.

Whyte, John H. 1974. Ireland: Politics Without Social Bases. In *Electoral Behaviour: A Comparative Handbook*, edited by Richard Rose, 619–51. New York: The Free Press.

4

Regulatory governance

Jonathan Westrup

Introduction

Perhaps the most significant change to the formal institutions of Irish governance over the past decade has been the establishment of independent regulatory
agencies. These agencies are designed to be independent or non-majoritarian
– they have been delegated specific regulatory powers for which the traditional
hierarchical institutions of government are considered to be inappropriate.[1] They
are significant in terms of governance because of the decision of political actors
to delegate important policy-making powers to agencies outside their immediate control and for the consequent challenge of how to reconcile the apparent
paradox of preserving independence while maintaining accountability to the
political system.

The focus of this chapter is on the evolution of these new regulatory actors
and the gradual emergence of regulatory governance as a distinctive form with its
own pattern of interaction between state and private actors. It argues that regulatory governance has taken time to evolve and that its uneven path can only be
understood by reference to Ireland's existing configuration of institutions and the
corresponding preferences of key actors. In particular, the combination of a high
concentration of executive authority, a corporatist style of policy-making, and a
parliament with little interest in oversight has posed significant challenges to the
emergence of a new regulatory regime. Indeed, the failure of the financial regulatory system to prevent the collapse of the domestic banking system in 2008 asks a
fundamental question about the capability of a regulatory regime to operate within
the constraints of Irish institutions and preferences of the key political actors.

However, an examination of the institutional constraints that confronted the
regulators does serve the purpose of illuminating a wider set of questions about
governance in the Irish political system and the system's ability to adapt to the
demands and preferences of a broader range of both public and private actors.

The initial decision to create regulatory actors was in the Irish case prompted
largely by the demands of EU legislation that prevented the government from
both owning and regulating utilities.[2] The result, particularly in the case of
Telecom – where the state has sold its entire stake – is an obviously important

shift in the role of the state, from owner to regulator. However, the decision to delegate powers to regulators, initially made somewhat reluctantly in the case of the utilities, has proven to be increasingly attractive to political actors, so that regulatory governance has emerged as an increasingly popular institutional choice.

Thus what has emerged in terms of the functions of the state is what Rhodes describes as a 'hollowing out', as the state chooses to divest itself of direct responsibility for a series of regulatory functions (Rhodes 1994). Osborne and Gaebler describe the result of delegation as a shift in the role of the state from 'rowing to steering' (Osborne and Gaebler 1992).

Analytical Framework

As Table 4.1 indicates, a plethora of regulators and agencies with significant regulatory responsibilities have been created over the past fifteen years.[3] The chapter focuses upon three particular cases of regulatory reform: telecoms, energy, and financial markets. The rationale behind the choice of these cases is firstly their importance in a modern economy, meaning that state and private actors can be assumed to have highly developed interests and policy preferences. The second

Table 4.1 Irish regulators

Sector	Agency/regulator	Year created
Accounting	Irish Auditing and Accounting Supervisory Authority (IAASA)	2003
Aviation	Commission for Aviation Regulation	2001
Competition	Competition Authority	1991
Electricity	Commission for Energy Regulation (CER) (originally the Commission for Electricity Regulation)	1999
Environment	Environmental Protection Agency (EPA)	1992
Financial Markets	Irish Financial Services Regulatory Authority*	2002
Food Safety	Food Safety Authority of Ireland	1998
Pharmaceuticals	Irish Medicines Board	1995
Taxis	Commission for Taxi Regulation	2004
Telecommunications	Commission for Communications Regulation (ComReg) (originally Office of the Director of Telecommunications Regulation, ODTR)	1996

Source: compiled by author

* Merged back into the Central Bank in October 2010 to become the Central Bank Commission.

rationale is methodological in that the evolution of these interests and policy preferences can be assessed over time, which allows for process tracing.

In the cases of telecoms and energy, a regulatory regime was created from scratch, whereas in financial regulation, a new single regulator was created that replaced existing actors. The analysis uses a principal–agent framework whereby the principals are the government and the Oireachtas and the agents are the regulators. This approach allows for an identification of the shifting preferences of the key actors over time. It also allows for an analysis of what Kathy Thelen has identified as the need for institutions to maintain and nurture political support if they are to evolve and flourish (Thelen 2004).

History of independent regulators

The concept of an agency with a specific regulatory mandate but separate status from the hierarchical institutions of government was traditionally an American phenomenon that dates back to the end of the nineteenth century (Eisner 2000). As Shipan describes, the initial rationale for an independent regulatory commission came from the 'scientific management school' that argued that to achieve optimal policy outcomes, politics and administration needed to be separated, and that the creation of agencies that were outside both the executive and the legislative branches was the most appropriate means of achieving such an objective (Shipan 2006). The political appeal of these new actors saw the creation of a bundle of agencies during the twentieth century, with a particular peak at the time of the New Deal (Eisner 2000).

The Thatcher government in Britain is credited with being the first government to create regulatory agencies with similar-type powers outside the United States. The need for these new institutional actors followed the Conservative government's decision to privatize previously publicly owned utilities, notably British Telecom and British Gas. Privatization meant that a regulator independent of government was required to oversee the firms, due both to the state's continued ownership of significant stakes but also because of the firms' continued monopoly or at best duopoly status. The paradoxical result was, as Steven Vogel pointed out, that the Conservative government's ambition to deregulate and liberalize utility markets actually resulted in re-regulation and the creation of what became new and powerful regulatory actors (Vogel 1996).

From an Irish perspective, the passing of the Single European Act in 1986, with its objective of a single market by 1992, proved to be particularly significant in the evolution of regulatory policy. The result of the SEA was a swathe of directives across a broad range of policy areas that led to what Mark Thatcher describes as 'a rapid and sustained expansion of regulation in Europe' and the emergence of what Majone has described as the emergence of the EU as a 'regulatory state' (Majone 1996; Thatcher 2002). It was therefore 'top-down'

Europeanization, understood as the mechanisms by which EU policies and directives affect the domestic policies and institutions of member states, that has proven important in explaining the emergence of much of Ireland's regulatory policy (Börzel 2005; Radaelli 2000). The institutional implication of the Europeanization of regulatory policy has depended upon the 'goodness of fit' with member states' existing regulatory architectures (Schmidt 2002). With respect to utility regulation, for the Irish case, like the majority of EU states, it meant the creation of new regulatory agencies with a significant level of independence from the existing hierarchical government structure (Thatcher 2002). However, in the case of financial and other important areas of regulation, the EU has not mandated any particular institutional design or level of independence from government, so member states have had the freedom to implement directives to suit their particular institutional preferences. As a result, Gilardi has found evidence of considerable variation in terms of regulatory design and independence (Gilardi 2002). But the result of the emergence of the EU as a regulatory state is that for Ireland, as for all EU member states, regulation is firmly, in Putnam's terms, a two-level game, played out at both an EU and a domestic level (Putnam 1988). However, it is important to emphasize that the decision to delegate regulatory responsibility is not just a result of Europeanization but reflects other political incentives.

Why independent?

Why do politicians decide to delegate important powers to actors that are beyond their immediate control? There is, not surprisingly, a great deal of academic debate regarding the apparent paradox as to why political actors should voluntarily choose to weaken their powers. Three rationales are pointed to. First is to ensure the credibility of a regulatory decision, also called the credible commitment rationale (Kydland and Prescott 1977; Levy and Spiller 1996). If, it is argued, the market recognizes that regulatory decisions will be overturned due to changes in public opinion or government, the result will be uncertainty and ultimately a less desirable policy outcome. The credible commitment rationale is key to the argument as to why central banks are given autonomy in terms of monetary policy, where it is claimed that the outcome is lower rates of inflation than a monetary policy regime directly influenced by partisan concerns could provide (Cukierman, Webb and Neyapti 1992; Grilli, Masciandaro and Tabellini 1991). The argument also conveniently gives a reason for politicians to tie the hands of future governments by making it difficult for them to overturn existing policies.

The second rationale for why delegation occurs is that it insulates politicians from the fallout of unpopular decisions by shifting the blame to the regulator (Egan 2004; Weaver 1987). By definition, regulators must adjudicate on important policy issues with significant distributional outcomes, so it can be of obvious political advantage for governments to avoid taking responsibility for decisions that could alienate important interest groups and potential voters.

The third rationale is to ensure a high level of expertise in the making of regulatory decisions. It is argued that regulation frequently involves policy issues of high technical complexity that pose significant difficulties for existing government departments due to their lack of sufficient expertise (Majone 1997, 2001). The creation of a regulatory agency therefore allows for the cultivation of such expertise, both in terms of allowing for high levels of staff specialization and in the ability to recruit outside of normal public service guidelines.

How to hold regulatory actors accountable

If there are clear arguments as to why governments should consider delegating powers to regulatory agencies, there is a thriving academic literature analysing how government and legislative actors can ensure agencies remain accountable to the political system. Democratic theory assumes that at a certain level there should be a link between the citizens of a country and its policies. There is also an assumption that in most cases citizens must delegate responsibility to elected politicians to create and enact policies, and that if citizens do not like them, they can choose to vote their elected representatives out of office. The creation of agencies that are, to some degree, outside the control of politicians but responsible for important decisions, obviously serves to weaken further the direct link of delegation. The political challenge is therefore how to minimize the trade-off between the advantages of independent agencies and the apparent threat to the normal process of democratic accountability.

The most widely applied theoretical framework used to analyse this trade-off is that of principal–agent, derived largely from economics of organizations, where the government and the legislature are considered the principals and the regulator is considered the agent (Epstein and O'Halloran 1999; Moe 1984; Weingast and Moran 1983).[4] The principals are assumed to seek to minimize 'agency losses', defined as a situation where agents act contrary to the preferences of the principal, because of 'shirking', where agents act to pursue their own preferences. The degree of independence is shaped therefore by *ex ante* mechanisms such as the legislative mandate that describes the role and objectives of the regulator and by a series of *ex post* mechanisms requiring the regulator to report on its actions to the principals. In terms of *ex post* mechanisms, McCubbins and Schwarz describe how legislative committees can choose between two styles of oversight: 'police patrols' or 'fire alarm'. In the case of police patrol, regulatory oversight is 'centralized, active and direct' and includes legislative hearings and special inquiries, whereas fire alarm is less active and indirect, and encourages citizens to bring agency discretion to the attention of principals (McCubbins and Schwartz 1984).

While the principal–agent framework has limitations – notably in the European context in identifying exactly who are the regulatory principals given the important role of EU institutions – it is a useful lens by which to analyse the incentives of the different actors that make up the domestic regulatory regime and the success or otherwise of the accountability structure.

The Irish context

Before laying out the details of the telecom and electricity cases, it is important to emphasize that prior to the establishment of the regulators – given the state's long-term ownership of both monopolies – there was no explicit regulatory policy or objective. Instead the state had a diverse set of policy preferences that included employment generation and regional development, often at the expense of efficiency and profit (Guiomard 1995). The result was that policy outcomes tended to reflect the interests of producers rather than consumers, and given the importance that state actors placed upon social partnership during the 1990s, challenging the entrenched interests in both firms had proven to be difficult. They also reflected the institutional design of the partnership process, where there was no explicit role for the interests of consumers (OECD 2001).

In terms of political institutions, the predominance of producer interests reflected the incentives predicted by a PR electoral system, as suggested by Lijphart and Crepaz (Lijphart and Crepaz 1991). It also reflected the preferences of state actors, focusing upon employment growth following the economic turmoil of the 1980s, and the need to satisfy the requirements of the Maastrict criteria.

Telecoms

The immediate catalyst for the creation of an independent regulator was the government decision to sell a stake in Telecom in 1996 to a foreign consortium, KPN Telia. This was motivated largely by the need to invest in Telecom's infrastructure, but the government was constrained by the obligations of the Maastricht criteria from doing so from its current spending (Chari and McMahon 2003).

The sale of the stake prompted the passing of the Telecoms Miscellaneous Provisions Act (1996), the Act that set up the Office of the Director of Telecoms Regulation (ODTR). While the state had obtained derogation in terms of opening up the domestic market to full competition, the EU, through a range of directives, had a stated ambition to end national monopolies and ensure competition. Telecom's monopoly was clearly coming to at an end (Thatcher 2002). Once the decision was made to sell a stake in the firm, EU directives demanded the creation of a regulator independent from government.[5] However, from a government perspective, the other rationales described earlier were also clearly important. First, in terms of credible commitment, KPN Telia as the new owner of the significant minority stake was unlikely to agree to a situation where the state continued to be both a shareholder and the de facto regulator. Second, given the increasing complexity of telecoms as a policy issue, there was also an obvious need for expertise. Third, telecoms policy was politically controversial so blame-shifting can also be seen as a further attraction. While telecoms pricing was always contentious in an Irish context, issues such as levels of competition and the need to encourage technological innovation were also becoming controversial in a way that further explains an incentive to shift the responsibility for decisions.

However, the 1996 legislation – the crucial *ex ante* mechanism – neglected to signal any formal objectives for the ODTR either in terms of promoting competition or performing a social welfare function. The legislation stipulated that the ODTR was to be 'independent in the course of its functions', but did not clarify how the new regulator was to interact with the legislature (ODTR 1996). It also contained no requirement to set up a consumer panel, which was the usual mechanism for ensuring a formal role for consumers in the formulation of policy.

The most immediate result was a major controversy that erupted when the Director of the ODTR refused to appear before an Oireachtas committee in January 1998 on the grounds that it could compromise the agency's independence. This prompted a political furore, with the relevant committee changing its terms of reference to compel the director to appear. However, the controversy sparked broader questions about accountability when the then Attorney General stated: '[L]egislators should not stand over any system which takes away the rights of citizens to hold to account individuals that affect their everyday lives' (Byrne 1998).

The other damaging implication of the 1996 legislation was the lack of powers it gave to the ODTR to take firms, particularly Telecom, to task for their tardiness in implementing the requirements of various EU directives. Consequently, decisions of the ODTR were consistently appealed to the judicial system, resulting in long delays and the subsequent hindrance of competition. The result was high prices for telecom services, as Telecom maintained a virtual monopoly in fixed lines and a duopoly in mobiles, and consequently low levels of innovation, with long delays in the unbundling of the local loop (OECD 2001).

However, despite its clear inadequacies as a regulator, the creation of the ODTR can be seen, in retrospect, as a turning point in terms of Irish governance. First, the creation of a regulator with statutory powers did mean a formal shift away from traditional governance structures to a rule-oriented, arms-length style of governance, emblematic of the regulatory state. Second, it meant a change in the way that policy was formulated. This included formal requirements for the ODTR to consult with relevant private actors; transparency, where the

ODTR had to publish consultation papers; and finally, justification, where the ODTR had to explain its decisions. These changes in the way that regulatory policy was made can be understood to affect different actors' strategic options in terms of how they chose to interact with the regulator. Third, the decision to fund the ODTR from a levy imposed on the regulated firms, as opposed to a ministerial budget, gave it an important degree of financial independence that allowed it, over time, to build up its resources and expertise.

The government's sale of its remaining stake in Telecom in 1999 did serve to reduce the conflict of interest with regards to regulation. This was made possible by an agreement between the government and the Telecom unions a year previously to an Employee Share Ownership Programme, under which the employees purchased fifteen per cent of the firm.

Commission for Energy Regulation

The Commission for Electricity Regulation (as it was originally termed) was formally established in 1999, following the 1996 EU directive that opened up domestic electricity markets to competition. The directive not only allowed for a certain level of third-party access to the electricity network but also ended the domestic monopoly rights for the construction of power lines and power stations (Eising and Jacbo 2001). The result was again that a regulator was required under EU legislation to ensure the development of a market. However, unlike the telecom case, there was no change in the status of the Electricity Supply Board, which remained firmly under the ownership of the state.

If Europeanization was the undisputed key explanatory variable, the decision to create the CER fulfilled other political aims. The need to encourage other firms into the Irish market meant that the credible commitment rationale was clear, as was the need for regulatory expertise, and an interest in shifting the blame to the regulator for responsibility for energy costs. In terms of the accountability structure, the CER legislation did learn one lesson from the mishaps of telecoms regulation in so far as the obligation to appear in front of the Oireachtas was explicitly stated. However, no formal objectives for the regulator were established and no consumer panel was mandated (Westrup 2002). The result was again a regulatory policy that appeared to favour the interests of the incumbent producer at the expense of increased competition.

The government chose to expand the CER's remit to include gas regulation and changed its name to the Commission for Energy Regulation in 2002 but left its underlying remit unaffected.

Financial regulation

With respect to financial regulation, the important institutional difference from the utility cases was that prior to reform there already existed a range of regulatory actors, the most important of which was the Central Bank.[6] There was also a clear difference in the role of a financial regulator from that of a utility regulator. A financial regulator has two distinct objectives: first, to avoid a systemic failure of the banking system given its crucial role in allocating credit, and second, to counter the particular problem of asymmetric information where the consumers of financial services have difficulty assessing the risks and returns of products.

While the Central Bank's regulatory responsibilities were increased by successive governments during the 1980s and 1990s as a result of the need to implement a range of EU directives, there were some unusual features unique to the Irish regulatory regime. In particular was the lack of a specific regulator to oversee the securities markets, a responsibility that was delegated to the British Securities and Investment Board until 1995 when the Central Bank was given the task (Westrup 2005). This gap was surprising given how the scope and significance of financial regulation had grown during the 1990s as financial services had evolved into a key sector of the economy, and was given additional impetus from the success of the Financial Services Centre (MacSharry and White 2000).

The catalyst for regulatory reform was a series of financial failures and scandals which suggested that the Central Bank was struggling to cope with increasingly consumer-focused issues of regulation. An advisory group, appointed by the government in 1998, recommended that a regulator be established that was completely separate from the Bank, arguing that due to its monetary policy independence it could not be sufficiently accountable to the political system (McDowell 1999). However, the report set off a clamour from the banks and other financial services firms arguing for the retention of the Bank as regulator. The government, after deliberating for nearly two years, decided in 2001 upon a curious hybrid – the new regulator was established as part of a newly constituted Central Bank.[7] Given that the decision was at odds with the recommendations of the expert group, it proved to be controversial, particularly as during the period in which the government was deliberating, the Oireachtas report on the Deposit Interest Retention Tax scandal was published, suggesting that the Central Bank's regulatory oversight of the banking sector had been far from robust.

So why did the government decide to reject the advice of its own advisory group and opt for such an unconventional regulatory design? What is clear is that neither the key state nor private actors wanted a change in the Central Bank's regulatory role. The close relationship between the Department of Finance and the Central Bank was typified by the almost automatic appointment of the First Secretary of the Department to be Governor of the Bank. The result was reluctance by these key state actors to have a regulator created that was outside their control. The aggressive lobbying by the banks and the financial firms located in the International Financial Services Centre (IFSC) confirmed their resistance to change in the regulatory status quo (Westrup 2005).

Despite its peculiar relationship with the Central Bank, the new financial regulator, which finally opened its doors in May 2003, signifies an important break with the previous regulatory regime. For the first time, the regulator was given an explicit mandate to protect the interests of consumers.[8] Again as in the utility cases, the decision-making processes of the regulator were open to greater scrutiny, as consultation documents and the responses of firms were to be published. Finally, the explicit funding of regulation by levies on financial firms rather than from the revenues of the Central Bank allowed for a more transparent form of funding.

Initial misgivings

An overview of all three cases provides important common insights from the perspective of a principal–agent framework. The initial pattern of regulatory policy-making was characterized by a distinct reluctance by state actors to delegate sufficient powers to the utility regulators to allow them to challenge the positions of the incumbents. An analogy can be drawn with the case of financial regulation, where the existing regulator, the Central Bank, in conjunction with powerful private actors, was able to persuade the government to make an incremental reform rather than the decisive one recommended. The interests of producer groups, adept at using the existing institutional configuration to pursue their preferences, clearly remained predominant. In all three areas of policy there was evidence of a significant level of what Stigler identified as 'regulatory capture', where the regulatory regime reflected the interests of the regulated industry rather than the interests of consumers (Pelzman 1976; Stigler 1971). Indeed, in the case of the utility regulators, there was no formal recognition of the interests of consumers, while in the case of financial regulation they were recognized but very belatedly. The result was distinct policy outcomes that resulted in the continuation of comparatively high telephone, energy and banking charges and relatively constrained choices for consumers (Competition Authority 2004; OECD 2001).

In terms of principal–agent theory, we see initial reluctance by the key principal, state actors, to grant significant powers to regulators that were outside their immediate control. Indeed, in the case of the utilities, it is possible to argue that without the requirements of Europeanization, despite the other political benefits that accrued from delegation, the state would have chosen not to create independent regulators. The counterfactual is underpinned by the government's decision not to create regulators prior to EU requirements and, once created, the reluctance to specify objectives and delegate sufficient powers to them to allow them to challenge the interests of the incumbent firms.

The oversight role of the other principal, the Oireachtas, despite protestations at the ODTR's initial refusal to appear, subsequently proved to be very limited. Indeed a study has indicated that the pattern of Oireachtas committee hearings with regulators in all three cases was infrequent and marked by long gaps

(Westrup 2002). The comparative weakness of the committee system in terms of resources, allied with Gallagher's finding of the lack of political incentive to pursue an oversight role, meant that in McCubbins and Schwarz's terms, the Oireachtas has certainly not pursued a police patrol style of oversight (Gallagher 2010). While the fire alarm metaphor is a more accurate description, even that assumes a certain institutional capability which, despite the attempts of individual members, the Oireachtas committee system struggles to provide.

The result of the actions of both principals is that the initial stage of regulatory reform resulted in limited change in policy-making and very little change in policy outcomes. The creation of new regulatory institutions was therefore not sufficient to challenge the existing patterns of policy-making that were conditioned by the broader configuration and preferences of political actors and institutions.

Regulatory change

However, if it is possible to identify an initial period of regulatory reform that began with the set-up of the ODTR in 1997, characterized by the continuation of existing patterns of policy-making despite the efforts of the new regulatory actors, there is also evidence of a second period, beginning in or around 2002, that has seen regulatory agencies gradually emerge as actors with significant powers and political influence. This change reflects a gradual evolution in the preferences of key regulatory actors, particularly those of the state.

First, and perhaps most significantly, there has been a realization that the regulatory outcomes that resulted from the initial period of reform were in conflict with the state's broader economic development goals, particularly that of attracting technologically sophisticated international firms to Ireland. A lack of technological innovation in terms of the range of available telecom services and high telecom and energy costs are not attractive options for firms with many choices as to where to invest. A critical report by the OECD in 2001 that emphasized both the potential consequences of high telecom and energy costs and argued a key rationale was that 'consumer interests are not well represented in policy debate and deliberation in Ireland, which remains dominated by producer interests' was particularly influential, judging by the policy response it evoked (OECD 2001).[9] Preferences of previously significant insiders such as Telecom and its union members were no longer as important as those of a wider range of private actors.[10]

Second, there was a realization by state actors initially suspicious of delegating power to regulators that the other rationales for delegation were proving to be increasingly politically attractive. The decision to create the Commission for Aviation Regulation to regulate airport charges in 1999 was a decision triggered not by Europeanization but by a combination of credible commitment, blame-shifting and the need for expertise. Indeed, the decision to create a taxi regulator in 2004, and subsequently a regulator to oversee the accountancy profession in 2005, is further evidence of the political appeal of this relatively new form of governance. This institutional innovation also provides evidence that senior civil servants had overcome much of their apparent aversion to change in terms of Irish governance, aided undoubtedly by the continued growth of the economy.

An indication of the changing preferences of state actors was a number of reports, high-level appointments and legislation designed to strengthen the efficiency of the existing regulatory institutions. The High Level Group on Regulation, appointed following the OECD report, produced a series of plans including *Towards Better Regulation* in 2002 that culminated in a White Paper in 2004 entitled *Regulating Better*. This document set out a commitment to pursue a key recommendation of the OECD which was to mandate regulatory impact assessments (RIAs) as a means of targeting the effects of regulation.[11] This reflected a government desire to ensure that regulation was both efficient but also proportional as business groups such as the Irish Business and Employees Confederation (IBEC) and the Financial Services lobby became increasingly vocal about the increased cost of compliance (IBEC 2004).

The first important legislative changes took place in 2002 when the government enacted many of the policy proposals first floated by the then Department of Public Enterprise in 2000 to improve the accountability and efficiency of the new regulatory regime (Department of Public Enterprise 2000). The legislation formulated broad objectives for the regulators that included promoting competition, increasing powers to fine firms, that regulatory decisions should stand while under judicial review, and a change in the executive format from a single director to a three-person commission. The Office of the Director of Telecom Regulation's name was also changed to the Commission for Communications Regulation (ComReg), reflecting the inclusion of responsibility for postal services made in 2000. However, the 2002 legislation still did not specify that an explicit forum for consumers be established, which was the norm in the majority of other EU and OECD states.

A further significant institutional response was the government decision to strengthen the mandate of the Competition Authority – the Competition Act of 2002 was described as 'a remarkable step forward' by its then chairperson (Fingleton 2004).[12] Given the apparent lack of competition that resulted from the initial round of utility regulation, the dramatic strengthening of the powers and budget of the Competition Authority was a further indication that political and state actors were serious in their intent to challenge the regulatory status quo.

If state and political actors were choosing to define and strengthen the role of regulators, the regulators themselves were also beginning to assert their institutional authority and to build up their institutional capacity. Coen has demonstrated how regulatory actors develop this capacity over time both from interaction with private actors and from institutional learning through member-ship in their relevant EU regulatory groups (Coen 2005). Given the important powers delegated to regulators and the particular style of policy-making charac-terized by a relatively high level of transparency and justification, Coen argues that firms and regulators have a mutual interest in exchanging information that develops the expertise of the regulator. Even if in the Irish case the initial regula-tory pattern resembled capture, the strengthening of the regulators' powers in the 2002 legislation, in conjunction with the greater political commitment to making the regime work, suggest that the institutional capacity of the regulators had increased. The result was their emergence as significant actors in the regula-tory game, with their own interests and preferences, developing an institutional clout that went beyond their delegated legal powers.

A further formal institutional change in the regulatory regime came in 2005 with the decision to create a National Consumer Agency with a specific man-date to promote the interests of consumers. While there has been an agency, the Office of the Director of Consumer Affairs, with responsibility for issues such as accurate display of prices, its mandate and resources have been very limited as compared to the stated objectives for the new agency. While consumers as a lobby group often suffer from a collective action problem, this was clearly exac-erbated by Ireland's particular institutional configuration. As we have seen, even the decision to create independent regulators did not lead to the establishment of consumer panels, as was usual in most EU states, to provide for the promotion of a consumer welfare function and some sort of balance to the interests of produc-ers. The decision to create a consumer agency was a recommendation of another High Level Regulatory Group but can also be seen as a result of both political and media pressure as Fine Gael was promoting its Rip-off Ireland campaign and high profile television exposés. However, such pressures were not sufficient to ensure the National Consumer Agency's survival as a stand-alone agency, fol-lowing the decision as a cost-saving measure to merge it with the Competition Authority in 2009.

But it is the dramatic failure of the financial regulatory system to prevent the collapse of the Irish banking system in 2008 that has raised the most funda-mental question about the future of regulatory governance. While other OECD states suffered banking failures following the credit crunch, in the Irish case it was what the Minister for Finance Brian Lenihan described as a 'classic property bubble' that ultimately led to the nationalization of Anglo Irish Bank, and the need for the state to underwrite the liabilities of five other financial institutions at an enormous cost (Honohan 2010). The two official reports commissioned by the government found that the particular configuration of political, property and business actors' interests led to regulatory capture and a situation where the Financial Regulator's capability to act in a broader national interest was critically compromised (Honohan 2010; Regling and Watson 2010). The Governor of the Central Bank, Patrick Honohan, found in his report that the regulator was overtly deferential to the financial institutions, lacking both the desire and the capability to enforce regulation effectively. In retrospect, it is clear that the regulator was not sufficiently independent to be able to perform its duties adequately. Whether this lack of independence was due to flaws in the design of its formal relationships with other regulatory and political institutions, or due to what the *Financial Times* describes as the culture of 'crony capitalism', remains open to debate (Peel and Barber 2009).

However, for political actors, the failure of the Financial Regulator to prevent the banking collapse did allow for initial blame avoidance. The resignation in early 2009 of the chief executive of the Office of the Financial Regulator allowed political actors to deflect attention from broader issues of regulatory policy, such as how the state allowed the situation to arise where such a concentration of lending to a small group of property developers could occur so as to imperil the financial viability of Ireland as a sovereign borrower. However, the Honohan and the Regling-Watson reports both point to the relationship between political actors and key banking figures as a crucial factor leading to the cataclysmic failure of the regulatory system.

So despite certain attempts to strengthen the regulatory institutions, there remains evidence that Ireland's regulatory outcomes are still characterized by signs of capture. While the financial regulatory case is compelling, the EU has also found evidence that in the cases of both energy and telecommunications, prices in Ireland are still comparatively high and levels of competition are low. The delays in opening up the ESB generation and distribution networks to competition, along with the state's continued ownership role, has meant that suspicions of continued conflict in the preferences of state actors persist.

Conclusion

The scale and impact of the failure of the financial regulatory system dominates any analysis of Irish regulatory governance. This chapter attempts to highlight important changes in the preferences of key actors since the initial demands of the EU saw the establishment of the ODTR in 1997. In theoretical terms, the evolution of Ireland's regulatory regime is a reminder that a formal decision to delegate powers does not automatically lead to the creation of powerful regulatory actors. Instead, policy regimes are slow to change, conditioned by existing institutional configurations, and as Thelen argues, require a continued exercise of political preference for the change to be sustained (Thelen 2004).

In terms of the wider issues of Irish governance, the introduction of independent regulatory agencies illustrates two important points. First, regulatory governance can only operate as a distinctive mode of governance within the overarching configuration of domestic political institutions and the consequent preferences of key actors. The result has been that issues of corporate governance, the promotion of competition and consumer choice, have struggled to find a place on the political agenda. Second, and as a direct consequence, it highlights the continued weakness of the Oireachtas in the pursuit of an oversight role. As regulatory governance continues to become a more important part of the way the state operates, such a gap promises to become even more significant. The weaknesses in legislative oversight on the part of the Oireachtas may be compensated for in part by other actors, but in normative terms, the paucity of democratic accountability remains a significant issue for the future evolution of Irish governance.

The failure of the financial regulatory regime between 2001 and 2007 to prevent the emergence of a massive property bubble has meant that as a state, Ireland has paid a particularly large price for its failure to develop more robust regulatory institutions. Notwithstanding such a failure, regulatory governance is likely to become an even more important part of Irish politics. This reflects not only the demands of the European Union, which ensures that regulation will remain a multi-level game as actors use both the European and the Irish political processes to argue for their interests, but also reflects the continued attraction of regulators to political actors at a time when the traditional hierarchical institutions of government are struggling to cope with the increasing complexity and visibility of many policy issues. Blaming the regulator looks set to remain a popular political game.

Notes

1 Coen and Thatcher define a non majoritarian regulator as 'an unelected body that is organizationally separate from governments and has powers of regulation of markets through endorsement or formal delegation by public bodies'. see Coen, David and Mark 2005: 330.

2 However, as Charles Shipan has described, the Environmental Protection Agency was given a level of independence from the Department of the Environment in 1993, see Shipan 2006.

3 Deciding upon a list of agencies with regulatory responsibilities is obviously a subjective task as a wide range of government and private agencies possess certain regulatory powers. Indeed, it could be argued that agencies such as the EPA and the Medicines Board should be distinguished from regulators such as the CER and ComReg because they carry out a range of functions that do not entail regulation.

4 However, in a Westminster-style government, the government and the legislature can often be considered as a single principal, as the government party virtually always has a majority in both the legislature and on the relevant parliamentary committee. See Gallagher 2010 for further discussion.

5 Independence of the regulator from the shareholder is an EU requirement set out in Directive 90/388/EEC and amplified by the Court of Justice.

6 The regulator for the insurance sector was the Department of Enterprise, Trade and Employment.

7 The new regulatory structure was unique in terms of its design in the EU and the OECD as states either decided upon a stand-alone single regulator, as in Germany or the UK, or to maintain the role of the Central Bank as in France, Spain and Italy. See Masciandaro, 2005.

8 The legislation also created a consumer panel with which the regulator had to consult and fund.

9 The Department of the Taoiseach immediately held a press conference to announce the setting up of the High Level Group on Regulation made up of senior civil servants and regulators to respond to the OECD report. see www.betterregulation.ie/index. asp?docID=41.

10 The comments of the Taoiseach, Bertie Ahern, in 2004 are a confirmation of this change in view: 'For too long, producer interests have shaped the policy agenda.' see Ahern, 2004.

11 The government had previously committed itself to such a process in 1999 with the Regulating Red Tape initiative, but the 2001 OECD Report argued that the process was not followed through with sufficient rigour.

12 The Act established the Authority as a public body with its own budget and proceeded to play a high-profile role in examining a range of policy areas.

Bibliography

Ahern, Bertie. 2004. *Speech to PAI Regulating Ireland Conference, Dublin*. Dublin. Available at www.betterregulation.ie/index.asp?docID=68.

Börzel, Tanja A. 2005. Europeanization: How the European Union Interacts with its Member States. In *Member States and the European Union*, edited by Simon Bulmer and Christian Lequesne, 45-69. Oxford: Oxford University Press.

Byrne, David. 1998. *Speech to UCD Law Society, Dublin*. Dublin: Office of the Attorney General.

Chari, Raj and Hilary McMahon. 2003. Reconsidering the Patterns of Organized Interests in Irish Policy Making. *Irish Political Studies* 18 (1): 27–51.

Coen, David. 2005. Business-Regulatory Relations: Learning to Play Regulatory Games in European Utility Markets. *Governance* 18 (3): 375–99.

Coen, David, and Mark Thatcher. 2005. The New Governance of Markets and Non-Majoritarian Regulators. *Governance* 25 (3): 329–505.

Competition Authority. 2004. *Competition Policy and Regulatory Reform*. Dublin: Competition Authority.

Cukierman, Alex, S. Webb and B. Neyapti. 1992. Measuring the Independence of Central Banks: International Evidence. *World Bank Economic Review* 6 (3): 397–423.

Department of Public Enterprise. 2000. *Governance and Accountability in the Regulatory Process: Policy Proposals*. Dublin: Government Publications Office.

Egan, Michelle. 2004. *Creating a TransAtlantic Marketplace*. Manchester: Manchester University Press.

Eising, R. and M. Jacbo. 2001. Moving Targets: National Interests and Electricity Liberalisation in the European Union. *Comparative Political Studies* 34 (7): 742–67.

Eisner, Marc Allen. 2000. *Regulatory Politics in Transition*. Baltimore, MD: Johns Hopkins University Press.

Epstein, David and Sharyn O'Halloran. 1999. *Delegating Powers: A Transaction Cost Politics Approach to Policy Making Under Separate Powers*. Cambridge: Cambridge University Press.

Fingleton, John. 2004. *Is the Competition Act 2002 the Last Step Forward?*. Dublin: Competition Authority.

Gallagher, Michael. 2010. The Oireachtas: President and Parliament. In *Politics in the Republic of Ireland*, edited by John Coakley and Michael Gallagher, 198-239. London: Routledge.

Gilardi, Fabrizio. 2002. Policy Credibility and Delegation to Independent Regulatory Agencies: A Comparative Empirical Analysis. *Journal of European Public Policy* 9 (6): 873–93.

Grilli, Vittorio, Donato Masciandaro and Guido Tabellini. 1991. Institutions and Policies: Political and Monetary Institutions and Public Financial Policies in the Industrial Countries. *Economic Policy* 6 (13): 341–92.

Guiomard, Cathal. 1995. *The Irish Disease and How to Cure it: Common-Sense Economics for a Competitive World*. Dublin: Oak Tree Press.

Honohan, Patrick. 2010. *The Irish Banking Crisis: Regulatory and Financial Stability Policy 2003-2008. A Report to the Minister for Finance from the Governor of the Central Bank*. Dublin: Central Bank. Available at http://www.centralbank.ie/frame_main.asp?pg=n ws%5Farticle%2Easp%3Fid%3D518&nv=nws_nav.asp.

IBEC. 2004. *The Costs of Regulation*. Dublin: IBEC.

Kydland, E.E. and E.C. Prescott. 1977. Rules Rather than Discretion: The Inconsistency of Optimal Plans. *Journal of Political Economy* 85 (1): 473–91.

Levy, B. and P. Spiller. 1996. *Regulations, Institutions and Commitment*. Cambridge: Cambridge University Press.

Lijphart, Arend and Marcus Crepaz. 1991. Corporatism and Consensus Democracy in 18 Countries: Conceptual and Empirical Linkages. *British Journal of Political Science* 21 (2): 235–46.

MacSharry, Ray and Padraic White. 2000. *The Making of the Celtic Tiger: The Inside Story of Ireland's Boom Economy*. Dublin: Mercier Press.

Majone, Giandomenico, ed. 1996. *Regulating Europe*. London: Routledge.

Majone, Giandomenico. 1997. From the Positive to the Regulatory State: Causes and Consequences of Changes in the Mode of Governance. *Journal of Public Policy* 17 (2): 139–67.

Majone, Giandomenico. 2001. Two Logics of Delegation: Agency and Fiduciary Relations in EU Governance. *European Union Politics* 2 (1): 103–22.

Masciandaro, Donato, ed. 2005. *Handbook of Central Banking and Financial Services in Europe*. Cheltenham: Edward Elgar.

McCubbins, Matthew and Thomas Schwartz. 1984. Congressional Oversight Overlooked: Policy Patrols versus Fire Alarms. *American Journal of Political Science* 28 (1): 165–79.

McDowell, Michael. 1999. *Report of the Implementation Advisory Group on the Establishment of a Single Regulatory Authortiy for the Financial Services Sector.* Dublin: Government Publications.

Moe, Terry. 1984. The New Economics of Organization. *American Journal of Political Science* 28 (4): 739–77.

OECD. 2001. *Regulatory Reform in Ireland.* Paris: OECD.

Office of the Director of Telecoms Regulation (ODTR) 1996. Telecommunications (Miscellaneous Provisions) Act 1996.comReg. Available at www.comreg.ie/–file upload/publications/Act34of1996.pdf.

Osborne, David and Ted Gaebler. 1992. *Reinventing Government: How the Entrepreneurial Spirit is Transforming the Public Sector.* Reading, MA: Addison-Wesley Publishing.

Peel, Quentin and Lionel Barber. 2009. End to Crony Capitalism. In *Financial Times*, 17 March London.

Pelzman, S. 1976. Towards a More General Theory of Regulation. *Journal of Law and Economics*: 19 (2): 211–40.

Putnam, Robert. 1988. Diplomacy and Domestic Politics: The Logic of Two-Level Games. *International Organization* 42 (3): 427–60.

Radaelli, Claudio. 2000. Policy Transfer in the EU: Institutional Isomorphism as a Source of Legitimacy. *Governance* 13 (1): 25–43.

Regling, Klaus and Max Watson. 2010. *A Preliminary Report on the Sources of Ireland's Banking Crisis.* Dublin: Government Publications Office. Available at www.bank inginquiry.gov.ie/Preliminary%20Report%20into%20Ireland's%20Banking%20Cri sis%2031%20May%202010.pdf.

Rhodes, R.A.W. 1994. The Hollowing Out of the State: the Changing Nature of the Public Service in Britain. *Political Quarterly* 65 (2): 138–51.

Schmidt, Vivien A. 2002. Europeanization and the Mechanics of Economic Policy Adjustment. *Journal of European Public Policy* 9 (6): 894–912.

Shipan, Charles. 2006. Independence and the Irish Environmental Protection Agency: A Comparative Perspective. Policy Institute Blue Paper 20. Dublin: Trinity College Dublin.

Stigler, George J. 1971. The Theory of Economic Regulation. *Bell Journal of Economics* 2 (1): 3–21.

Thatcher, Mark. 2002. Delegation to Independent Regulatory Agencies: Pressures, Functions and Contextual Mediations. *West European Politics* 25 (1): 127–47.

Thelen, Kathleen. 2004. *How Institutions Evolve: the Political Economy of Skills in Germany, the United States, and Japan.* Cambridge: Cambridge University Press.

Vogel, Steven. 1996. *Freer Markets, More Rules: Regulatory Reforms in Advanced Industrial Countries.* Ithaca, NY: Cornell University Press.

Weaver, Kent. 1987. *The Politics of Blame Avoidance.* Washington DC: Brooking Institute.

Weingast, Barry and Michael Moran. 1983. Bureaucratic Discretion or Congressional Control? Regulatory Policymaking by the Federal Trade Commission. *Journal of Political Economy* 91 (5): 765–800.

Westrup, Jonathan. 2002. Financial Regulatory Reform in Ireland: the Accountability Dimension Policy Institute Blue Paper 5. Dublin: Trinity College Dublin.

Westrup, Jonathan. 2005. The Case of Ireland. In *Handbook of Central Banking and Financial Services in Europe*, edited by Donato Masciandaro, 355–70. Cheltenham: Edward Elgar.

5

Governing the Irish economy: a triple crisis

Sebastian Dellepiane and Niamh Hardiman

Introduction

During the 1990s and 2000s, Ireland experienced an unprecedented spell of economic growth and rising living standards, job creation and export perform-ance that pulled it away from the southern periphery of the EU with which it had long been bracketed. Lauded by the OECD, featuring on cover stories of *The Economist* newspaper, the 'Celtic Tiger' seemed set to rival its Asian counterparts as a global role-model. But the international financial crisis of 2008 hit the Irish economy particularly hard, with a severe drop in growth and employment, and the sudden emergence of a sizeable fiscal deficit. By the late 2000s, it seemed appropriate to many to classify Ireland once again alongside southern European economies with large fiscal deficits and mounting public debt, in what some have termed the PIGS: Portugal, Ireland, Greece and Spain (Dadush 2010).

This chapter explores the policy underpinnings of the rapid change in Ireland's fortunes. Unlike Greece, where fiscal mismanagement underlay the crisis and where the principal problem by 2009 was the risk of sovereign debt default, Ireland's economic crisis was mainly due to a mismanaged financial sector which, by over-lending to property developers and house-purchasers, con-tributed to a classic property bubble. The housing boom had further effects on policy choices, since it underlay the distortions that were permitted to develop in the public finances. And the inflationary effects of cheap credit and rising house prices in turn contributed to competitiveness losses. The three facets of crisis – financial, fiscal and competitiveness – are interlinked in their origins. In the fallout from international crisis after 2008, it slowly became apparent that the banks were not merely suffering liquidity problems, but risked insolvency. The Irish government response, to guarantee not only all deposit-holders but most bondholders, in effect socialized the losses of the private sector, resulting in an enormous public debt liability. In November 2010, Ireland was obliged to enter an EU–IMF multi-year loan programme, a symbolically significant loss of national economic autonomy (O'Rourke 2010a). This entailed onerous austerity obligations on taxpayers, with no corresponding losses for bank bondholders. The Irish crisis had become part of a rolling European crisis, the resolution of which would depend on the evolution of European decision-making capacity. How had things come to this pass?

The first section of this chapter outlines the main features of the Irish growth model and the scale of the shock it underwent from 2008 onwards. The second section analyses the elements of domestic policy that underlie the triple crisis in financial, fiscal and competitiveness performance. The third section considers the significance of European monetary union for Ireland's policy choices.

The Irish growth model

Irish political economy combines features of two rather distinct models of political economy. The institutional features of Ireland's systems of production place Ireland clearly within the Anglo-American liberal market model of capitalism (Hall and Soskice 2001). Industrial policy depends heavily on foreign direct investment, and tax incentives proved a crucial attraction for inward capital flows (Barry 1999). This consistent policy stance made Ireland a disproportionate beneficiary of inward investment in general and American capital in particular, following the completion of the European single market in 1992. The principal exporting sectors in the Irish economy, both in manufacturing (especially pharmaceuticals and chemicals, and information and communications technology) and services (especially software design and financial services), are dominated by foreign-owned firms (Central Statistics Office 2010).[1] About four-fifths of all manufacturing enterprises, almost all of them Irish-owned, employed fewer than 50 people in 2005. Of the larger firms, over four-fifths were foreign-owned, and they generated 93 per cent of total turnover in industry. In services, almost all firms were small or very small, often family-run; but the 2 per cent of larger firms accounted for about half of all employment and half of all turnover in the sector (Central Statistics Office 2008b). Although the domestic sector remains small by comparison, the presence of the foreign-owned sector has been credited with creating opportunities for upskilling and innovation there too (Barry, Bradley and O'Malley 1999; O'Malley and O'Gorman 2001). Consistent with its 'liberal' features, Ireland rates relatively highly in business-friendly practices such as minimizing delays in transacting official business and labour market flexibility (OECD 2007).

At the same time, as one of the most open economies in the world, Ireland also experienced incentives to manage its economic fortunes more actively than the market-conforming liberal model might suggest. This gave it something in common with the small European countries that had built up distinctive growth models during the more protectionist post-war decades. Scandinavia, the Low Countries, and the 'Alpine states' of Austria and Switzerland, had developed different variants of a similar approach whereby state management of export-oriented industrial policy secured their growth prospects, while corporatist structures facilitated domestic growth-sharing through bargained agreements rather than overt conflict (Katzenstein 1985, 2003). Thus industrial policy in Ireland depended not only on tax-friendly incentives, but also on activist state agencies to promote and facilitate investments. But Ireland's openness and its support for lightly regulated capital and labour markets also made its industrial policy quite different from the post-war European model, and different also from the highly statist developmental strategies of Asian late industrializers, causing Ó Riain to term it a 'flexible' or 'networked' developmental strategy (Ó Riain 2004).

A persistent political bias toward concertation of economic interests is apparent in Ireland, contrasting with the British marginalization of trade unions since the 1980s (Hardiman 2005). Social partnership agreements were regularly negotiated between 1987 and 2009, and have been credited with facilitating fiscal policy adjustment out of the depression of the 1980s and stable management of the rapid growth of the 1990s and 2000s (Barry 2009; MacSharry and White 2000). They also provided a mechanism for linking pay and a range of non-pay issues including changes in the incidence of taxation, minimum wages, the labour market inspectorate, contractual relations, training and labour market activation measures (Hastings, Sheehan and Yeates 2007; Roche 2009).

The 'Irish model' became celebrated for its successes in creating very rapid growth with virtually full employment during the 2000s (Auer 2000; Daly 2005). The labour force grew rapidly partly through increases in activation rates, and partly through the influx of well-qualified workers from outside the country. Until the early 1990s, Ireland's growth profile relative to the EU average had resembled that of the southern European EU cohesion countries of Spain, Portugal and Greece, but it pulled away quite dramatically thereafter (Barry 2003; Bradley 2000; FitzGerald 2000). Ireland came fourth after Singapore, Hong Kong and Japan in a ranking of catch-up growth for the period 1960–98, and if we remove the two city states, only Japan outperformed Ireland (Knack 2003). Economists debated whether this was attributable to a catch-up with European averages that followed from new inputs and a better policy mix, or from the discovery of an FDI-led growth dynamic that would not necessarily encounter limits based on convergence (Barry 2005; Honohan and Walsh 2002). Either way, the sharp upturn was remarkable.

But the rapid turnaround in Irish growth and employment performance were very unlike those of Asian economies in one important respect: in the Asian high-growth states, the social effort involved in increased productivity was complemented or compensated by equality-increasing policies, especially in education provision and real efforts to secure equality of opportunity (Campos and Root 1996). In Ireland, economic prosperity loosened the patterns of social mobility somewhat (though social mobility is not really the same thing as equality of opportunity in any case (Breen 2010)). But the evidence suggests that this was principally due to the surge in economic activity and tight labour markets,

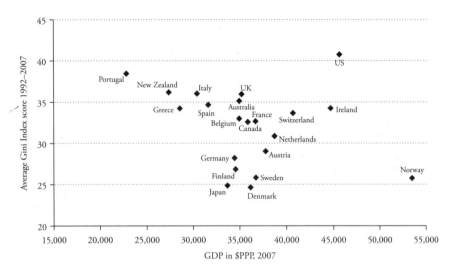

Source: UN Development programme *2009 Human Development Report.*

Figure 5.1 Growth and inequality, 1992-2007

which caused employers to look to criteria other than conventional ones such as educational attainments that tend to favour the reproduction of class advantage (Whelan and Layte 2006). Thus it seems that social mobility opportunities were less the consequence of equality-enhancing social policy or investments in social infrastructures to promote equality of opportunity, and rather more a consequence of the volatility of the economic boom itself.

There was a continuous fall in the most extreme levels of social deprivation, but this was achieved principally through the drop in aggregate unemployment. The meaning of relative income poverty rates of over 20 per cent might perhaps be questioned at a time of rising average incomes. But among those who remained at serious risk of poverty, income and lifestyle deprivation were severe (Nolan 2009; Whelan, Nolan and Maitre 2007). Those most adversely affected were households headed by someone who was not in work due to illness or disability, lone parents and those with low levels of education and skill attainments.

More generally, the boom years also saw levels of income inequality increase as the top section of the income distribution pulled away from the median. Figure 5.1 shows the profile of wealth and inequality across nations, showing inequality between 1992 and 2007 relative to wealth levels in 2007. This indicates that while Ireland's income per capita ranked among the highest in the OECD by 2007, the average levels of income inequality over the period of the boom remained stubbornly high. Indeed, this indicator reveals that on the inequality measure, Ireland's performance is similar to that of poorer southern European countries such Spain and Greece, and only slightly better than other liberal market economies (Britain, New Zealand and Australia), with Portugal and the USA being particular outliers in each of these groups.

These measures indicate that rapid growth and employment expansion, combined with ongoing commitment to social partnership processes, did not contribute either to a sustained reduction in domestic social inequalities or to an expansion in the extent of social or collective consumption. The expansion of public social spending that took place did not keep pace with market-driven living standards. As we shall see, the tax system favoured rather than contained the surge in higher income rewards. Redistributive spending, while it grew over time and especially during the 2000s, continued to be disbursed on a 'residual' model, involving often complex means-testing and eligibility assessments. As in the USA, tax breaks featured extensively as publicly funded supports to the acquisition of privately enjoyed benefits in areas such as pensions and health insurance (Hacker 2004, 2006). Many aspects of service provision had long been set up in a two-tier delivery structure with public and private target clienteles. But unusually, as Chapter 6 in this volume illustrates in the case of healthcare, the Irish system involved considerable cross-subsidy from the public to the private sector, whereby relatively modest fees and insurance premiums could ensure enhanced services on top of those provided by the public sector – a kind of inverse configuration of welfare services, an upside-down welfare state.

The institutional inheritance of welfare provision is only understandable with reference to the long path-dependent history of the role of the Catholic Church in Irish society and the dominance of the medical profession in healthcare (Barrington 1987; Fahey 1992).

Explaining the policy choices made under conditions of unprecedented prosperity during the 1990s and 2000s also requires us to consider the profile of the party political system, especially the electoral dominance of the highly pragmatic right-of-centre Fianna Fáil party, with its strong financial and personal network connections to the business and construction sectors (Clancy, O'Connor and Dillon 2010; Hardiman 2010a).

But two other factors must also be taken into account. The first concerns the limits to the influence the trade union movement was capable of exercising. Union membership was all but non-existent in the most productive, foreign-owned sector. Trade union density declined from almost half in 1990 to a little over one-third by 2007, as the newer sectors of employment, especially in private sector services and in retail trades, proved very difficult to organize. Union membership was heavily weighted toward public sector representation. The trade union movement found it considerably easier to engage with government on deals to do with tax cuts and disposable income, than to adopt 'solidaristic' policies on improved social services, let alone to take a coherent position on issues of income distribution (Hardiman 2006). Government's active promotion of social partnership agreements integrated both unions and employers into public policy process (Roche 2009). But the discourse of egalitarianism was noticeably enfeebled in Irish political life, and the legitimacy of market-driven outcomes was scarcely challenged.

The second and related factor underlying the market-friendly features of political life in Ireland is related to the extent of its economic openness and to the way Ireland was positioned in the web of international economic relationships. Ireland's trade openness index was at almost 100 per cent of GDP and almost 120 per cent of GNP during the 1990s and 2000s. But what was distinctive about Ireland's position in the international economy was that it was becoming increasingly exposed to three export markets, the demands of which imposed rather contradictory policy pressures on Ireland. Britain, which had been virtually the sole export destination for the Irish economy in 1960, was declining in relative importance, but was still a significant trading partner. The extent of FDI and export reliance on the US market kept Ireland attuned to the culture of American economic life. Membership of the EU had facilitated the access to the wider European market which non-European investors prized. Thus as currency stabilization and eventually monetary union moved up the EU agenda, Ireland found itself positioned between three currency zones. But the full extent of the difficulty of functioning within the Eurozone, without the possibility of an independent interest rate policy or scope for relative cost adjustment through devaluation, would not become apparent until after the crisis had hit.

What policy choices and constraints are implied by the Janus-faced features of the Irish growth model that are associated with having a large FDI-based sector as well as indigenous firms? For some commentators, the extent of reliance on foreign capital investment permitted very little domestic policy autonomy, and the role of governments in supporting social partnership should best be understood in terms of the 'competition state', or even as 'corporate takeover' (Adshead, Kirby and Millar 2008; Allen 2007; Kirby 2004; O'Hearn 2001). For others, the relatively stable institutionalization of social partnership was a sign not of exploitation or subordination but of insider access to influence on the part of trade unions and civil society organizations, the 'partnership state' (O'Donnell 2008; O'Donnell and Thomas 2006). For others again, no single paradigm encompasses all these priorities, and state policy has to be understood as a complex of 'competing projects', each of which has distinctive core policy constituencies that overlap only minimally (Ó Riain 2008).

The approach of the remainder of this chapter draws on the classic resources of political economy, considering not only the nature of domestic interests and how they are configured in Irish society, but also the international situation of the Irish economy and the policy constraints emanating from membership of the EU and from Ireland's situation in the globalized context of production more generally (Gourevitch 1986, ch. 1; Hall 1986, chs 8 and 9). Only in this context can we make sense of the scale of the crisis between 2007 and 2009, and

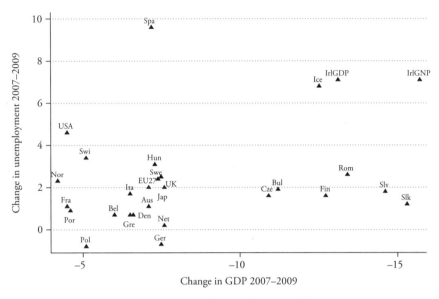

Sources: Eurostat, Irish Central Statistics Office

Figure 5.2 The crisis in growth and employment, 2007–09

attempt to trace the underlying weaknesses that gave rise to the dramatic change in economic fortunes.

A triple crisis

Between 2007 and 2009, Ireland's previously enviable combination of steady growth and virtually full employment suddenly came to an end. The economy contracted sharply and unemployment shot up, as profiled in Figure 5.2. This graph provides two measures of the contraction in Ireland's growth, as the drop in GNP was more severe than that of GDP. This reflects the fact that the foreign-owned heavily export-oriented sector was less severely hit than the domestically owned and more labour-intensive sector. The difference between GNP and GDP is principally accounted for by profits that are taxed at the low level of 12.5 per cent in Ireland, then transferred back to the home country headquarters of the exporting firm.

The implications for Irish public finances were equally sudden and severe. Figure 5.3 shows that Ireland was in fiscal surplus when the crisis hit in 2007, but that its deficit was already more severe than Greece's by 2009. Ireland's public debt had shrunk as a proportion of GDP during the years of very rapid growth. But the rapid accumulation of borrowing obligations for current spending quickly increased consolidated debt obligations, and the government rescue

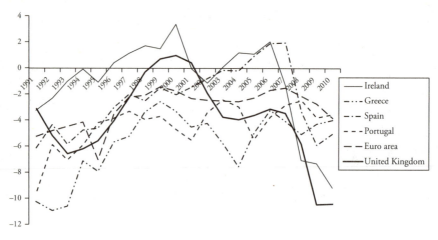

Source: OECD Economic Outlook 85 database

Figure 5.3 General government cyclically adjusted balances

of the banking sector increased both deficit obligations and debt totals during 2009–10.

Figure 5.4 shows that the European countries with the largest consolidated general government debt were Italy, Greece and Belgium. Italy and Belgium had long found it difficult to restrain their public indebtedness, but their capacity to service existing borrowing was not in serious question. In contrast, Greece's problems with fiscal discipline were not solved by the time they were admitted to membership of the single European currency, and became worse over time. Ireland's gross government debt exposure was not among the worst in 2010. But its general government deficit was particularly problematic, and the prospects for rapid debt accumulation were clear. The principal component of the government's primary fiscal deficit amounted to about 14 per cent of GDP in 2009, an extraordinarily large problem in the context of Ireland's commitment under the terms of the Stability and Growth Pact to restore the deficit to under 3 per cent by 2014.

The government's blanket guarantee to the banking sector in October 2008 was offered before the full scale of the banks' liabilities had become clear. Estimates of the full sum required have crept steadily upward to approximately €70bn required to stabilize the financial sector (albeit spread over a number of years), some two-thirds of this attributable to Anglo-Irish Bank alone. This brought the total budget deficit to some 32 per cent of GDP for 2010, an astonishing and quite unprecedented sum.

The government undertook to deal with the collapse of the banking sector through the creation in 2009 of a 'special purposes vehicle', the National Asset

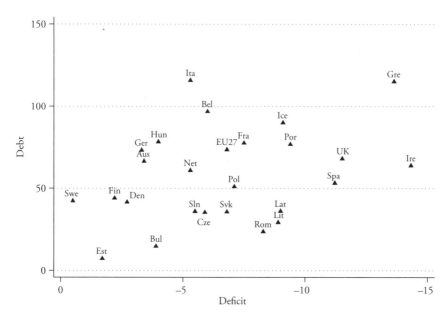

Source: General government deficit, general government debt, Eurostat

Figure 5.4 Debt and deficit as % GDP, 2009

Management Agency (NAMA). This was to deal with the now severely depreci-
ated assets of the bankrupt developers and builders, loans to whom had gravely
over-extended the banks, by swopping them for government-backed bonds.
NAMA proved to be an unwieldy and expensive instrument, but the government preferred this to the alternative of nationalization as a prelude to direct
public recapitalization. This worsened both the government deficit and implied
a greatly increased debt exposure once the NAMA process was completed. Table
5.1 gives an indication of the early estimates of the scale of taxpayer exposure to
liabilities arising from banking failure.

Disentangling the various elements of economic crisis, we might say that
Ireland succumbed to three simultaneous crisis: a financial crisis due to the collapse of the banking system; a fiscal crisis because of the rapidly widening gap
between current expenditure and revenues; and a competitiveness crisis resulting
from the runaway domestic cost structures that had developed during the boom
years.

Financial crisis

The suddenness and the severity of the economic fall from grace took many
by surprise. Ireland's banks were the first casualty of the international financial
crisis. But the principal explanations for Ireland's woes were not to do with the

Table 5.1 **Euro-area public interventions in the banking sector, % GDP**

	Approved	Effective
Austria	32.8	8.7
Belgium	92	26.7
Finland	27.7	0
France	18.1	5.6
Germany	24.4	9.1
Greece	11.4	4.6
Ireland[a]	231.8	229.4
Italy	1.3	0
Netherlands	52	25.4
Portugal	12.5	3.3
Slovenia	32.8	0.4
Spain	12.1	5
Euro Area	25.4	11.5
EU27	31.2	12.6

[a] Mostly guarantees on blank liabilities

Note: Approved: Amounts approved in state aid decisions by the Commission under state aid rules. Effective: Amounts from schemes effectively implemented, for example capital effectively injected in banks or state guarantees effectively granted to banks on their issuance of liabilities.

Data covers approved measures from June 2008 to 17 July 2009 and effective measures from June 2008 to mid-May 2009.

Source: European Commission. 2010. *Annual Report on the Euro Area 2009: European Economy 6*, Table 2.1, p.46

banks' exposure to risky investment products: Ireland was relatively untouched by US sub-prime lending.

The main source of the Irish banks' problems was their over-exposure to property-based loans and the close personal as well as financial links between bankers, property developers, builders and politicians, especially in the dominant Fianna Fáil party. Between 1997 and 2007, 'housing prices rose 175 percent in the United States, 180 percent in Spain, 210 percent in Britain, and 240 percent in Ireland' (Krugman and Wells 2010). Many commentators had warned that Ireland was in the grip of an asset price bubble – an enormous and clearly unsustainable construction boom and soaring house prices (Kelly 2009). The international crisis exacerbated but did not cause the underlying banking crisis in Ireland.

The contribution to Ireland's crisis of ruinously bad lending practices, increasing reliance on short-term international lending and over-reliance on poorly

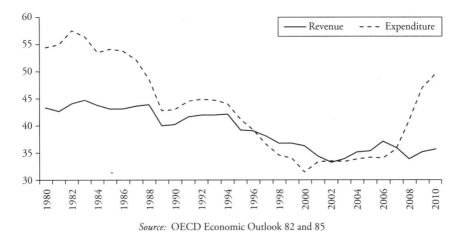

Source: OECD Economic Outlook 82 and 85

Figure 5.5 Ireland's fiscal profile, % GDP, 1980-2010

monitored loan collateral, and poor regulation of the banking sector, is by now well established. Ireland experienced a 'plain vanilla' banking crash due to over-reliance on loans to construction in an unsustainable bubble economy. Banking regulation was too light to make any appreciable impression on banks' pursuit of profits through increasingly risky lending practices (Honohan 2010; Regling and Watson 2010; Ross 2009). For a time, this yielded large profits for banks and large bonuses for the bankers: the privatization of gains. The government's bank guarantee, on the other hand, resulted in the nationalization of losses.

The fiscal profile

A fiscal crisis implies a gap between public spending and state revenues: it is not a priori an issue of over-spending, but of a mismatch between spending commitments and the capacity to fund them. The historical profile of revenue and expenditure in Figure 5.5 shows that the large deficits of the 1980s had not only been stabilized, but by the mid-1990s were replaced by fiscal surpluses, in the context of a very rapidly growing economy. The devastating fall-off in revenues and the soaring increase in expenditure graphed here are exaggerated by the fact that GDP itself shrank by some 15 per cent between 2007 and 2009.

But what these data suggest is that that there were underlying weaknesses in both revenue-generating capacity and in spending patterns in Ireland. The impact of the crisis that had its origins in international conditions was intensified by weaknesses in domestic economic management (Hardiman 2010a, 2010c). This is apparent in the growing relative reliance on public investment and public spending to sustain economic activity, and in the increasing reliance on cyclical revenue sources to meet continuing spending commitments.

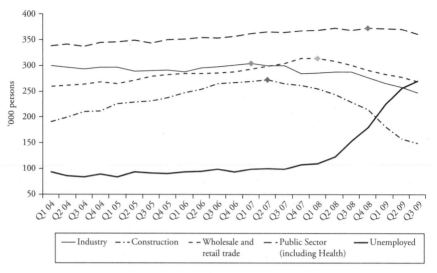

Note: 'Industry' = NACE codes B-E; 'Construction' = NACE code F; 'Wholesale and Retail Trade' =
NACE code G; 'Public Sector' from CSO Public Sector Database.
Markers show maximum point in trend.

Source: CSO Quarterly National Household Survey, Employment by NACE Sector; CSO Database
Direct, Employment and Earnings in Public Sector

Figure 5.6 Employment profiles, 2004–09

From the early 2000s on, warning signs were emerging over the sustainability
of Ireland's economic path. While capital stock soared by 157 per cent in real
terms in 2000–08, housing accounted for almost two-thirds of the increase. So
far from investing in the 'smart economy', which became a byword in the late
2000s, Ireland was busy building a 'concrete economy'. Of the rest, economist
Rossa White notes that it was mostly related to the state or semi-state sectors
(including road-building), not driven by private enterprise (White 2010). The
public sector had taken over as the motor of employment too: Figure 5.6 shows
that the peak point of employment in industry, sales, and even in construction
preceded the arrival of the crisis, yet public sector employment continued to
grow steadily until after the effects of the crisis were felt and public spending
retrenchment began to be imposed.

Figure 5.7 shows that the volume of tax revenue shrank rapidly with the
onset of the crisis. But long before the crisis hit, the composition of revenue
had become ever more exposed to property-related sources, whether in the form
of stamp duty (transaction tax) or capital gains tax. At a time of severe asset-
price inflation, increasing reliance on such a volatile base was problematic. And
property-related investment incentives that were constructed through the tax

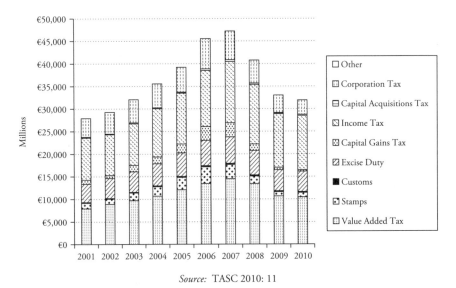

Source: TASC 2010: 11

Figure 5.7 Composition of taxation in Ireland, 2001–10

code further fuelled the asset-price bubble while it was at its peak (TASC 2010). Despite the turn toward tax simplification and creation of a broad tax base in the late 1980s, Irish policy-makers had a persistent tendency to use tax incentives to shape behaviour. Although these started to be reversed again in the mid-2000s, they were very costly (Callan, Walsh and Coleman 2005). And the long-standing reliance on low corporation tax remained a fixed commitment for all governments (Hardiman 2004).

Meanwhile, the significance of personal income tax in the overall revenue mix – that 'great engine of finance', as Gladstone termed it – had been permitted to decline. Fianna Fáil, in coalition with the liberal Progressive Democrats, had embarked on a more vigorous programme of tax reduction in 1997. Minister for Finance Charlie McCreevy evinced a strong ideological commitment to reducing the incidence of personal income tax: it was he who reduced the top rate of tax and halved capital gains tax between 1997 and 2003, measures which not only benefited higher earners disproportionately, but which also introduced a sharp increase in disposable incomes at just the time when access to cheap credit suddenly widened, with the advent of the Euro.

The social partnership-based pay agreements had also come to centre on tax concessions in exchange for wage moderation. This produced real benefits for trade union members in the form of increased personal disposable income. The tax burden on all forms of household and at all wage levels became steadily lighter to the point at which Irish employees were among the most lightly taxed in the whole OECD region, outdone only by Korea and Mexico (OECD 2009:

51). Yet the revenue stream was not yet visibly compromised. New revenue sources were sought in so-called 'stealth taxes' – indirect taxes such as VAT, and fees and charges for public services. Indirect taxes tend to be inequitable in their impact on household budgets; they add directly to inflationary pressures, as they increase the costs of a host of everyday transactions. For several years though, it seemed as if Ireland could have it all: lower direct taxes as well as increased spending, all fuelled by a spell of very rapid growth. And so the Irish revenue base was systematically weakened, through the scale of tax expenditures, increased dependence on property-related transactions and decreased reliance on direct income taxation.

Irish tax policy during the 2000s fed into inflationary pressures, both directly through consumption and transaction taxes, and indirectly through the incentivizing effects on the construction boom. But this was not balanced by spending policies that would contain such pressures. Rather, Ireland has experienced a consistent bias toward pro-cyclical spending policies, notoriously captured by Fianna Fáil Finance Minister Charlie McCreevy's comment in the early 2000s that 'when I have it, I spend it'. During periods of rapid growth, governments have tended to increase spending, and especially current spending; in a downturn, they are left with little option but to impose contractionary measures to contain the emergent deficit (Lane 1998, 2003, 2009). Public spending increased rapidly in the late 1990s and especially in the run-up to the election of 2002. Following another Fianna Fáil-dominated electoral victory, McCreevy sought to control spending commitments somewhat; but electoral unpopularity quickly resulted in a resumption of a more relaxed stance on expenditure.

Ireland, unlike Britain, was part of the Eurozone system of fiscal discipline from 1992 onwards. Conformity with the conditions of the Stability and Growth Pact was meant to be domestically enforced and subject to sanction by the European Central Bank. However, it quickly became apparent after 2000 that the era of cheap credit, one of the anticipated benefits of the single currency, was a potent force for destabilizing fiscal disciplines in countries with growth rates that were more buoyant than the large core economies of Germany and France.

The domestic institutional context of budget formation varies across European countries. Hallerberg, Strauch and von Hagen suggest that there are two modes of achieving stable fiscal policy: one based on bargained pre-commitments by coalition partners binding government to specific targets, the other based on strong and autonomous decision-making by the finance minister (Hallerberg, Strauch and von Hagen 2007, 2009). The latter model is more characteristic of the executive-dominated policy-making processes of Britain and Ireland, notwithstanding Ireland's greater propensity to form coalitions. But what is not captured by the model is the variation within liberal market economies in the political motivation for ministers to engage in tight budgetary controls. And indeed Britain, despite having independent control over monetary and exchange rate policies, and an independent central bank from 1997 on, incurred a growing fiscal liability throughout the 2000s and found itself by 2010 among the four European countries with the highest fiscal deficits. In Ireland, too, the autonomy of the finance minister permitted a good deal of leeway, but was not conducive to running a consistent counter-cyclical stance. Periods of fiscal surplus were relatively short-lived and proved vulnerable to electoral pressures for increased spending during an upturn.

Real public spending continued to increase until the crisis was well under way. At that point, the Fianna Fáil–Green coalition government that had taken power in 2007, just before the crisis broke, began its corrective measures. Once convinced of its necessity, the government possessed the institutional resources to take strong and decisive action. But once again, the government adopted a fiscal stance that intensified the underlying cyclical trend in the economy. This time though, the pro-cyclical approach was contractionary in its effect. Arguing that the revenue base was now too precarious to attempt to increase taxes, and against the recommendations of the recently published Commission on Taxation report, the government sought to implement its fiscal adjustment entirely through spending cuts (Commission on Taxation 2009).

The institutional processes of budget formation in Ireland had been strengthened as a consequence of its membership of the Euro, since the European Central Bank, under the terms of the Stability and Growth Pact, required systematic reporting on budget targets and multi-annual forecasting. And the political autonomy available to the Minister for Finance, similar to the British system of strong executive dominance, should have entailed a strong capacity to adhere to a coherent fiscal stance. But in fact it is clear that Ireland followed a markedly expansionary fiscal policy in aggregate over the period 1992 to 2003 (Hallerberg *et al.* 2009: 180). Under conditions of extraordinary growth, Ireland might have been better advised to accumulate large fiscal surpluses, as was the case in Sweden and Finland. But domestic factors pushed in the opposite direction. Short-term electoral pump-priming prevailed over longer-term planning that would resist such populist pressures (Hardiman 2009).

Competitiveness challenges

The cost base of the Irish economy suffered deterioration over time relative to the core European economies, particularly Germany, as Figure 5.8 shows. Given the fixed exchange rate, the most prominent economists in Ireland recommended that the principal means by which competitiveness could be restored was through a decrease in real wage levels (Bergin, Conefrey, FitzGerald and Kearney 2009). But competitiveness has many contributory elements to it: supply-side factors in areas such as education and skill attainment contribute to competitiveness; so also do infrastructural investments in transport, broadband connectivity and

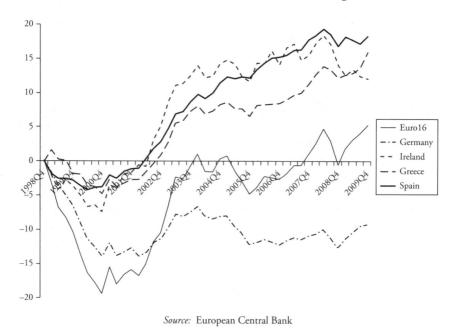

Source: European Central Bank

Figure 5.8 Harmonized competitiveness indicator, % change, Q4 1998=100

energy costs. In many of these areas, Ireland has particular weaknesses (National Competitiveness Council 2009). Ireland ranked 29th of 139 countries in the international 2010/11 Global Competitiveness Report, but in some crucial areas the scores were much worse. On 'Public trust in politicians', for example, Ireland ranked 65th, and on 'Wastefulness of government spending' it came in at 93. While 'Cooperation in labour–employer relations' ranked at 35, on the 'Flexibility of wage determination' it was 128th (World Economic Forum 2010).

Wage flexibility is not the same as cost competitiveness, but Ireland along with Spain, and closely followed by Greece, experienced the most marked relative deterioration in relative cost structures. In contrast, Germany's relative cost base had been held firmly under control, even during the unstable conditions of 2002–3. Within the Eurozone of course, the smaller, weaker countries were unable to weaken their relative exchange rates to recover competitiveness; equally, Germany was now unable to do what it had frequently done in the past, and revalue its currency relative to others. Within the 'one size fits all' currency regime, inability to adjust through relative cost changes was likely to result in increased domestic unemployment.

The role of wages in the total cost base of Irish economic activity is highly differentiated because of the structure of the economy. Yet although there are no formal mechanisms for extending the coverage of pay agreements, pay deals were capable of penetrating more extensively than the numbers might suggest. Union membership comprised some 34 per cent of the labour force in the late 2000s (Central Statistics Office 2008a). Union membership was perhaps at 80 per cent in the public service, which means virtually 100 per cent coverage. Membership was about 15 per cent in the private sector; firms in which there was at least some union presence were likely to observe the terms of pay agreements for all their employees. Virtually none of the most profitable, export-oriented firms, either in manufacturing or services, was unionized, but the foreign-owned companies tended to shadow the terms of the pay agreements, while also varying pay rates through bonuses and other flexible adjustments methods (D'Art and Turner 2005; Gunnigle, Collings and Morley 2005; Roche 2001). A study of workplace bargaining in the late 2000s concluded that multinational corporations adopting national wage agreements that were designed:

> to protect employment in indigenous companies with lower productivity levels, are able to set wages at levels well below what would normally be the case than if bargaining was undertaken by trade unions at the business-level or where individuals negotiated directly with their employer. (McGuinness, Kelly and O'Connell 2010: 593)

Some sectors that might otherwise be difficult for unions to organize were subject to mandatory industry-wide agreements – most strikingly in the construction industry. And when issues arose concerning the monitoring and implementation of statutory labour market protections, the unions pressed the issue through social partnership networks to ensure better monitoring of compliance standards. Thus the governance of the labour market was more pervasive than might first seem to be the case (Hardiman 2006).

Aggregate unit wage costs in Ireland showed some relative deterioration, as Figure 5.9 suggests. But the effects were unevenly felt, since in the modern, export-oriented sector, labour costs constituted a relatively small portion of total costs; the capital intensiveness and high productivity levels of both manufacturing and services meant that unit labour costs were not problematic in most exporting sectors (Breathnach 2010).

Social partnership institutions provided the context for pay bargaining continuously between 1987 and 2009. Both union and employer representatives had been committed during the 1990s to securing the conditions for Euro membership; the Maastricht criteria were internalized into domestic political priorities. Within the trade union movement, public sector unions were particularly strong. Over the decades a complex set of differentials and relativities had developed in the public sector that was capable of generating recurrent cycles of pay claims above and beyond those agreed by the partnership process. A 'benchmarking' agreement in 2004 aimed to bring these 'special' pay claims to an end and to secure industrial peace in the public sector. But the efficiency arguments

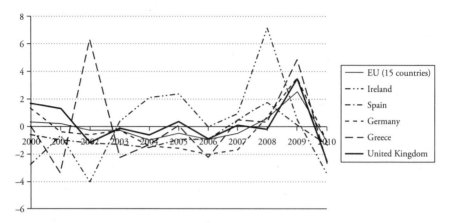

Source: Eurostat. Growth rate of the ratio: compensation per employee in current prices divided by GDP in current prices per total employment

Figure 5.9 Unit wage costs

for the agreement were less clear. Thus by the late 2000s, there was some evidence, albeit contested, that any misalignment between public and private sector pay now tended to favour the former, particularly at the top (Kelly, McGuinness and O'Connell 2009).

As domestic inflationary pressures began to gather pace in the early 2000s, employers sought to build in new safeguards against inflationary wage demands by strengthening the role of social partnership's overseeing National Implementation Body. But the economic governance capabilities of social partnership were not put to any severe test until 2008/9. Until then, buoyant growth meant that hard distributive trade-offs could still be accommodated, and higher spending and lower taxes could, for the time being, be sustained. However, the foresight capacities of social partnership institutions had proved quite limited. The challenge of negotiating a deflationary pay deal under extreme pressure during 2009 proved extremely difficult. Eventually, centralized pay determination fell apart as government imposed a series of unilateral public sector pay cuts as part of its deficit-reducing strategy, and private sector employers pulled out of pay talks. Market disciplines were to be reasserted to manage adjustment to hard times. But some reliance on consultative processes persisted. In a new form of concession bargaining, government secured union acquiescence to its fiscal strategy: public sector reform and flexibility in work practices in exchange for a stay on further pay cuts (Stafford 2010).

Relative competitiveness encompasses more than wage costs though. Nominal unit labour cost compresses a variety of contributions to competitiveness into a single measure. The capital intensity of production, and the extent of self-

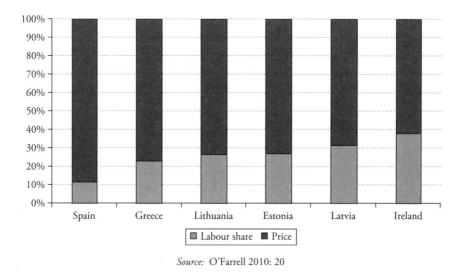

Source: O'Farrell 2010: 20

Figure 5.10 Components of loss of competitiveness

employment and especially professional self-employment, affect measures of productivity. The volume of credit available in the economy and the way fiscal policy is used either as a countervailing or augmenting influence may have a significant effect on the changing relative costs of factor inputs. In a comparative analysis of the EU member states that had suffered the greatest competitiveness losses, a European Trade Union Institute economist argued that changes in competitiveness were more significantly affected by product market than labour market, as illustrated in Figure 5.10 (O'Farrell 2010: 21).

Neither unit wage costs nor relative exchange-rate-based competitiveness measures can be understood without understanding government's own contribution to inflationary pressures. Government reliance on consumption and non-income-based taxation, and government unwillingness to take measures to control the explosion in property prices, combined to push up the cost base of the Irish economy. This in turn drove wage demands among employees who, in spite of rising real incomes, found the cost of housing rising out of reach, even for dual-earner households in the ever-expanding outlying commuter belt. Thus the Irish domestic cost base of production was driven by problems with controlling spending, and as in Spain, a house price boom injected inflationary expectations into the system.

The European context of economic governance

We have considered the domestic origins of Ireland's economic crisis, in particular the respects in which pre-existing policy and institutional weaknesses paved the way for a financial crisis, a fiscal crisis and a competitiveness crisis. But we cannot consider the decline in the relative competitiveness position of Ireland, Greece, Spain and Portugal, without reflecting on the other side of the comparison, which is the relative competitiveness gain experienced by Germany since 1998, and what this reveals about structural imbalances between European economies within the single currency area.

The domestic origins of different pathways to economic crisis therefore have to be placed in the context of the design of the Euro itself (Dellepiane and Hardiman 2010). The adoption of the Euro was a 'political' project from the outset, in the sense that a system of rules was created through treaty agreements that was intended to foster the development of greater convergence at the level of domestic economies. During the 1970s and 1980s, closer European integration came to seem all but inevitable as a solution to the uncertainties and the conflicts of national interest – especially between France and Germany – associated with managed exchange rates. Against those who held that real convergence between European economies was a prerequisite of a viable European currency, the view prevailed that nominal unity through a shared system of money would enforce closer alignments of policy and of economic performance (Marsh 2009).

But two major design problems made this difficult. The first is that while Germany retained its capacity to discipline domestic costs effectively over time, the same was not true in other Eurozone member countries with very different political institutions and organized interests. Inflation control had long been prioritized in Germany through the role of its strong and independent Bundesbank, and the signalling mechanisms from the Bank that any relaxation of fiscal disciplines, or any sign of inflationary wage settlements, would be controlled through increases in interest rates (Franzese and Hall 2000; Hall 1994).

The second problem was that the 'one size fits all' interest rate regime had proven woefully unsuited to countries with very different growth rates, and interest rates were set low to benefit the needs of the largest states. Convergence on low German interest rates was one of the signal benefits expected to result from Economic and Monetary Union (EMU). But the unanticipated consequences of EMU for the smaller and more peripheral Eurozone countries was that credit was suddenly much cheaper than their higher growth potential would warrant. Ireland and Spain in particular both experienced a massive surge in the availability of consumer credit. Lacking the capacity to increase domestic interest rates, national governments proved unable or unwilling to exercise fiscal disciplines on a scale that would have made any appreciable difference (Conefrey and FitzGerald 2010). The tsunami of low-interest credit was particularly problematic for what had previously been the 'cohesion' states of southern Europe and Ireland (Blavoukos and Pagoulatos 2008).

The implication is that fiscal crisis and competitiveness loss were not problems that existed in Ireland in isolation. Stable solutions ultimately implied some reconsideration of the design of the Eurozone itself (Gros 2010). For Ireland, the experience of both fiscal and competitiveness crisis was very painful. For any individual country, with a particular profile of borrowing requirements and of both private and public debt burdens, the need to secure loans on international markets brings with it subjection to risk assessment of its sovereign debt liabilities on the part of the international ratings agencies. Thus the most vulnerable countries are constrained to adopt those policies that will secure their credibility with the bond markets. This has required strategies for reducing government borrowing requirements that have centred on visible spending cuts, combined with promissory action to reduce costs to improve export capabilities and alter their balance of payments profile. But austerity for all risks reinforcing a deflationary bias in a form of generalized beggar-my-neighbour strategy (Baldwin, Gros and Laeven 2010; Blanchard and Cottarelli 2010; O'Rourke 2010b). Furthermore, these very austerity measures in turn caused a downgrading of the peripheral economies' sovereign debt ratings, as the markets concluded that the capacity to service debt was compromised by the harshness of the adjustment strategy – a Catch-22 for the peripheral economies.

The foundations of the Euro were badly shaken by the near sovereign debt default by Greece in mid-2010, which revealed further design flaws in the Euro itself: breaches of the Stability and Growth Pact due to fiscal crisis could not be fixed by imposing further fiscal sanctions. Bond market instability created growing difficulties for peripheral European states to continue to service their national debts. And yet the European political response continually lagged behind the rolling economic crisis. New European oversight mechanisms for national economic governance were belatedly under consideration (Task Force on Economic Governance 2010). New European loan mechanisms, devised in conjunction with the International Monetary Fund (IMF), were slow to develop, contentious in design and limited in reach (Baldwin *et al.* 2010).

The EU–IMF loan agreement which the Irish government finally agreed in November 2010 was shaped by a variety of competing objectives, among them the need to protect European Central Bank liquidity, prevent broader European financial sector losses, and limit German taxpayer exposure to the need to 'bail out' weaker economies (Hardiman 2010b). Ireland's national economic autonomy was thus highly restricted for the duration of the loan agreement. It remained unclear whether the conventional remedies of deflation and painful domestic devaluation would be politically tolerable if imposed as severely as seemed to be required.

Conclusion

The sudden and calamitous end to Ireland's phase of relative prosperity came as a shock. In retrospect though, the institutional configurations and policy choices that made the Irish reaction to crisis all the more severe were already in place. The liberal structure of the economy, and the small-state propensity to seek protective policy solutions, stood in uneasy relationship to one another. Ireland's development stance based on FDI meant that a major plank of tax policy, the rate of corporation tax, was non-negotiable for any party in power. A business-friendly legal environment provided additional encouragement to foreign investment.

But much of Ireland's growth during the 2000s was based on the domestic sector, particularly on an unsustainable reliance on construction. Tax incentives favoured property-owners, developers, builders, and bankers, who were in turn strong supporters of Fianna Fáil. The reliance on 'light-touch regulation', and trust in the banks not to over-extend themselves, proved fatally flawed policies: a form of 'crony capitalism' Irish-style.

Adopting the Euro fundamentally altered economic governance conditions during the 2000s. Within a single currency regime, the only policy choices under domestic control are fiscal policy and relative cost adjustment, and Ireland proved signally weak at both. National economic policy was subsumed into a European-level adjustment strategy; any national economic recovery strategy would similarly depend as much on international conditions as on national policy choices.

Note

1 The 'modern' sectors in Irish industry include NACE 20 Chemicals and chemical products, 21 Basic pharmaceutical products and preparations, 26 Computers, electronic and optical products, 27 Electrical equipment, 1820 Reproduction of recorded media, 3250 Medical and dental instruments and supplies.

Bibliography

Adshead, Maura, Peadar Kirby and Michelle Millar. 2008. Ireland as a Model of Success. In *Contesting the State: Lessons from the Irish State*, edited by Maura Adshead Peadar Kirby and Michelle Millar, 1–23. Manchester: Manchester University Press.

Allen, Kieran. 2007. *The Corporate Takeover of Ireland*. Dublin: Irish Academic Press.

Auer, Peter. 2000. *Employment Revival in Europe: Labour Market Success in Austria, Denmark, Ireland and the Netherlands*. Geneva: ILO.

Baldwin, Richard, Daniel Gros and Luc Laeven. 2010. *Completing the Eurozone Rescue: What More Needs To Be Done?*, London: Centre for Economic Policy Research. Available at: www.voxeu.org/index.php?q=node/5194.

Barrington, Ruth. 1987. *Health, Medicine and Politics in Ireland 1900-1970*. Dublin: Institute of Public Administration.

Barry, Frank, ed. 1999. *Understanding Ireland's Economic Growth*. Basingstoke: Macmillan.

Barry, Frank. 2003. Integration and Convergence in the Cohesion Countries. *Journal of Common Market Studies* 41 (5): 897–921.

Barry, Frank. 2005. Future Irish Growth: Opportunities, Catalysts, Constraints. *ESRI Quarterly Economic Commentary* (Winter 2005): 1–25.

Barry, Frank. 2009. Social Partnership, Competitiveness and Exit from Fiscal Crisis. *Economic and Social Review* 40 (1): 1–14.

Barry, Frank, John Bradley and Eoin O'Malley. 1999. Indigenous and Foreign Industry. In *Understanding Ireland's Economic Growth*, edited by Frank Barry, 45–74. Basingstoke: Macmillan.

Bergin, Adele, Thomas Conefrey, John FitzGerald and Ide Kearney. 2009. Recovery Scenarios for Ireland. ESRI Research Series 007. Dublin: ESRI. Available at www.esri. ie/publications/latest_publications/view/index.xml?id=2774.

Blanchard, Olivier and Carlo Cottarelli. 2010. Ten Commandments for Fiscal Adjustment in Advanced Economies. *Vox*, 28 June. Available at www.voxeu.org/ index.php?q=node/b3.

Blavoukos, Spyros and George Pagoulatos. 2008. The Limits of EMU Conditionality: Fiscal Adjustment in Southern Europe. *Journal of Public Policy* 28 (02): 229–53.

Bradley, John. 2000. The Irish Economy in Comparative Perspective. In *Bust to Boom? The Irish Experience of Growth and Inequality*, edited by Brian Nolan, Philip J. O'Connell and Christopher T. Whelan, 4-26. Dublin: IPA.

Breathnach, Proinnsias. 2010. *The Importance of Exports to the Irish Economy*. Available at http://irelandafternama.wordpress.com/.

Breen, Richard. 2010. Social Mobility and Equality of Opportunity. *Economic and Social Review* 41 (4): 413–28.

Callan, Tim, John Walsh, and James S. Coleman. 2005. Tax Expenditures. In *Budget Perspectives 2006*, 47–60. Dublin: ESRI.

Campos, José and Hilton L. Root, eds. 1996. *The Key to the Asian Miracle: Making Shared Growth Credible*. Washington DC: Brookings Institution.

Central Statistics Office. 2008a. *Quarterly National Household Survey: Union Membership*. Dublin: Available at www.cso.ie/releasespublications/documents/labour_market/ current/qnhsunionmembership.pdf.

Central Statistics Office. 2008b. *Small Business in Ireland*. Dublin: CSO. Available at www.cso.ie/newsevents/pr_smallbusireland08.htm.

Central Statistics Office. 2010. *Industrial Production and Turnover*. Dublin: CSO. Available at www.cso.ie/releasespublications/documents/industry/current/prodturn.pdf.

Clancy, Paula, Nat O'Connor and Kevin Dillon. 2010. *Mapping the Golden Circle*. Dublin: TASC. Available at www.tascnet.ie/upload/file/MtGC%20ISSU.pdf.

Commission on Taxation. 2009. *Report of the Commission on Taxation*. Dublin: Government Publications Office. Available at www.commissionontaxation.ie/down-loads/Commission%20on%20Taxation%20Report%202009.pdf.

Conefrey, Thomas and John FitzGerald. 2010. Managing Housing Bubbles in Regional Economies Under EMU: Ireland and Spain. *National Institute Economic Review* 211 (1): 91–108.

D'Art, Daryl and Thomas Turner. 2005. Union Recognition and Partnership at Work: A New Legitimacy for Irish Trade Unions? *Industrial Relations Journal* 36 (2): 121–39.

Dadush, Uri. 2010. *Paradigm Lost: The Euro in Crisis*. Washington DC: Carnegie Foundation. Available at http://carnegieendowment.org/publications/special/misc/EuroCrisis/.

Daly, Mary. 2005. Recasting the Story of Ireland's Miracle: Policy, Politics or Profit? In *Employment 'Miracles': A Critical Comparison of the Dutch, Scandinavian, Swiss, Australian and Irish Cases versus Germany and the US*, edited by Uwe Becker and Herman Schwartz, 133-56. Amsterdam: Amsterdam University Press.

Dellepiane, Sebastian and Niamh Hardiman. 2010. The European Context of Ireland's Economic Crisis. *Economic and Social Review* 41 (4): 471–98.

Fahey, Tony. 1992. Catholicism and Industrial Society in Ireland. In *The Development of Industrial Society in Ireland*, edited by John H. Goldthorpe and Christopher T. Whelan, 241-64. Oxford: Clarendon Press.

FitzGerald, John. 2000. The Story of Ireland's Failure – and Belated Success. In *Bust to Boom? The Irish Experience of Growth and Inequality*, edited by Brian Nolan, Philip J. O'Connell and Christopher T. Whelan, 27-57. Dublin: IPA.

Franzese, Robert J. and Peter A. Hall. 2000. Institutional Dimensions of Coordinating Wage Bargaining and Wage Policy. In *Unions, Employers, and Central Banks*, edited by Torben Iversen, Jonas Pontusson and David Soskice, 174-204. Cambridge: Cambridge University Press.

Gourevitch, Peter. 1986. *Politics in Hard Times: Comparative Responses to International Crises*. Ithaca, NY: Cornell University Press.

Gros, Daniel. 2010. All Together Now? Arguments for a Big-bang Solution to Eurozone Problems. *Vox*, 5 December Available at www.voxeu.org/index. php?q=node/5892.

Gunnigle, Patrick, David G. Collings and Michael Morley. 2005. Exploring the Dynamics of Industrial Relations in US Multinationals: Evidence from the Republic of Ireland. *Industrial Relations Journal* 36 (3): 241–56.

Hacker, Jacob S. 2004. Privatizing Risk Without Privatizing the Welfare State: The Hidden Politics of Social Policy Retrenchment in the United States. *American Political Science Review* 98 (2): 243–60.

Hacker, Jacob S. 2006. *The Great Risk Shift: The Assault on American Jobs, Families, Health Care and Retirement and How*. Oxford: Oxford University Press.

Hall, Peter A. 1986. *Governing the Economy: the Politics of State Intervention in Britain and France*. Oxford: Oxford University Press.

Hall, Peter A. 1994. Central Bank Independence and Coordinated Wage Bargaining: Their Interaction in Germany and Europe. *German Politics and Society* (31): 1–23.

Hall, Peter A. and David Soskice. 2001. An Introduction to Varieties of Capitalism. In *Varieties of Capitalism: The Institutional Foundations of Comparative Advantage*, edited by Peter A. Hall and David Soskice, 1–70. Oxford: Oxford University Press.

Hallerberg, Mark, Rolf Strauch and Jürgen von Hagen. 2007. The Design of Fiscal Rules and Forms of Governance in European Union Countries. *European Journal of Political Economy* 23 (2): 338–59.

Hallerberg, Mark, Rolf Rainer Strauch and Jürgen von Hagen. 2009. *Fiscal Governance in Europe*. Cambridge: Cambridge University Press.

Hardiman, Niamh. 2004. Paying for Government. In *Dissecting Irish Government: Essays in Honour of Brian Farrell*, edited by Tom Garvin, Maurice Manning and Richard Sinnott, 82-103. Dublin: University College Dublin Press.

Hardiman, Niamh. 2005. Politics and Markets in the Irish 'Celtic Tiger'. *The Political Quarterly* 76 (1): 37–47.

Hardiman, Niamh. 2006. Politics and Social Partnership: Flexible Network Governance. *Economic and Social Review* 37 (3): 347–74.

Hardiman, Niamh. 2009. The Impact of the Crisis on the Irish Political System. Working Paper 2009/32. Dublin: UCD Geary Institute. Available at http://geary.ucd.ie/images/Publications/WorkingPapers/gearywp200932.pdf.

Hardiman, Niamh. 2010a. Bringing Domestic Institutions Back Into an Understanding of Ireland's Economic Crisis. *Irish Studies in International Affairs* 21: 73–89.

Hardiman, Niamh. 2010b. Firestorm and Contagion: How Ireland Got Burned. In *Crooked Timber*. Available at http://crookedtimber.org/2010/12/01/firestorm-and-contagion-in-the-eurozone-how-ireland-got-burned/.

Hardiman, Niamh. 2010c. Institutional Design and Irish Political Reform. *Journal of the Statistical and Social Inquiry Society of Ireland* XXXIX (November): 53–69.

Hastings, Tim, Brian Sheehan and Padraig Yeates. 2007. *Saving the Future: How Social Partnership Shaped Ireland's Economic Success*. Dublin: Blackhall Publishing Ltd.

Honohan, Patrick. 2010. *The Irish Banking Crisis: Regulatory and Financial Stability Policy 2003-2008. A Report to the Minister for Finance from the Governor of the Central Bank*. Dublin: Central Bank. Available at www.centralbank.ie/frame_main.asp?pg=nws%5Farticle%2Easp%3Fid%3D518&nv=nws_nav.asp.

Honohan, Patrick and Brendan Walsh. 2002. Catching Up With the Leaders: The Irish Hare. In *Brookings Papers on Economic Activity* 2002(1): 1–57. Washington, DC: Brookings Institution.

Katzenstein, Peter J. 1985. *Small States in World Markets: Industrial Policy in Europe*. Ithaca, NY: Cornell University Press.

Katzenstein, Peter J. 2003. Small States and Small States Revisited. *New Political Economy* 8 (1): 9–30.

Kelly, Elish, Seamus McGuinness and Philip O'Connell. 2009. Benchmarking, Social Partnership and Higher Remuneration: Wage Setting Institutions and the Public-Private Wage Gap in Ireland. *Economic and Social Review* 40 (3):339–70.

Kelly, Morgan. 2009. The Irish Credit Bubble. UCD Center for Economic Research Working Paper. Dublin: University College Dublin. Available at www.ucd.ie/t4cms/wp09.32.pdf.

Kirby, Peadar. 2004. Development Theory and the Celtic Tiger. *The European Journal of Development Research* 16 (2): 301–28.

Knack, Stephen. 2003. *Democracy, Governance, and Growth*. Princeton, NJ: Princeton University Press.

Krugman, Paul and Robin Wells. 2010. The Slump Goes On: Why? *New York Review of Books* 57 (14).

Lane, Philip. 1998. On the Cyclicality of Irish Fiscal Policy. *Economic and Social Review* 29 (1): 1–16.

Lane, Philip. 2003. The Cyclicality of Fiscal Policy: Evidence from the OECD. *Journal of Public Economics* 87 (12): 2661–75.

Lane, Philip. 2009. A New Fiscal Strategy for Ireland. *Economic and Social Review* 40 (2): 233–53.

MacSharry, Ray and Padraic White. 2000. *The Making of the Celtic Tiger: The Inside Story of Ireland's Boom Economy.* Dublin: Mercier Press.

Marsh, David. 2009. *The Euro: The Politics of the New Global Currency.* New Haven, CT: Yale University Press.

McGuinness, Seamus, Elish Kelly and Philip J. O'Connell. 2010. The Impact of Wage Bargaining Regime on Firm-level Competitiveness and Wage Inequality: The Case of Ireland. *Industrial Relations* 49 (4): 593–615.

National Competitiveness Council. 2009. Annual Competitiveness Report. Dublin. Available at www.competitiveness.ie/media/ncc090818_acr_2009.pdf.

Nolan, Brian. 2009. Policy Paper – Income Inequality and Public Policy. *Economic and Social Review* 40 (4): 489–510.

O'Donnell, Rory. 2008. The Partnership State. In *Contesting the State: Lessons from the Irish Case,* edited by Maura Adshead, Peadar Kirby and Michelle Millar, 73–99 Manchester: Manchester University Press.

O'Donnell, Rory and Damien Thomas. 2006. Social Partnership and the Policy Process. In *Social Policy in Ireland: Principles, Practice and Problems,* edited by Sean Healy, and Brigid Reynolds, 117–46 Dublin: The Liffey Press.

O'Farrell, Rory. 2010. *Wages in the Crisis.* Brussels: ETUI. Available at www.etui.org/research/activities/Employment-and-social-policies/Reports-and-working-papers/WP-2010.03.

O'Hearn, Denis. 2001. *The Atlantic Economy: Britain, the US and Ireland.* Manchester: Manchester University Press.

O'Malley, Eoin and Colm O'Gorman. 2001. Competitive Advantage in the Irish Indigenous Software Industry and the Role of Inward Foreign Direct Investment. *european Planning Studies* 9 (3): 303–21.

O'Rourke, Kevin. 2010a. Letter From Dublin. *Eurointelligence,* 2 December. Available at www.eurointelligence.com.

O'Rourke, Kevin. 2010b. What Do Markets Want? *Eurointelligence,* 3 June. Available at www.eurointelligence.com.

Ó Riain, Seán. 2004. *The Politics of High Tech Growth: Developmental Network States in the Global Economy.* Cambridge: Cambridge University Press.

Ó Riain, Seán. 2008. Competing State Projects in the Contemporary Irish Political Economy. In *Contesting the State,* edited by Maura Adshead, Peadar Kirby and Michelle Miller, 165–85. Manchester: Manchester University Press.

OECD. 2007. *Economic Survey: Ireland 2006.* Paris: OECD.

OECD. 2009. *Taxing Wages 2007–8.* Paris: OECD.

Regling, Klaus and Max Watson. 2010. *A Preliminary Report on the Sources of Ireland's Banking Crisis.* Dublin: Government Publications Office. Available at www.bankinginquiry.gov.ie/Preliminary%20Report%20into%20Ireland's%20Banking%20Crisis%2031%20May%202010.pdf.

Roche, William K. 2001. Accounting for the Trend in Union Recognition in Ireland. *Industrial Relations Journal* 32 (1): 37–54.

Roche, William K. 2009. Social Partnership: From Lemass to Cowen. *Economic and Social Review* 40 (2): 183–205.

Ross, Shane. 2009. *The Bankers: How the Banks Brought Ireland to its Knees.* Dublin: Penguin Ireland.

Stafford, Peter. 2010. The Croke Park Deal and the Death of Partnership. *Political Reform Blog* 14 June. Available at http//politicalreform.ie.

TASC. 2010. *Failed Design? Ireland's Finance Acts and their Role in the Crisis.* Dublin: TASC. Available at www.tascnet.ie/.

Task Force on Economic Governance. 2010. *Strengthening Economic Governance in the EU.* Brussels: European Commission. Available at www.consilium.europa.eu/uedocs/cms_data/docs/pressdata/en/ec/117236.pdf.

Whelan, Christopher T. and Richard Layte. 2006. Economic Boom and Social Mobility: The Irish Experience. *Research in Social Stratification and Mobility* 24 (2): 193–208.

Whelan, Christopher T., Brian Nolan and Bertrand Maitre. 2007. Consistent Poverty and Economic Vulnerability. In *Best of Times? The Social Impact of the Celtic Tiger*, edited by Tony Fahey, Helen Russell and Christopher T. Whelan, 87-104. Dublin: Institute of Public Administration.

White, Rossa. 2010. Irish Macro Comment: Years of High Income Largely Wasted. In *Research Report: Irish Economy*. Dublin: Davy Research. Available at www.davy.ie.

World Economic Forum. 2010. *Global Competitiveness Report 2010/11*. Available at http://gcr.weforum.org/.

6

Creating two levels of healthcare

Claire Finn* and Niamh Hardiman

Introduction

The system of healthcare provision in Ireland came to a crossroads in the early twenty-first century. Problems of capacity constraints reached a critical level during the years of rapid economic growth and population expansion of the 1990s and 2000s. Provision of both primary and acute healthcare was no longer adequate to the needs of a growing population whose expectations were also rising. The challenge seemed especially daunting in the hospital sector, where overcrowding in Accident and Emergency units was a persistent phenomenon, and where waiting lists for surgical procedures were a very visible measure of the mismatch between need and availability of services.

How best to manage these problems became not just a matter of levels of public funding, but also involved consideration of the role of the private sector, and the management of the complex interrelationships between public and private sectors. Public spending on healthcare provision grew at unprecedented rates during the late 1990s and early 2000s. Policy documents published during the 1990s reiterated support for the public system, providing equitable access to and quality healthcare for all. Yet at the same time government was offering new incentives and supports to private sector initiatives in healthcare provision. Ireland appeared to be at a critical juncture in the governance of healthcare, between intensifying public provision on the one hand, and increasing its reliance on the private sector on the other.

In this chapter we examine some of the implications of this dual system, with particular reference to the acute hospital sector. First we outline the main features of the Irish system that differentiate it from other countries that have private as well as public healthcare. Second, we suggest that the insurance system developed in Ireland resulted in inequitable access to most consultant care and to hospital care for surgical procedures. Third, we consider how best to explain the evolution and persistence of the current system. We suggest that the nature

* Claire Finn wishes it to be noted that this chapter is written in her personal capacity and does not reflect the views of the National Economic and Social Council.

of consultants' contracts is intimately bound up with the continuity of the two-tier system. Finally, we argue that the uneasy dual-track policy in fact entailed an unacknowledged bias toward growing reliance on private healthcare and a reinforcement of established inequities.

Perspectives on public and private healthcare

Healthcare has become one of the most important areas of public policy in modern states. Citizens expect to have access to affordable treatment appropriate to their condition, and where this does not exist, this is generally viewed as a problem where policy intervention is appropriate. Many of the wealthier OECD countries combine a public and a private sector in acute healthcare, though the mechanisms for funding and delivery vary considerably. There is no optimal amount any country might spend on healthcare. As Barr notes, somewhat facetiously perhaps, 'if we spent nothing on health, some people would die unnecessarily from trivial complaints; if we spent the whole national income on healthcare there would be no food and we would all die of starvation' (Barr, 1998: 279).

Like education, healthcare is an example of a publicly provided private good, paid for to a large extent by the public purse, where the marginal cost of an additional other user is substantial, and once the resource has been used it cannot be used elsewhere. There are both efficiency and equity arguments for state intervention in the market for healthcare. Healthcare is associated with numerous market failures and government intervention is seen as necessary to correct these problems. But in addition, healthcare is an example of a merit good, which should be available to all regardless of ability to pay, so that access to essential medical attention is not debarred by reason of inadequate means. This, as with all equity-related decision-making by a society, is a normative judgement. Redistribution from the better-off to the less well-off through a benefit-in-kind (such as public healthcare) rather than a cash transfer, ensures that resources are spent for the purposes intended (Barr 1998).

Nevertheless, some powerful arguments have been put forward in favour of private provision and financing in healthcare. Chief among these is that it reduces the burden on the public sector and thereby improves both access to the public sector and the quality of the service it can offer (Besley and Coate 1991). Indeed, redistributive benefits can even be shown to occur, under certain conditions, where a private alternative exists. If the quality of the public sector is kept at a level that induces those who are better off to leave the public sector and seek private treatment, this will free up space in the public sector for those who remain (Besley and Coate 1991). Patients with low waiting costs will choose public treatment. Waiting time induces patients with high waiting costs to choose private treatment, thereby reducing the cost of public healthcare that

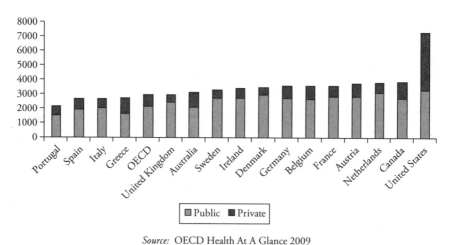

Source: OECD Health At A Glance 2009

Figure 6.1 Health expenditure per capita, US$, public and private, 2007

everyone pays for (Hoel and Saether 2003). So the existence of a private sector may free up resources, thereby helping to reduce waiting lists in the public sector; and it may offer choice by allowing those who are willing to pay to seek treatment elsewhere. But these assumptions only hold if public and private sectors are strictly alternative paths of treatment. And it depends on the public sector being seen as the default option, catering to the great majority, and resourced to a level that maintains broad-based satisfaction with the system. As we shall see, all of these assumptions turn out to be problematic in the Irish case.

The nature and extent of the role of private funding varies greatly across the OECD, but in most western European countries, government plays a key role in healthcare provision, and free or subsidised healthcare is available to a significant majority of citizens. Healthcare at a certain quality level is provided and paid for through public funds, though the relative balance of tax and social insurance funding may vary. However despite the availability of this public healthcare, in most countries citizens also have the right to choose or alternate between varying combinations of public and private healthcare, if they wish to do so. The decision to purchase private care is often prompted by an individual's desire to bypass perceived public sector inflexibilities and to access treatment with a quality level higher than that offered by the public system.

Although Ireland spends rather less than the average amount on healthcare relative to GDP, Figure 6.1 shows that total per capita spending on health was not unusually low compared with other OECD countries.[1]

While the particular combination of public and private in the Irish healthcare system is distinctive, the existence of a private alternative, offering a quality level higher than that of the public sector, is not unique. Many wealthy countries have

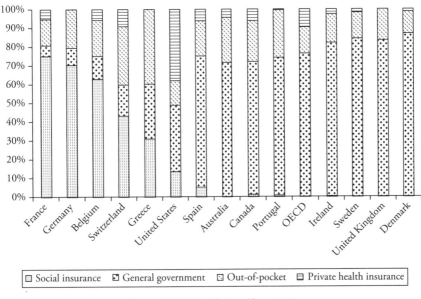

Source: OECD Health At A Glance 2009

Figure 6.2 Composition of total health expenditure, 2007

some role for private insurance. Countries tend to cluster in their funding patterns. Figure 6.2 shows that not only the mix of public and private in total health spending varies, but that within the public sector, the contribution of public social insurance as opposed to spending from general government revenues can vary a lot too. Almost 80 per cent of total spending on healthcare provision in Ireland comes from public sources and, like Britain and Sweden, this is mostly funded through general taxation (Nolan 2008. 302).

Consistent with Esping-Andersen's well-known typology of welfare states, continental European countries are strongly insurance-based in their health funding, and Scandinavian countries fund their welfare spending from general revenues (Esping-Andersen 1990; Esping-Andersen, Gallie, Hemerijck and Myles 2002). The USA stands out in that, for a wealthy country, a much smaller proportion of total health spending is channelled through public provision.

The Irish 'duplicate' system

Delving further, the OECD classifies the Irish system as a 'duplicate' system, that is, one where insurance complements and supplements but also duplicates provision offered by the public system. In duplicate systems, private health insurance typically provides a level of care, choice and speed of access above that offered by the public system (OECD 2004). Currently, along with Australia, Ireland has the largest duplicate market in the OECD. Approximately half the population in both countries holds private health insurance.

The Irish system features universal entitlement to public care, but there are important limits to this in practice. Public out- and in-patient hospital services are heavily subsidized by the state for those who are not eligible for medical cards (that is, means-tested entitlement to a range of benefits such as free medical care and prescriptions), hence justifying Ireland's classification as a 'universal' system. Charges in the public sector are subject to means-testing, and non-medical card holders can incur significant user fees as they access medical care. But the capacity of the healthcare system to provide access to appropriate medical care entails a strong reliance on private sector provision. The trends in eligibility for free public medical services on the one hand, and consumption of private health insurance on the other, throw up some explanatory puzzles. The proportion of the population with medical cards stood at about 38 per cent in 1977, and varied only a little until 1987. By 2001 though, it had fallen to 31 per cent (Wren 2003: 375), and was below 30 per cent in April 2008 (*Dáil Debates*, Vol. 654, 15 May 2008, Deputy Mary Harney, Written Answer 19025/08). But entitlement to free hospital care, subject to a nightly charge, was extended to the whole population in 1991. Access to free GP care was broadened to all those aged over 70 (albeit concluded on controversial terms) in 2001, though rescinded in 2008 with a return of a means test as a result of budgetary pressures associated with the economic downturn. And partial cover for primary care (covering GP visits only) was extended to more low-income families in 2005.

Yet just as we see entitlement to both hospital and primary care expanding, the proportion of the population taking out private health insurance shows a marked increase. The proportion of the population with private health insurance was 18 per cent in 1977, a figure that rose to about 30 per cent in 1982. This had further grown to 35 per cent in 1990, and continued to grow thereafter to 46 per cent in 2001 (Wren 2003: 375); the 2009 figure was about 52 per cent (Burke 2009: 15; Thomas, Normand and Smith 2006). The reasons for the expansion of private health insurance, in parallel with the extension of public sector cover, need to be explored further.

The incentives to take out private health insurance can be traced to the long-standing government policy of facilitating arrangements for private healthcare as a means of augmenting the resources and capacity available for acute sector healthcare (Department of Health and Children 1999). A central tenet of the argument supporting this policy is not just the cost saving to the public system when patients seek treatment in the private sector, thereby forgoing their public entitlements, and in theory, freeing up resources in the public sector for those that remain. A further consideration is that patients opting for private treatment often receive their treatment in public hospitals. This means that their insurance pays the public hospital as well as the consultants for their treatment: thus public hospitals have an incentive to treat private patients (Finn and Harmon 2006). Indeed, government policy actively supports insurance take-up as a means of boosting the hospitals' resource base.

Private insurance in Ireland is said to facilitate equitable treatment because the cost of insurance was governed from the outset by principles of community rating. Notwithstanding some qualifying conditions, and some recent complexities arising from the need to comply with EU competition requirements, private health insurance premiums were not weighted by individual characteristics such as age or health status of the policy-holder. The risk is thereby pooled across all policy-holders, though because the scheme is voluntary, 'risk-pooling' does not have the society-wide reach of universal insurance schemes. The private health insurance system in Ireland was established in 1957 and was provided by a state-owned, non-profit, monopoly insurer, Voluntary Health Insurance (VHI). This was designed to cater for the top 15 per cent of earners who, at the time, were excluded from an entitlement to free or subsidised public health services. It was set up principally to provide cover for acute hospital care and typically covers all or most in-patient hospital expenses. Private out-patient hospital appointments are paid by the user on a pay-per-visit basis, on the same basis as private GP services. Insurance schemes make a relatively low contribution to them.

Private health insurance cover in Ireland therefore continued to be strongly associated with acute hospital in-patient care, and the bulk of the claims discharged involved costs associated with surgical procedures requiring a hospital stay. Direct subsidies such as tax relief on private health insurance premiums are justified on the grounds that they 'allow those with chronic health conditions to benefit from insurance at a reasonable cost' (Department of Health and Children 1999).

From 1987 on, sharp cuts were made in healthcare spending as part of the drive to curb public spending and to reduce high levels of public indebtedness. The investment deficits at this time resulted in lasting under-resourcing of the public sector in comparative terms, with a legacy of a lower ratio of beds to population, and lower numbers of specialist consultants in relation to population than other OECD countries. We must not assume any intention to roll back the welfare state, analogous to retrenchment policies then gathering momentum across continental Europe. Rather, a relatively under-developed healthcare system had suffered restrictions before a full high-quality public system had been put in place. Public spending on healthcare in fact subsequently increased under every combination of party in power. From 2000, spending on healthcare grew at unprecedented rates, much faster than in other OECD countries. But spending per capita on most indicators still lagged behind EU rates (Tussing and Wren 2006: ch.1). The legacy of the cutbacks and of the restrictions on infrastructural investments throughout the difficult years of the 1980s persisted in the form of capacity constraints throughout the system. Rapidly increasing public spending translated into much slower improvement in service delivery.

Problems of sustaining a public–private mix

We have already noted the arguments in favour of public policy support for a private sector health alternative. But there are two problems with this argument. The first is that the existence of a strong private sector may have the opposite effect – it may result in draining resources from the public sector, thereby reducing public sector quality and restricting access (Besley, Hall and Preston 1999; Iversen 1997). The second is that the targeting of benefits toward the least well-off, to achieve the best results in alleviating need, may actually be counter-productive if the primary aim is social equity, as it may intensify the flight into the private sector.

Policy feedback and quality slippage

If individuals are to forgo public sector entitlements and pay for private sector treatment, whether out of pocket or through insurance schemes, the public sector must be of a quality that is lower than the private alternative. From the point of view of equitable access to services, this may be problematic. The quality of the public sector may be 'too' low, resulting in significantly worse experiences for those depending on public provision.

Among the considerations that weigh upon governments in the allocation of public spending, electoral pressures are always likely to loom large. Private health sector users may be able to exercise disproportionate influence over the allocation of resources in healthcare provision both directly through lobbying and voting behaviour, and indirectly by participating in or opting out of the public provisions on offer (Blomquist and Christiansen 1999). Once an individual is privately insured they cease to be concerned about public sector waiting lists, which is generally taken as an indicator for public sector quality (Besley, Hall and Preston 1998; Besley *et al.* 1999). If the intensity of demand for public services can be alleviated by siphoning it off to the private sector, the pressure on policy-makers to improve public sector quality – measured in terms of waiting list length and duration – may be diminished. Moreover, private users may favour a smaller role for the state as a matter of principle (Propper and Burckhardt 1999). If attitudes are further affected by use, then an expansion of private healthcare may mean a further diminution in support for public provision and for the taxation required to fund it: 'Government may under-fund public services in areas with high private insurance coverage' (Siciliani and Hurst 2003). It may be that those who opt for private insurance are among the most affluent and articulate and are more successful at political lobbying than other groups. Since better public services and shorter waiting lists are not a priority for them, political pressure on these issues is reduced, and electoral and lobbying support for private sector alternatives is correspondingly strengthened. British research offers some support for these hypotheses. Besley and his co-authors, for example, suggest that:

regions in which many are privately insured appear to put fewer resources into keeping waiting lists short . . . From a public choice perspective, resource allocation is influenced by wilful political acts. If more individuals choose to opt out of certain NHS services by taking out private insurance this can affect the way in which resources are allocated. (Besley *et al.* 1998: 496)

In the British experience, investigators have found that patterns of use and the political articulation of policy preferences tend to go together:

> On the one hand, the private alternative reduces the demand on the public system, thereby reducing costs, to the benefit of users of the public system. On the other hand, the loss of clientele to the private sector can be expected to reduce public support for a high quality public service, at least among those who do not use the public alternative. This is particularly true if those with the highest demand for quality are the first to opt out of the public system. (Epple and Romano 1995: 298)

These findings are not uncontested. Propper, for example, argues that many health service users in Britain tend to use both public and private in varying combinations, depending on circumstances and geographical location (Propper and Burckhardt 1999). Many services are in any case not normally available through the private sector – Accident and Emergency, most notably.

It is possible that these patterns are not as readily investigable in the Irish case. In Britain, the public and private health sectors constitute two distinct sectors with separate organizational structures. But even at that, it has been estimated that only about 1 per cent of total NHS admissions in 2001 were through the private sector (National Economic and Social Forum 2002: 38). In Ireland, in contrast, the interpenetration makes the distinction less stark and less immediately visible. But private insurance cover does offer the kind of choices which Besley, Propper and others have been concerned to investigate in the British case. So it is at least plausible that some comparability of findings might be anticipated in the Irish case.

The paradoxes of targeting

Targeting benefits and services through means-testing is often held to be the best way to achieve redistribution and to ensure that those in need receive most help. However, taking the above arguments one step further, a number of analyses of the welfare state have pointed out that governments may be able to build up electoral coalitions of support behind a universal model of provision, not primarily by appealing to the altruism of the wealthiest, but by ensuring that every income group sees benefits in the scheme for itself. Korpi and Palme argue that 'institutional structures affect the ways in which citizens come to define their interests and preferences' (Korpi and Palme 1998: 664). Welfare state institutions are shaped by different interest groups. Once these institutions are in place, they tend to influence the way citizens perceive their interests and the kinds of political alliances that are most appealing to them. Welfare state institutions themselves therefore have feedback effects on distributive processes. Universal care is undoubtedly more expensive to provide than targeted care. But paradoxically, electoral support for higher taxation and higher spending is likely to be stronger where entitlements are universal, and where everyone therefore has some grounds for believing that they are 'all in the one boat' (Rothstein 1998).

Although hospital care is in principle available to all in Ireland, the Irish healthcare system has many of the characteristics of a targeted system. The risk is, as Titmuss noted, that welfare for the poor is poor welfare (Titmuss 1958). As Levi notes, support from the middle class from a public sector is based on 'contingent consent', whereby government must offer benefits at a quality level that keeps voters broadly happy (Levi 1998: 88). The rise in demand for private insurance suggests dissatisfaction with public provision in Ireland. But more seriously than that, survey evidence indicates much greater levels of dissatisfaction with healthcare provision in Ireland than in almost all other OECD countries. In a Eurobarometer survey reported in the OECD's Health Data Report for 2008, respondents in Finland, Belgium and France topped the poll in recording favourable verdicts on their national healthcare systems that were between two and three times greater than the negative ones. Only 20 per cent of Irish respondents reported judgements that were at all positive, and 72 per cent reported that their healthcare arrangements required 'fundamental changes' or needed to be 'completely rebuilt'. This level of dissatisfaction was topped only by Greece's 78 per cent and Portugal's 80 per cent (OECD 2008).

Equity issues in a two-tier system

The Irish dual system created two levels of healthcare according to insurance status and therefore ability to pay. For most procedures against which it is possible to insure, it is normal to find that separate waiting lists are maintained for public and private patients, resulting in variations in waiting time that depend on means rather than clinical need. This is one of the most visible aspects of inequitable treatment in the Irish healthcare system, and probably the issue that generates most resentment. Furthermore, instead of the public and private sectors each having their own funding stream, and contrary to the incentive systems facing hospitals to treat private patients in public hospitals, in fact the Irish acute care system is based on massive subsidies flowing from the public system to the private.

The profile of those with private insurance

We now turn to consider the socio-economic and household characteristics of those who buy private health insurance, and their motivations for doing so.

In Ireland, about 52 per cent of the population in 2008 had private insurance,

27 per cent had free access on grounds of low income, and about 25 per cent had neither medical cards nor private insurance. 70 per cent of those not qualifying for the free public care under the means-tested medical card scheme opted for private health insurance (Finn and Harmon 2006). And some with medical card entitlements still took out private insurance, generally on account of a chronic or acute health condition (Burke 2009: 15). But recent work examining the impact of individual and household characteristics on the probability of buying private insurance shows that the better educated, wealthier and healthier are much more likely to insure themselves. There is a clear disparity between those with and those without private health insurance across both income and education levels. Nearly 60 per cent of those in the top income quartile are insured compared to 18 per cent of those in the lowest quartile. Of those people with no educational qualifications or who only attended primary education, only 20 per cent have health insurance. Among those with third-level education (which is a category that has expanded rapidly over the last 30 years, and accounts for up to half of those in the younger age categories), almost four-fifths (79 per cent) are privately insured. Those with third-level education have a 43 per cent higher probability of having private health insurance compared with those with no qualifications or primary education only. Those with the strongest propensity to have private insurance are not those with the greatest incidence of current health needs. Only 26 per cent of those with poor health are privately insured. Of those with good health, almost double this proportion, 47 per cent, have private health insurance. The effect of poor health on propensity to insure is in fact negative – those with poor health status have a 10 per cent less probability of being insured than those with good health (Finn and Harmon 2006; Harmon and Nolan 2001) And we can also show that health status itself is inversely related to income and education (Finn and Harmon 2006).

Irish public policy is aimed at promoting the take-up of private health insurance as a means of improving the supply and quality of healthcare. It does so through incentives such as community rating and tax reliefs. But it now seems that this is primarily successful at encouraging take-up among people at the higher ends of the income and education distributions, and those who already enjoy better health (Layte and Nolan 2004).

A majority of people cite a concern with quality as the most important consideration in their decision to insure. Typically private health insurance buys an individual a higher standard of accommodation (private or semi-private) and hotel-style facilities (i.e. TV, phone, meal menus). But access clearly looms largest in people's motivations for taking out private insurance. Chief among people's concerns about public sector quality is not the standard of accommodation facilities once in hospital, but the ability to avoid queueing for out-patient appointments and for surgical procedures (Harmon and Nolan 2001; Williams, Kinsella and Watson 1996).

Evidence about differential access is hard to come by. No central record of waiting list statistics is kept anywhere in the Irish health system, and the National Patient Treatment Register only provides information on waiting times for public patients for procedures in public hospitals. Indeed the time spent between referral from a general practitioner and an initial consultant appointment in the public sector often considerably exceeds the time spent between being recommended for a surgical procedure and admission to hospital (Wren 2003). The National Economic and Social Forum (NESF) found that following referral for a procedure, about a quarter of those without insurance, but no-one with private insurance, waited for more than one year for hospital-based treatment. (National Economic and Social Forum 2002: 55–9). Furthermore, 'going private', whether through out-of-pocket payments or using private health insurance, also ensures choice of consultant and guaranteed treatment by a consultant rather than a member of the hospital doctors' team, neither of which is guaranteed for public patients.

Cross-subsidies from public to private

Take-up of private insurance is therefore skewed along lines of relative social advantage, which means that access to healthcare is differentially available depending on ability to pay. But in addition to this, the private system is so intricately bound up with the public system of healthcare provision in Ireland, that private patients, or rather their insurers, do not pay anything like the full economic cost of their care. Those who are privately insured benefit not only from direct fiscal incentives, but also from cross-subsidies from the public sector to private medicine. As these are not distributed equally across the population, healthcare funding contributes to inequalities in access and quality of provision between public and private patients.

The cost of tax relief on medical insurance premiums and health expenses that was offset against income tax was reported by the Revenue Commissioners as €225 million in 2002 and €273 million in 2003 (Revenue Commissioners 2006: Table IT6). Total current health spending in 2002 was €8.2 million, of which rather less than half went to hospitals (Wren 2003). Tax relief on health was scaled back over time in line with the objective of broadening the tax base and reducing the use of fiscal instruments to achieve policy objectives, and health insurance relief was made available only at the standard rate of 20 per cent. But this would still be a considerable benefit to those with private insurance, and a sizeable contribution from the public purse to private health treatment.

The ownership structure of Irish hospitals is complex, and meshes public and private in ways that derive from the origins of healthcare in Ireland as a mixture of religious charitable institutions on the one hand, and highly targeted, means-tested public care on the other. Some of the more recently established hospitals are owned and controlled by the public authorities (originally Regional

Health Boards; the Health Services Executive since 2005) under the auspices of the Department of Health and Children. Others continue to have the status of 'voluntary' hospitals, owned and controlled by religious orders, though now almost entirely publicly funded. All of these hospitals treat both private and public patients. However, hospitals do not charge insurance companies the full economic costs of treatment of private patients in public hospitals. Nolan and Wiley, looking at areas of direct subsidy such as the difference between the actual accomodation cost of a private patient and that charged to the insurer, estimated in 2000 that insurance payments came to about 50 per cent of total actual costs (Nolan and Wiley 2000). In 2003, charges were raised by a very sizeable 67 per cent to take account of medical inflation, but they still paid between half and 60 per cent of total costs (Tussing and Wren 2006: 139). Furthermore, hospitals do not charge fees for use of public hospital equipment and premises when treating private patients. We may also note that the public system absorbs the cost of professional training, public hospital development, and indeed Accident and Emergency costs. Considerable subsidies can be shown to flow from the taxpayer to private hospitals and private patients in public hospitals (Commission on Financial Management and Control Systems in the Health Service 2003: 72).

Patients with private insurance can be treated in what are primarily public hospitals because consultants' contracts engage them for a specific number of hours' commitment to public patients per week, on top of which they may engage in private practice (either on-site or off-site, depending on type of contract). Since most hospitals not only permit this but rely on the income from private patients, this mixed system has flourished. Not more than 20 per cent of bed capacity is meant to be occupied by patients admitted from consultants' 'private' waiting lists. But Nolan and Wiley showed that while there was 'substantial crossover of private patients to public beds', the flow in the opposite direction was much smaller (Nolan and Wiley 2000). In practice it is acknowledged that it is very difficult to monitor or maintain the 20 per cent limit to private patient admissions, as bed management is mainly managed by consultants themselves rather than by hospital managers. Two-thirds of private beds were in public hospitals in 2007, and Dublin public hospitals had up to 40 per cent private patients (Burke 2009: 16, 118). And about two-thirds of all admissions to acute in-patient care come via Accident and Emergency rather than through scheduled elective surgery.

The development of a dedicated private for-profit hospital sector added extra capacity to the Irish healthcare system, and they accounted for some 12 per cent of acute in-patient beds and elective surgery in 2000 (Tussing and Wren 2006: 98). There were two in 1988, and 18 in 2008 (Burke 2009: 216). But a new category of private hospital appeared to be favoured by the Fianna Fáil-Progressive Democrat coalition during the first decade of the twenty-first century: that is, for-profit private hospitals, co-located on the grounds of existing public or voluntary hospitals. Eight were planned in 2008 (Burke 2009: 216–21), though public spending cutbacks postponed the implementation of the commitments. This ran counter to the planned rationalization of the hospital sector outlined in the Hanly Report. But in addition, there is a considerable hidden cost to the Exchequer. Tax reliefs to private hospitals have been estimated to amount to approximately 40 per cent of the total costs of these facilities, without even considering the value of the land on which they are built (Burke 2009: 207; Tussing and Wren 2006: 106). Only those insured or willing to pay out of pocket have access to private hospital facilities.

A final aspect of subsidization of the private sector by the public concerns the National Treatment Purchase Fund (NTPF). The Minister for Health and Children initiated the scheme in 2002 to alleviate excessive waiting time of public patients for specific procedures. From a starting number of fewer than 2,000 patients in 2002, the Fund had treated some 150,000 in total by 2009. Undoubtedly the scheme has been of immense assistance to its beneficiaries. But the logic of using public money to buy treatment in the private sector raises further issues of both equity and efficiency. The NTPF spent over €40 million on direct patient care in 2004. The Comptroller and Auditor-General found that some 44 per cent of these procedures were carried out in a public hospital – and the majority of these were treated by the same consultant who had referred them from their own public patient lists to the NTPF (Office of the Comptroller and Auditor-General 2004: 133–4). He also noted that there seemed to be little standardization of the costs of procedures at that point, though these practices were subsequently addressed (Office of the Comptroller and Auditor-General 2004: 137). In effect the NTPF, while remedying some urgent treatment needs, worked by transferring public sector resources into the private sector to treat public sector patients.

In summary, this policy of subsidization of the private sector through taxpayer money is justified by the argument that those who choose to be treated privately forgo their public sector entitlement for which they have already paid (through their tax bill). The case may be made that they are entitled to better quality treatment and access should they choose to pay more – analogous to paying for an upgrade on an airplane perhaps. But we have noted two principal counter-arguments. One of these is that that access based on insurance status is inequitable. If equitable access is the benchmark, it may be argued that healthcare is not like plane seats, and access ought to be organized on grounds of clinical need rather than ability to pay. The other is that the Irish system effects a considerable resource transfer in the form of a variety of subsidies from the public to the private sector.

The evolution of the two-tier system

The organization of healthcare in Ireland, with its distinctive public–private mix, proves to be somewhat problematic when it comes to equitable access and indeed efficiency of resource allocation and utilization. Why then has this system been maintained, when government policy documents reiterated the commitment of every major party to the improvement of the quality of public sector health care, major improvements in public primary care and in the public acute care system, and a progressive drive to reduce the proportion of private to public hospital beds (Department of Health and Children 2001: 93–107)?

The process through which decisions are made can be complex. Breyer and Schneider note that:

> In health economics . . . there is a large gap between policy recommendations often made quite unanimously by academic experts and the measure eventually taken by political decision makers. (Breyer and Schneider 1992: 267)

Among the most urgent requirements for governments is the need to be re-elected. And increasingly competition for power takes place over the allegiances of a growing number of weakly aligned or non-aligned voters. It may even be argued that:

> Policymaking is motivated not by the efficiency criteria of welfare theory, but rather by the desire to design policy which can obtain a majority in the voting process. (Blomquist and Christiansen 1999: 17)

Private patients benefit from private insurance. In the absence of any clear pathway to a significantly better quality of provision in the public sector, it is quite likely that a large proportion of the electorate would favour continuing with the existing system of private insurance.

The particular mix of public and private in Irish public hospitals was made possible because of the structure of specialist care provision in hospitals, based on a 'consultant-led' service, not 'consultant delivered'. The contemporary system is the result of several phases of change and attempted change, firstly in the late 1940s, then in the late 1970s, and most recently in 2008.

Post-war reform initiatives

The late 1940s saw a surge of reform initiatives in Ireland, parallel to the drive to reform healthcare provision right across Europe in the aftermath of the Second World War. Prior to this, two-tier healthcare provision had been the norm, with private care provided by self-employed consultants for the wealthier, and a separate system of public care for the less well-off. A change in public mood meant that governments sought to establish integrated schemes for hospital treatment and access to primary care, based on clinical need and equally available to all. Ireland was no different, and political parties shared broadly similar objectives. Fianna Fáil in 1947 was as committed to expanding free primary care as was Noel Browne, with the 1951 Mother and Child Bill. This would have provided free acute and primary medical care for expectant mothers and for all children up to age 16, through bringing self-employed doctors onto the public payroll.

Quite a variety of schemes were eventually introduced across Europe. Doctors do not necessarily hold a trump card in negotiations with government. In a study of the health reform initiatives in Sweden, Switzerland and France, Ellen Immergut argued that institutional 'veto points' mattered more than pressure group power in shaping outcomes. Swedish consultants were unable to prevail against a strong and unified majority government decision. In Switzerland, in contrast, the outcome was the most favourable to private medicine, and government was confined to providing subsidies for private insurance. A united medical profession was able to use referendums in local regions to fragment public opinion and weaken government's ability to act (Immergut 1992: 58).

The conflict over health reforms in Ireland in 1951, widely understood at the time as a stand-off between Church and State, has been reinterpreted as primarily a conflict between private medicine and health policy reformers. Doctors were able to mobilize a powerful player – Catholic bishops, and specifically John Charles McQuaid of Dublin – on their behalf (Barrington 1987). These had ready access to the ear of government; and a weak and divided coalition was especially poorly equipped to hold a firm line against the expressly articulated preferences of the Catholic hierarchy (Inglis 1998; McCullagh 1998).

The net effect of governments' failure to introduce their preferred measures was a greatly reduced government appetite for reform, and the introduction, as in Switzerland, of public subsidies to private insurance, in the form of the 1957 Voluntary Health Insurance Act. This was aimed at the 15 per cent of the population outside the means-tested hospital access introduced in 1953 (Barrington 2003: 106). Public funding replaced the charitable or sweepstake-based funding of the 'voluntary' hospitals. Yet these hospitals were not nationalized as their British counterparts had been.

The 1979 changes

As the 'public' hospitals were upgraded, the need to rationalize conditions of work across the sectors grew more urgent. This resulted in the introduction by a Fianna Fáil government of the 1979 'common contract' in which the combination of public and private was entrenched. This was an attempt to create some commonality in conditions of work for specialists who had previously worked under widely varying conditions. A two-tier career structure then obtained, in which some consultants were full-time salaried employees of the regional health boards, and others received no salary or pension from the state, but worked in the 'voluntary' hospital sector, earning fees from private patients, and gaining some recompense for treating non-fee-paying patients from the hospitals from the grants they received from the Department of Health (Barrington 1987: 107). But neither clinical accountability of consultants nor any coherent system for monitoring their work-time was adequately built in to the consultant contract.

Between 1979 and 2008, consultants' contracts required them to offer 33 hours a week to the public sector, between running clinics, undertaking procedures and ensuring administrative efficiency of their caseloads, but it did not specify the extent of their personal time commitment to public patients. In practice, public patients were likely to be attended to by non-consultant hospital doctors whose salaries are also paid from public health sector finances. This facilitated many specialists to concentrate on their private patients. Until 1997, it was possible for consultants to have one of two types of contract: one which paid a salary but with some 'abatement' of the rate payable, and which permitted them to engage in private practice in addition to public employment; and another which permitted only work in the public sector on a salaried basis, and which paid a somewhat higher standard salary in recognition of private earnings forgone. The latter option – only held by 47 consultants in 2003 – was abolished in 1997 on the recommendation of a Review Body on Higher Remuneration in the public sector (Commission on Financial Management and Control Systems in the Health Service 2003: 66). This further liberalized the consultant's contract and expanded the scope of the public–private mix, while simultaneously providing some saving in public salary expenses. About three-fifths of consultants in 2008 had 'Category 1' contracts that permitted them to treat private patients within the public hospital in which they were employed. Just over one-third of the consultants, mostly in Dublin and Cork, had 'Category 2' contracts that permitted them to treat patients privately off-site as well as within their main place of work. The method of reimbursement thus entrenched is known to have significant effects on the behaviour of medical professionals (Propper, Croxson and Shearer 2002). Consultants are salaried employees for their public sector work. But they are paid on a fee-per-patient basis by their private patients. There is an opportunity cost to consultants of working in the public sector – that is, reimbursement in the private sector (Rickman and McGuire 1999: 54) As two experts in this area have noted:

> Public health systems have done little to alter the underlying incentives whereby those with the greatest control over the conditions of supply are rewarded rather than penalised for maintaining waiting lists. (Street and Duckett 1996)

The public–private mix itself may therefore be seen to contribute directly to excessive waiting in Ireland (Tussing and Wren 2006: 115).

Yet the anomalies of Ireland's 'mixed' rather than 'hybrid' system grew over the decades that followed. The Brennan Report concluded bluntly that 'the opportunity to earn additional monies through private practice, combined with the ability to delegate public work to other staff, is not in the best interests of the Irish taxpayer' (Commission on Financial Management and Control Systems in the Health Service 2003: 66). This report argued that the only solution to the perverse incentives built in to the system, from the point of view of a high-quality public health service, would be the complete separation of public and private practice:

The existing arrangements for mixing public and private treatments are inherently unsatisfactory from a management and control perspective. They result in a conflict of interest for Consultants between meeting clinical obligations to public patients on the one hand and, on the other, the prioritisation, treatment and the use of publicly provided infrastructure and resources in public hospitals for private patients. They also raise issues of fair competition with private hospitals in that the resources used are not charged for fully. They severely limit the time the majority of clinicians have to pursue resource management. Ultimately, these issues can only be resolved fully by completely separating public and private practices. (Commission on Financial Management and Control Systems in the Health Service 2003: 71).

Consultant contracts in the 2000s

It is generally acknowledged that there is a significant shortfall in the number of consultants relative to population size, compared with other developed countries. In Ireland in 2005, non-consultant hospital doctors (NCHDs) outnumbered consultants by about 2.3 to 1 (just under 2,000 consultants, and a little over 4,000 NCHDs), and hospital services depend on these doctors working long overtime hours (Tussing and Wren 2006: 23). Government policy adopted the recommendations of the various consultancy reports that the health service be consultant-delivered, not consultant-led. A new consultant contract was finally negotiated in 2008 as a precondition to hiring more consultants. This involved a commitment to work for 37 hours in the public system, in return for a significant increase in the remuneration package – making Irish consultants the best-paid in Europe by a considerable margin. The Brennan Report recommended that 'all new Consultant appointments, covering new posts and the replacement of existing Consultants, should be on the basis of contracting the Consultants to work exclusively in the public sector' (Commission on Financial Management and Control Systems in the Health Service 2003: 67). But only about a quarter of consultants had signed up for the public-only option on offer this time. The rest remained free to develop their private practice. The new consultant contract 'reinforces rather than deconstructs the two-tier system of hospital care', resulting in a system in which Sara Burke has argued that 'apartheid in Irish healthcare was official government health policy' (Burke 2009: 117). Consultants sought to protect both existing members' rights and the rights of new appointees to continue to practise privately.

The capacity of the public sector to deliver adequate services remained well below the level of actual demand in the system. And the health sector had long been characterized by fragmented management in unclear lines of accountability, such that overall system coordination presented major challenges. Capacity constraints can be identified across a range of measures. Bed availability and extraordinarily high rates of bed occupancy are highly visible indicators that inflame popular feeling, especially when people see severely ill patients lying on trolleys waiting for diagnosis, admission and treatment (Tussing and Wren 2006: 182–90). Bed occupancy was regularly at or in excess of 100 per cent of capacity, compared with international norms closer to 85 per cent (Burke 2009: 106).

The abolition of the regional health boards and the creation of the Health Services Executive (HSE) in 2005 represented a decisive move in the direction of centralization, with a view to achieving greater coordinating capacity and therefore greater efficiency. However, problems of managing the new structures generated significant new problems. Most importantly, the relationship between the Department of Health and Children on the one hand, and the Health Services Executive on the other, had not been fully specified at the time the legislation was enacted, and produced real uncertainty over domains of responsibility, initiative and financial accountability (Tussing and Wren 2006: 305–20). Spending control in a very large and diverse system was a real challenge. But opportunities to deliberate on resource allocation had been progressively reduced over time (Barrington 2003: 116). Accountability within hospitals remained severely under-defined. Indeed, weak financial controls within hospitals were specifically identified as a problem in the Brennan Report, which recommended that 'where they do not already exist, chief executive officers in all hospitals should immediately establish an Executive Management Committee', to agree the hospital Service Plan, monitor performance against budget, agree corrective measures and advise on policy matters (Commission on Financial Management and Control Systems in the Health Service 2003: 68).

Organizational reform of the Irish health system was thus pushed toward centralization of decision-making, though with a crucial lacuna in accountability and decision-making at the centre. This went against the trend in many other European societies, which had begun to experiment with decentralization, creation of internal markets and fostering of competitive opportunities to try to achieve cost savings and efficiencies. Michael Moran has argued that this is not inconsistent with continuing government oversight and management:

> Closely integrated oligarchies dominated by professional and corporate interests, operating with a substantial degree of independence from the core institutions of the state, are being replaced: by looser, more open, more unstable networks; by networks in which professional and corporate elites still exercise great power but in a more contested environment than hitherto; and by an institutional setting in which the core institutions of the state exercise much tighter surveillance and control than hitherto. This is the sense in which to speak about the rise of the market and the retreat of the state is a great oversimplification. (Moran 1999: 178)

A broad political and policy consensus appeared to exist in Ireland that market-based solutions in a small market would not be beneficial (Wiley 2000: 922). Perhaps the real issue, though, is the weak political capacity displayed to date to manage organizational change effectively.

But the problem at the core of the system – the intermingling of public and private – was not centrally addressed by any of these structural changes. The consultant contract goes hand in hand with entrenched differentiated entitlements of those with and without private insurance. Nominal commitment to the public sector notwithstanding, successive governments presided over the expansion of a two-tier health care system.

Conclusion

Irish health care policy in the early twenty-first century was approaching a decisive point. Electoral pressures to reform and improve the many deficiencies in health services were strong. The quality of provision in the public sector needed to be improved significantly. All governments pledged themselves to do this – to reduce waiting lists, reduce trolley-based waiting time for admission, make hospitals cleaner and safer places, and introduce the sort of evidence-based practice assessment that improved patient outcomes but that could only be delivered in a modernized health delivery system.

Key to doing all this was the employment of a great many more front-line medical personnel, which would involve increasing the role of consultants and redesigning the role of non-consultant hospital doctors. But the great majority of consultants already had private practice commitments. Much of the delivery of services took place through private practice structures, whether in public or private hospitals. A slight majority of the population was equipped with private insurance cover.

Under these conditions, successive governments seemed unable to decide where their priorities for healthcare reform lay. And while they spoke of their commitment to public sector quality, in effect private sector incentives were, if anything, strengthened. Ireland was no longer in the early or foundational stages of constructing a national integrated health service, as so many European countries were in the years following the end of the Second World War. At that point, decisive policy changes were perhaps more easily undertaken. But reform of a developed healthcare system can be likened to rebuilding the ship while already at sea. A variety of problems in health sector governance have remained unresolved. At the heart of it lies the conundrum of the intermeshing of public and private. Some commentators, as we have noted, recommend a complete separation of the two. Quite how to do this, in a system that relies so heavily on the private sector to deliver central parts of its services, is unclear. How it might be initiated, and by whom, given the complex relationships within the Health Services Executive, and between the HSE and the Department of Health and Children, remains a puzzle.

Irish politicians claimed to wish to strengthen public sector provision, yet acted to strengthen private sector rewards and incentives. But if governments fail to take decisive action for long enough, inaction or indecision itself becomes a policy when it is pursued over time in a fairly consistent way (Korpi and Palme 1998). The public–private mix in Irish healthcare is a good example of policy evolution along unplanned lines, following contradictory imperatives, where non-decisions eventually become de facto decisions.

Note

1 Comparative data can be difficult to compare with confidence. Irish health spending appears lower than it really is because, unlike other countries, GDP was higher than GNP in Ireland during the 1990s and 2000s. Also, the Irish population had a lower rate of age dependency, which should keep demand lower than elsewhere. On the other hand, at least two of the seven categories of Irish health spending are 'social spending' in OECD terms: community care of the elderly, and disability support (Nolan 2008; Tussing and Wren 2006).

Bibliography

Barr, Nicholas. 1998. *The Economics of the Welfare State.* Oxford: Oxford University Press.

Barrington, Ruth. 1987. *Health, Medicine and Politics in Ireland 1900–1970.* Dublin: Institute of Public Administration.

Barrington, Ruth. 2003. Governance in the Health Services. In *Governance and Policy in Ireland,* edited by Dónal de Buitléir and Frances Ruane, 105–22. Dublin: IPA.

Besley, Timothy, and Stephen Coate. 1991. Public Provision of Private Goods and the Redistribution of Income. *The American Economic Review* 81 (4): 979–84.

Besley, Timothy, John Hall and Ian Preston. 1998. Private and Public Health Insurance in the UK. *European Economic Review* 42: 491–7.

Besley, Timothy, John Hall and Ian Preston. 1999. The Demand for Private Health Insurance: Do Waiting Lists Matter? *Journal of Public Economics* 72: 155–81.

Blomquist, S. and V. Christiansen. 1999. The Political Economy of Publicly Provided Private Goods. *Journal of Public Economics* 73 (1): 31–54.

Breyer, F. and F. Schneider. 1992. Political Economy of Hospital Financing. In *Health Economics Worldwide,* edited by Peter Zweifel, and H.E. Freh, 267–85. Dordrecht: Kluwer.

Burke, Sara. 2009. *Irish Apartheid: Healthcare Inequality in Ireland.* Dublin: New Island.

Commission on Financial Management and Control Systems in the Health Service. 2003. *Report of the Commission on Financial Management and Control Systems in the Health Service (The Brennan Report).* Dublin: Stationery Office.

Department of Health and Children. 1999. *White Paper on Private Health Insurance.* Dublin: Stationery Office.

Department of Health and Children. 2001. *Quality and Fairness: A Health System for You.* Dublin: Stationery Office.

Epple, Denis and Richard Romano. 1995. Ends Against the Middle: Determining Public Service Provision When There Are Private Alternatives. *Journal of Public Economics* 62: 297–325.

Esping-Andersen, Gøsta. 1990. *Three Worlds of Welfare Capitalism*. London: Polity.

Esping-Andersen, Gøsta, Duncan Gallie, Anton Hemerijck and John Myles. 2002. *Why We Need a New Welfare State*. Oxford: Oxford University Press.

Finn, Claire and Colm Harmon. 2006. A Dynamic Model of Demand for Private Health Insurance. Discussion Paper 2006/12. Dublin: UCD Geary Institute.

Harmon, Colm and Brian Nolan. 2001. Health Insurance and Health Service Utilisation in Ireland. *Health Economics* 10: 134–45.

Hoel, M. and E.M. Saether. 2003. Public Health Care with Waiting Time: The Role of Supplementary Private Health Care. *Journal of Health Economics* 22: 599–616.

Immergut, Ellen. 1992. The Rules of the Game: The Logic of Health Policy-Making in France, Switzerland, and Sweden. In *Structuring Politics: Historical Institutionalism in Comparative Perspective*, edited by Sven Steinmo, Kathleen Thelen and Frank Longstreth, 57–89. Oxford: Westview.

Inglis, Tom. 1998. *Moral Monopoly: The Rise and Fall of the Catholic Church in Ireland*. Dublin: University College Dublin Press.

Iversen, Torben. 1997. The Effect of a Private Sector on the Waiting Time in a National Health Service. *Journal of Health Economics* 16: 381–96.

Korpi, Walter and Joakim Palme. 1998. The Paradox of Redistribution and Strategies of Inequality: Welfare State Institutions, Inequality and Poverty in the Western Countries. *American Sociological Review* 63 (5): 661–87.

Layte, Richard and Brian Nolan. 2004. Equity in the Utilisation of Health Care in Ireland. *Economic and Social Review* 35 (2): 111–34.

Levi, Margaret. 1998. A State of Trust. In *Trust and Governance*, edited by Valerie Braithwaite and Margaret Levi, 77–101. New York: Russell Sage Foundation.

McCullagh, David. 1998. *A Makeshift Majority: the First Inter-Party Government, 1948–51*. Dublin: Institute of Public Administration.

Moran, Michael. 1999. *Governing the Health Care State: A Comparative Study of the UK, the US and Germany*. Manchester: Manchester University Press.

National Economic and Social Forum. 2002. *Equity of Access to Hospital Care. Forum Report No. 25*. Dublin: NESF.

Nolan, Anna. 2008. Health: Funding, Access and Efficiency. In *The Economy of Ireland: National and Sectoral Policy Issues*, 10th edn., edited by John W. O'Hagan and Carol Newman, 297–316. Dublin: Gill and Macmillan.

Nolan, Brian and Miriam M. Wiley. 2000. Private Practice in Irish Public Hospitals. *General Research Series 175*. Dublin: ESRI.

OECD. 2004. *Private Health Insurance in OECD Countries: The OECD Health Project*. Paris: OECD.

Office of the Comptroller and Auditor-General. 2004. *Annual Report*. Dublin.

Propper, Carol, Bronwyn Croxson and Arran Shearer. 2002. Waiting Times for Hospital Admissions: The Impact of GP Fundholding. *Journal of Health Economics* 21 (2): 227–52.

Propper, Carol and Tania Burckhardt. 1999. Does the UK have a Private Welfare Class? *Journal of Social Policy* 28 (4): 643–65.

Revenue Commissioners. 2006. *Revenue Commissioners' Statistical Report, 2005*. Dublin: Revenue Commissioners.

Rickman, Neil and Alistair McGuire. 1999. Regulating Providers' Reimbursement in a Mixed Market for Health Care. *Scottish Journal of Political Economy* 46 (1): 53–71.

Rothstein, Bo. 1998. *Just Institutions Matter: The Moral and Political Logic of the Universal Welfare State*. Cambridge: Cambridge University Press.

Siciliani, Luigi and Jeremy Hurst. 2003. Explaining Waiting Time Variations for Elective Surgery Across OECD Countries. *OECD Health Working Paper 7*. Paris: OECD.

OECD. 2008. *Health Data 2008*. Paris: OECD. Available at www.ecosante.org/ OCDEENG/67.html.

Street, Anders and S. Duckett. 1996. Are Waiting Lists Inevitable? *Health Policy* 36 (1): 1–15.

Thomas, Stephen, Charles Normand and Samantha Smith. 2006. *Social Health Insurance: Options for Ireland*. Dublin: Adelaide Hospital Society. Available at www.adelaide.ie.

Titmuss, Richard M. 1958. *Essays on 'The Welfare State'*. London: Allen & Unwin.

Tussing, A. Dale and Maev-Ann Wren. 2006. *How Ireland Cares: The Case for Health Care Reform*. Dublin: New Island Press.

Wiley, Miriam F. 2000. Ireland. *Journal of Health Politics, Policy and Law* 25 (5): 915–24.

Williams, James, Ray Kinsella and Dorothy Watson. 1996. Perceptions of the Quality of Health Care in the Public and Private Sectors in Ireland. Research Series No. BMI 163. Dublin: Economic and Social Research Institute.

Wren, Maev-Ann. 2003. *Unhealthy State: Anatomy of a Sick Society*. Dublin: New Island Press.

7

The governance of the environment: handling the waste mountain

Brigid Laffan and Jane O'Mahony

Introduction

Concern about the environment and pressure for enhanced environmental protection emerged as a political and policy issue in Ireland in the 1970s. Although the first Green party TD was not elected until 1989, environmental concerns became part of the political agenda from the 1970s onwards. Furthermore, membership of the European Union in 1973 had a major impact on the evolution of environmental policy and law. Prior to membership, there were a number of laws that addressed environmental concerns, notably the Foreshore Act (1933), the Forestry Act (1946) and the Local Government (Planning and Development) Act of 1963. Notwithstanding this, Ireland's system of environmental regulation was one of the weaker national regulatory regimes when Ireland joined the Union (Flynn 2003, 2006). The weaknesses related to the regulatory framework, institutional capacity, enforcement and policy responsiveness. Consequently, EU membership and the evolving environmental *acquis* was a major driver of policy change. During the 1970s and 1980s, there was a flurry of legislative activism with the enactment of a myriad of laws in this field. Many of the laws were intended to give effect to EU directives. Moreover, Ireland faced growing problems of environmental sustainability, particularly in relation to waste management.

The focus of this chapter is on the evolution of governance in the environmental sphere in Ireland since the 1990s. Waste management, a critical issue for sustainable development, offers a lens to explore the political and institutional challenges that have arisen in the governance of the environment in Ireland. There have been changes in policy, institution-building, law-making, investment in infrastructure and the mediation of deep conflicts about the location of such infrastructure. Public authorities were under sustained pressure because of the growing problem of waste and presence of the European Commission with its demands to strengthen the regulatory framework, diversify the range of waste management infrastructures and enhance enforcement and compliance. Ireland's waste problem was greatly exacerbated by the growth of the Irish economy from the mid 1990s onwards (see Figures 7.1 and 7.2). The political and institutional

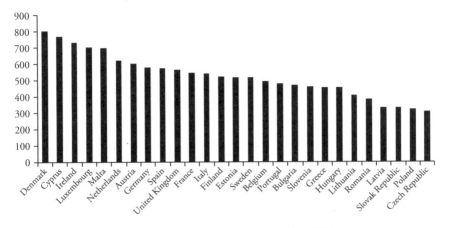

Source: European Environment Agency online, 2011

Figure 7.1 Waste generation in EU countries: municipal waste in kg per capita, 2008

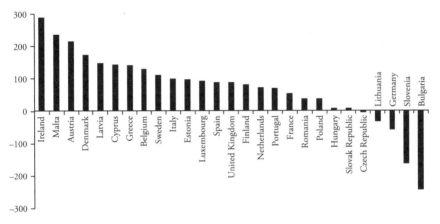

Source: European Environment Agency online, 2011

Figure 7.2 Increase in municipal waste generation per capita, EU, 1995-2006

system of environmental governance, however, has struggled to manage the multiple pressures in this policy field. The chapter begins with a brief overview of the problem of waste.

The waste mountain

Since the early 1990s, successive governments and environmental ministers have struggled to come to terms with a growing waste mountain. Prior to the establishment of the Environmental Protection Agency (EPA) in 1993, reliable statistics on waste generation in Ireland were not available. Following its establishment, the EPA maintained a national database on waste that shows significant increases in the generation of municipal waste, industrial waste, hazardous waste and construction waste in the 1990s. The downside of high levels of economic growth in the 1990s was pressure on the existing infrastructure for waste management; there was also evidence of widespread illegal dumping.

In its 2001 Millennium Report on Ireland's environment, the EPA reported that almost 80 million tonnes of waste was generated in 1998. In the period 1998-2001 there was an overall increase of 31.5 per cent in municipal waste, an average increase of 10.5 per cent per annum (Environmental Protection Agency 2003). Traditionally, municipal waste collection in particular was the responsibility of local authorities (29 county councils and five urban authorities). However, the role of local authorities changed from 1996 and the private sector became increasingly involved in the provision of waste collection services in all local authority areas. According to the EPA, 'a simple system involving almost complete reliance on landfill as the sole waste management option with local authorities as the main service providers has been replaced by a sophisticated and intricate waste management network involving both the public and private sector' (Environmental Protection Agency 2005). Since 2005, both domestic and commercial users have been charged for waste disposal in Ireland. Waste collection charges are paid to the local authority if it provides the waste collection services. Increasingly local authorities have allowed private operators to contract directly with individual households for waste collection services at freely fixed rates. One consequence of this development has been an increased incidence of unauthorized waste activity.

Prior to 2005, unauthorized waste activity primarily consisted of the illegal dumping of waste. For example, a large number of illegal dumps were found in Wicklow adjacent to Dublin. In August 2001, Wicklow County Council staff discovered an illegal dump on land owned by a private landowner, and the investigation of this dump led to the subsequent discovery of many other illegal dumps in the area, including one on land owned by a major Irish company, CRH. The investigation of the dumps found that there was 'systematic illegal dumping' and 'illegal dumping on a commercial scale' in Wicklow (quotes from Mr Edward Sheehy, Wicklow County Manager, in evidence to the Joint Committee on the Environment and Local Government, 5 February 2003). The waste found included hazardous waste from Dublin hospitals, construction and demolition waste, and household waste. Given the scale of the problem (88 illegal sites) and the nature of the waste that was dumped there, Wicklow County Council used the courts to get those responsible to deal with the waste and restore the sites. In addition, the Gárda National Bureau of Criminal Investigations was called in to investigate the criminal dimension of the illegal activity.

In 2003, the Office of Environmental Enforcement (OEE) was established within the EPA to ensure the implementation and enforcement of environmental legislation in Ireland, including waste legislation and prosecutions for breaches of such legislation. According to a 2005 EPA report on the nature and extent of unauthorised waste activity, such large-scale illegal dumping was quickly stamped out. Instead, however, the EPA encountered significant illegal movement of waste to Northern Ireland. In addition, the increased cost of waste management, driven largely by increases in landfill gate fees, contributed to unauthorized practices such as ad hoc fly-tipping and backyard burning of waste (Environmental Protection Agency 2005; OECD 2008).

As the domestic system struggled to come to terms with the emerging waste problem, the EU has been the main forum for the evolution of Irish environmental policy and regulation on waste management. A number of specific directives on packaging, waste oils, landfill of waste and incineration augmented the EU's 1975 Framework Directive on Waste. The Union's waste policy paradigm sought to minimize the generation of waste in the first instance, thereafter to encourage recovery and recycling and finally the disposal of waste safely. The paradigm was encapsulated in a waste continuum – prevention, minimization, reuse, recycling, energy recovery and disposal – extending from the most-to least-favoured policy option. Traditionally, the practice of waste management in Ireland relied heavily on landfill sites with limited recovery and recycling. In other words, there was a serious misfit between Ireland's practices of waste management and what was emerging in the EU as best practice. The literature of the domestic impact of European regulation emphasizes misfit between the demands of EU legislation and national policy as a source of adaptive pressures on the member state (Börzel and Risse 2003). It is argued that the need for policy adjustment is high when national policies differ from EU demands (Héritier, Kerwer, Knill, Lehmkuhl, Teutsch and Douillet 2001). Misfit is regarded as a necessary but not sufficient condition of domestic change. In waste management terms, Ireland was a laggard. See Figures 7.3 and 7.4 for a comparison between Ireland and the environmental leaders in the European Union on the management of waste.

Ireland recycled or composted relatively little of the waste it generated, and landfill accounted for over 80 per cent of waste disposal during the 2000s. There are no commercial incinerators in Ireland and on average just under half of all hazardous waste produced in Ireland is sent abroad for treatment and recycling (Environmental Protection Agency 2009). During the 1990s, landfill sites came under considerable pressure due to the growing volume of waste and the need to improve and upgrade existing sites that were poorly run and managed. Increasingly local environmental groups resorted to the courts to obtain closure or better management of landfill sites in their areas (O'Sullivan 2001). The Environmental Protection Agency warned in 2001 that landfill:

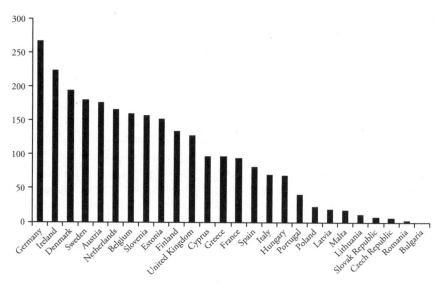

Source: European Environment Agency online, 2011

Figure 7.3 Municipal waste recycled in EU, kg per capita, 2008

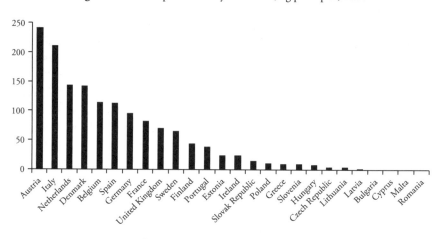

Source: Eurostat online statistics, 2011

Figure 7.4 Municipal waste composted in EU, kg per capita, 2009

would not be sustainable in the longer term given the quantities of waste being generated and the difficulty in providing new facilities due to public objections. In addition, targets set by EU directives and declared national policy preclude the continuance of the scale of reliance on this mode of disposal. (Environmental Protection Agency 2001)

The EU's 1999 Landfill Directive required a 25 per cent reduction of biodegradable waste going to landfill by 2006, rising to 65 per cent by 2016. During the 1990s, the growth of waste, the impending exhaustion of landfill sites and increased concern about waste disposal in the media meant that waste management emerged as a key priority and challenge to successive governments. As ministers sought to address the policy and implementation challenges, the Commission continued its pressure on the Irish public authorities. In early 2002, the Commission's Environment Commissioner, Margot Wallström stated that as far as the Commission was concerned, waste was the dominating environmental issue facing the Irish public. Speaking at a public meeting in Ireland, the Commissioner said:

> We prefer material recovery before energy recovery but we also put incineration before landfill. You have too many landfills and you also have illegal dumping. You'll have to decide on that . . . The Commission does not have one model that goes for all member states. You'll have to find an Irish model. (Commissioner Wallström, *Irish Times*, 25 January 2002)

The objective of this chapter is to explore and explain the institutional, policy and political dynamics that have moulded the evolution of Ireland's governance regime in waste management. The next section outlines the analytical framework adopted in this chapter.

An explanatory framework

The analytical framework adopted to explain the evolution of waste management in Ireland has a number of elements. The policy process is conceived as a process involving formal and informal goal-oriented actors operating within an institutional framework that establishes the norms, rules and opportunities within which the actors interact. A key characteristic of this policy field is the fragmentation of responsibility across governmental levels: the national, local and European. Given the nature of the waste problem identified above and sustained pressure from the European Commission, domestic actors are under pressure to promote a new policy paradigm, EU-driven, for waste management and to develop the political and institutional capacity to implement it. The evolution of waste management in Ireland required not just the implementation of new policy paradigms but also a strengthening of the organizations responsible for the policy area.

The concept of 'reform capacity' was developed by Héritier *et al.* to explore the impact of EU laws on the member states (Héritier *et al.* 2001). The study defines reform capacity as 'integrated political leadership, based on formal competences or factual consensus capacity'. The two facets of political leadership identified in this definition matter. First, the formal competences of the various actors in this policy domain mould their authority and their opportunities to achieve their goals. The second facet, 'consensus capacity', relates to the ability of those promoting change and new policy paradigms to achieve a coalition for reform. Waste management is however a highly contested issue. There is conflict about the underlying principle 'the polluter pays' and deep conflict about the nature and location of waste infrastructure. Further more, the capacity for reform is hampered by the presence of 'veto players' in the political system. Tsebelis distinguishes between institutional veto players and partisan veto players (Tsebelis 1995, 2002). Institutional veto players are akin to 'veto points' where there are constitutional or jurisdictional opportunities for particular actors to veto a particular law or policy. The Irish political system is not characterized by formal veto points. The authority of a government with a majority in parliament is strong, but the nature of the Irish electoral system (proportional representation by means of single transferable vote), on the other hand, promotes the mobilization of partisan and societal veto players – Laffan and O'Mahony have analysed the mobilization of agricultural veto players in an environmental issue (Laffan and O'Mahony 2008).

Those actors attempting to overcome the mobilization of veto players cannot rely on the sort of deeply rooted support for environmental sustainability in the political culture which has enabled executives to overcome opposition in other European jurisdictions. Historically, societal interest in and sympathy for environmental protection in Ireland was weaker than in many other EU states, although this is now changing, particularly amongst those with higher levels of education (Flynn 2003; Kelly, Tovey and Faughnan 2007). Attitude surveys during the 1980s revealed that Ireland was consistently at or near the bottom of the league in terms of concern for the environment, especially when the issue was a trade-off between economic growth and environmental protection (Coyle 1994). A study commissioned by the Department of the Environment published in 2000 concluded that Irish attitudes were characterized by a disjuncture between what people thought and how they behaved in relation to the environment. Figure 7.5 conveys the principal elements of this analytical framework.

Formal and informal actors

The key public actors with a role in the development and implementation of waste management policy in Ireland are:

- The Department of the Environment, Community and Local Government and the Cabinet with responsibility for framing the laws, developing policy, financing waste infrastructure and mediating between Dublin and Brussels; the department and minister are the key drivers of policy change in the domestic context. Ireland's Westminster system of government is characterized by strong executive power and relatively autonomous sectoral ministries.

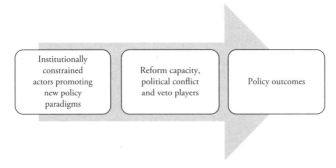

Figure 7.5 Reform capacity, political conflict and veto players

- The European Commission in its role of monitoring compliance with European directives and developing shared policy norms in this area. The Commission uses its role as guardian of European legislation to bring cases to the European Court of Justice against the member states for non-compliance.
- The Environmental Protection Agency (1993) as a key regulator of other actors and the source of authoritative information about waste. As mentioned above, as part of the EPA, the Office of Environmental Enforcement supervizes local authorities on issues of environment protection and enforces waste management law.
- Local Authorities with particular responsibilities under law in this area both as a regulator and provider of services.
- An Bord Pleanála, the national planning appeals board. An Bord Pleanála has responsibility for assessing landfill applications from local authorities and commercial incinerator applications.

In addition, private companies and households are important players as customers and suppliers of services. Waste is both a private and public goods issue with a high salience capable of being politicized with ease. The key institutional actors are driving policy change in a system that is institutionally and geographically fragmented. The capacity of different public agencies to engage in reform in this policy field has a major impact on policy outcomes. Moreover reform is being conducted in the context of a high level of civil society mobilization on questions of policy and location of waste infrastructure (OECD 2008). Given a high level of mobilization, the capacity of the system to mediate conflict and manage 'veto players' has a major impact on policy outcomes.

Tackling the problem

Central government under the guise of the Department of the Environment, Heritage and Local Government has primary responsibility for the 'national' development of a waste management strategy. Having adopted a series of ad

Table 7.1 **Central government response to the challenge of waste management**

Action and establishment of institutions	Legislation and guidelines
Regulatory framework	EPA Act 1992
	Waste Management Act 1996
	Waste Management Amendment Act 2001
	Protection of the Environment Act 2003
Institution-Building	Establishment of the EPA 1993
	Establishment of the Office of Environmental Enforcement 2003
New roles	Enhanced role for EPA in licensing
	Additional demands on local authorities
	New waste management planning system
New policy principles and policy documents	EU Waste Hierarchy
	Polluter Pays
	Changing Our Ways (1998)
	Delivering Change (2002)
	Waste Management – Taking Stock and Moving Forward (2004)
	National Overview of Waste Management (2004)

hoc legislative and institutional changes in the 1980s and the early 1990s, central government moved to reform Ireland's system of waste management. This involved changes to the regulatory framework, the establishment of new agencies, the granting of new roles to those agencies and the promotion of new policy principles. Rather than a one-off reform, there have been a series of incremental changes that together have amounted to significant change. See Table 7.1 for a summary of the governmental response.

Two key developments were the establishment of the Environmental Protection Agency (EPA) in 1993 and the enactment of the Waste Management Act in 1996, a law that came into force in 1998. The establishment of the EPA underlined the growing role of specialized agencies in Irish governance. Institution-building and law were combined to enhance the regulatory capacity of public authorities in this area. The Act was designed to provide 'a comprehensive and modern regulatory framework for the application of higher environmental standards, particularly in relation to waste disposal, in response to EU and national waste management requirements' (Department of the Environment and Local Government 2002). The Act integrated the key principles of EU waste management policy which were: (a) the precautionary principle – preventative action should be taken if serious risk exists; (b) the proximity principle – waste should be treated as close to its source as possible; and (c) the 'polluter pays'

> **Box 7.1 Summary: licensing regulations, Waste Management Act, 1996**
>
> **Local Authority**; shall collect or arrange for the collection of household waste within its functional area and may provide or arrange for recovery or disposal of commercial waste.
>
> **EPA**; licensing authority for all significant waste disposal and recovery activities.
>
> **The waste producer (domestic or commercial)**; is obliged to make source segregation of waste as required in local bye-laws enacted by the local authority.
>
> **Waste collection firms**; are obliged to achieve approval from the local authority through a waste collection permit and to conform to the conditions therein.
>
> **A waste recovery or disposal facility**; is obliged to obtain a waste licence from the EPA.

principle – the cost of waste management should be borne by those who produce the waste.

Its key provisions related to:

- a more effective organization of public authority functions in relation to waste management, involving new or redefined roles for the Minister, the EPA and local authorities;
- enabling measures designed to improve performance in relation to the prevention and recovery of waste; and
- a comprehensive regulatory framework for the application of higher environmental standards, in response to EU and national requirements.

See Box 7.1 for a summary of the licensing regulations.

The Act clarified the roles of the two main public actors responsible for the management of waste disposal, the Environmental Protection Agency and the local authorities. The EPA was assigned responsibility for licensing all significant waste recovery and disposal activities and for the planning, management and control of hazardous waste. It would continue to operate the Integrated Pollution Control (IPC) licensing system established by the EPA Act in 1993. In an important development, local authorities had for the first time to apply to the EPA for a licence on the basis of an IPC to operate recovery or waste disposal systems. The EPA, before granting a licence to a public or private operator, had to be satisfied that its criteria were met. Local authorities were thus subject to the regulatory reach of the EPA and were faced with additional responsibilities. Local authorities were responsible for:

- Waste management planning in relation to non-hazardous waste.
- Authorization of commercial waste collection activities.
- Control of waste movements.

Box 7.2 Government waste policy commitments by 2002

Establish a **National Waste Management Board** to coordinate, monitor, review and advise the Government on all aspects of waste management policy at all levels of the waste hierarchy;

Establish a **National Waste Prevention Programme** to achieve waste prevention and minimization;

Establish a **Core Prevention Team** within the EPA to drive the National Waste Prevention Programme;

Promote voluntary action and other initiatives to implement re-use systems and to implement the plastic bag levy;

Establish a **Recycling Consultative Forum** to act as a consultative and advisory body on all aspects of recycling;

Provide funds for waste recovery infrastructure including recycling infrastructure;

Introduce a landfill levy and implement landfill bans;

Establish a **Market Development Programme** to identify and promote markets for recyclable material;

Further promote or establish producer responsibility initiatives for packaging waste, end-of-life vehicles, waste electrical and electronic equipment, construction and demolition waste, newsprint, tyres and batteries;

Establish a **Producer Responsibility Unit** within the EPA;

Draw up a national strategy on biodegradable waste in the municipal waste stream and develop a public service waste management programme.

- Ensuring that adequate arrangements exist for the collection, recovery and disposal for household waste.
- Making by-laws in relation to the manner in which waste is presented for collection.

For local authorities, the two most significant aspects of the Act were (a) the provision requiring them to prepare local and regional waste management plans and (b) the provision that established the 'polluter pays' as a key principle that should govern waste management. The Minister for the Environment was given the power to specify the form and content of the local authority plans, and the power to compel them to coordinate their waste management plans.

Central Government continued its activism in this area with a major policy document on waste management: Box 7.2 outlines the sequence of its commitments. In October 1998, a policy statement on waste management – *Changing Our Ways* – was produced and addressed chiefly to local authorities. The document provided a national policy framework for waste management. It outlined the government's policy objectives and endorsed strategic waste planning on a regionalized basis and a reduction in reliance on landfill. Local authorities were obliged to prepare waste management plans providing for development of new waste infrastructure at the regional level. The 1998 policy statement identified landfill as the 'most fundamental issue to be addressed in the waste management area, and which should be the core objective of the current local planning process' (Department of Environment and Local Government 1998). The statement anticipated future EU directives in relation to landfill and drew attention to the ineffectiveness of previous waste plans. A new planning process was advocated with an emphasis on a regional approach and the use of more private operators in waste management. The politically sensitive issue of waste charges, flagged in the 1996 Act, was explicitly advocated:

> It is recognised that Ireland's waste management infrastructure has been consistently under-resourced and that significant capital investment will be necessary to achieve the radical improvements which are required . . . Local authorities must move rapidly towards full cost recoupment for the waste services they provide. As a matter of equity, and in order to directly incentivise waste reduction, the level of waste charges should vary according to usage. (Department of Environment and Local Government 1998: 11)

The possibility of adding incineration to the available waste infrastructure was suggested. Finally, the policy document established a series of targets for waste management to be achieved by 2013. The 1998 policy document was supplemented by an additional statement, Delivering Change, in 2002, which made provision for two new levies to finance an Environment Fund that would be used to assist waste recycling and other environmental initiatives. The policy statement also contained a number of further commitments and targets. The policy and legal framework was subject to additional change with the enactment of the 2003 Protection of the Environment Act amending the 1992 EPA Act, the 1996 Waste Management Act and the 1997 Litter Pollution Act. The focus of the Act was on further embedding the polluter pays principle in the regulatory framework. Finally, the 2004 publication 'Taking Stock and Moving Forward' completed the waste policy framework, focusing on the collection of accurate and up-to-date data on waste arising and ensuring more intensified and consistent enforcement of the law in relation to waste. The commitment to waste-to-energy thermal treatment facilities for municipal waste as one element in the integrated approach to waste management was reiterated (Department of the Environment, Heritage and Local Government 2004).

Delivering change?

It proved difficult to transform the new policy paradigm and regulatory framework from blueprint to implementation. Ireland has consistently failed to comply with its legal obligations. The Irish authorities were constantly in trouble with the EU authorities for compliance failures, as Table 7A in the Appendix shows.

Irish local government and politics has struggled, and in many cases failed, to achieve a consensus on waste management. An electoral system characterized by inter- and intra-party competition privileges the local over the national and allows groups in relatively small geographical areas to mobilize quickly and to have considerable influence on their local councillors. Councillors of all political parties are very unwilling to support unpopular actions because of the PR system; veto players emerge at local level with relative ease.

Local authorities were slow to draft waste management plans, and when they did, the plans were the subject of significant controversy. The drafting of the plans provoked considerable public interest and opposition, largely due to the inclusion of thermal treatment options and agreement on the plans proved impossible in a number of local authority areas. For example, in January 2000, Wexford County Council rejected the South East Regional Authority's waste plan and in September 2000, Roscommon County Council rejected the draft Connacht waste management plan, which provided for an incinerator and super-dump (*Irish Times*, 26 September 2000). The Galway, Longford and Louth County Councils also refused to adopt waste management plans for their counties. As a result of the difficulties encountered in the preparation of plans, the then Minister for the Environment, Noel Dempsey, reviewed the powers open to him to speed up the process of developing waste management plans and in fact rescinded the powers of local authorities in this area in March 2001. The minister's decision was later codified in the Protection of the Environment Act, 2003. This overcame one of the weak points in the transmission of policy by taking responsibility out of the hands of local politicians. But it did not necessarily overcome the problem. It merely transferred the pressure point to national politics. TDs face the same pressures as local councillors to promote and protect the local, however defined.

Even where waste management plans were agreed, implementation proved controversial. The implementation of the Waste Management Plan for the Greater Dublin Area illustrates the problems that have arisen. The Dublin regional waste management plan covers four county council areas: Fingal; Dublin Corporation (Renamed Dublin City Council); Dun Laoghaire-Rathdown; and South Dublin County Council. In 1996, when the waste management plan was first undertaken this region had a combined population of 1,056,666 (1996 Census). It was the most densely populated area of Ireland and thus in need of its own specific plan to resolve its household, commercial and industrial waste problems. Dublin's waste management plan was based on the premise that existing land filling rates of some 80 per cent to 90 per cent could not continue, and that new Irish and EU legislation must be met. In terms of the financing of waste disposal in the greater Dublin region, the costs of waste collection, treatment and disposal far exceeded the income generated through fees and charges. Apart from collection and disposal costs paid by the commercial sector there had been formerly little application of the 'polluter pays' principle. The domestic user of the services provided by the local authority paid only for disposal at civic amenity sites. Consequently, there was no economic incentive to householders to reduce their use of the service through waste prevention or minimization and diversion of waste from landfill to recycling. The cost of waste collection activities of the local authorities in the region was estimated at IR£15.6 million in 1997. Although this covered some trade collection, the majority of the cost could be attributed to the non-paying domestic sector. Local authority expenditure on household waste in Dublin represented 69 per cent of the overall annual operating expenditure. Waste treatment and disposal costs accounted for 19 per cent, and the remaining expenditure was due to administrative costs and waste reduction and recycling. Relative to investment in waste collection, treatment and disposal, the level of expenditure on waste reduction and recycling was low at 2 per cent of overall operational spend.

The Dublin Waste Management Strategy Study was undertaken in March 1997 and was followed by a two-month public consultation exercise. Copies of the draft report were given to libraries and other public buildings in the four-county region. While the public were keen to be involved in their area's waste management, assisted by local authority education, they were largely ignorant of the finances behind waste distribution. On a micro-level, they equated litter on the streets with waste, but not landfill and the expense of transporting waste out of the greater Dublin area. When the Local Authorities moved to recoup some of the cost with 'bin charges', extensive opposition to the charges emerged. In January 2001 Dublin City Council resolved that an Environmental Waste Charge be introduced for the city and the charges would therefore be legally payable (unless waived) in two instalments annually. Many councillors feared 'a public backlash over "double taxation"' (*Irish Times*, 4 January 2002) and Dublin saw massive anti-bin charge protests in 2003. By October 2003, all four Dublin local authorities had taken out legal injunctions to prevent further 'bin-tax' protests, by which time 15 protesters were in jail, including former MEP and now TD Joe Higgins and former Councillor and now TD Clare Doyle from the Socialist Party, for flouting injunctions preventing the obstruction of refuse collections. The Socialist Workers Party and Sinn Féin were also active in the campaign. The anti-bin charge movement began to lose its fervour in 2004, although a number of anti-bin charge candidates stood in the local elections. Some of the opposition was dissipated by moves to replace standard charges by a 'pay-by-volume' system. This is largely felt to be a more successful and popular implementation of 'polluter pays'. Put simply, a bin is only emptied if it is full, and the householder is not charged for a collection they do not require. Overt resistance to the charges dissipated but there remains a problem of non-compliance in some of Dublin's poorer areas, leading to illegal dumping and burning.

The bin charges were not the only flashpoint in Dublin to arise over the implementation of Irish waste management policy. A proposed municipal waste incinerator on the Poolbeg Peninsula in Dublin Bay has met with fierce resistance, not least from former Green Party Minister from the Environment John Gormley, charged with implementing the existing waste management strategy that includes a commitment to waste-to-energy thermal treatment. The dispute also has the potential to lead to fundamental changes in existing Irish waste management policy. When first proposed it was suggested that the Poolbeg mass burn incinerator would have a capacity to deal with up to 600,000 tonnes of non-recyclable waste per annum. At a public meeting in 2000, the then acting assistant city manager Mr Matt Twomey believed that 'thermal treatment was necessary if Dublin was to reduce its 90 per cent dependence on landfill to just 15 per cent within the next seven years. It was proposed to thermally treat 25 per cent of the waste and generate energy and electricity from it' (*Irish Times*, 23 February 2000). Chief opponents to the incinerator have included the Combined Residents Against Incineration (CRAI) group and the Irish Waste Management Association (on behalf of private waste disposal companies who would be in direct competition with the incinerator if it is completed).

In September 2004, Dublin city councillors voted against the incinerator but the vote was not regarded as having any weight by the then Dublin City Council Manager, Mr John Fitzgerald. The EPA eventually granted licence for a municipal waste incinerator in November 2008, with Minister for the Environment John Gormley coming under fire for the decision (the incinerator was to be located in his own constituency). The EPA licence granted was subject to more than 216 conditions relating to the environmental management, operation, control and monitoring of the facility and construction began in December 2009. However, on becoming Minister for the Environment in 2007, John Gormley wrote to Dublin City Council signalling that government policy on waste was likely to change and that incineration would no longer be its 'cornerstone' (Frank McDonald, *Irish Times*, 11 February 2010). Gormley challenged the construction of the incinerator in a number of ways. In late 2009, as work on the construction of the Poolbeg incinerator commenced, he indicated that, in light of conclusions from an international study he had commissioned on Irish waste management practice, which recommended a smaller level of incineration and favoured increased use of mechanical and biological treatment of waste, he intended to introduce a cap on incineration which would limit the amount of waste that could be burned on a regional basis. He also appointed a senior barrister to examine the financial liabilities of the contract awarded to the Covanta/Dong consortium for the Poolbeg incinerator. Speaking on RTE radio news on 14 December 2009, the minister stated that 'the local Council needs to consider its position . . . I think at this stage they need to understand an incinerator of this capacity is just not on'. In February 2010, Minister Gormley clashed publicly with Dublin City Manager John Tierney, who in turn claimed that he has a statutory obligation to go ahead with the incinerator and drew on an ESRI report on waste management commissioned by Dublin City Council in defence of the incineration project. The conflict richly illustrates the procedural difficulties in generating coherent policy priorities on sensitive issues.

The pattern of environmental governance

The case for reforming Ireland's approach to waste management is evident given the growing volume of waste and the problems of waste infrastructure. The system of environmental governance has not proved particularly robust when faced with the challenges. That said, there have been important changes since the early 1990s. Central government has focused on building up the regulatory framework through both legal measures and regulatory institutions. Irish law in the area of waste management is much stronger and more ambitious than it was and the EPA is maturing as an organization. In addition, central government attempted to shift the policy paradigm in new directions and to invest in waste infrastructure. With or without European Commission pressure, Irish central government would have had to tackle the growing waste mountain. EU deliberations and laws, however, provided a framework for policy in this field and the use by the Commission of sanctions was a resource to central government as it searched for solutions. European law is frequently used at domestic level for doing things that national governments would want or need to do anyway. Blaming Brussels or acknowledging the legal requirement to transpose and enforce European law is part of contemporary governance in Ireland. Considerable effort was devoted by successive ministers to drafting and enacting primary legislation and to developing overarching policy statements and problem-solving strategies. In line with the pattern of regulatory politics elsewhere, the Irish system was characterized by a reliance on law and regulatory institutions, notably the establishment of the Environmental Protection Agency (EPA) in 1992 and the development of its capacity in terms of expertise and staffing.

Local authorities are a central part of the delivery system. Their role, however, in relation to the environment is problematic as they face cross-cutting pressures from other responsibilities such as road-building and local economic development. Moreover, local councillors are far more open to local pressures than the experts working for the EPA. Under pressure from a mobilized public, local councillors become veto players in relation to environmental infrastructure. In relation to the environment, local authorities are responsible for implementing and enforcing national and EU legislation. They are the responsible authorities for physical planning, litter control and waste management. In other words, they are responsible for aspects of waste management that are not under the auspices of the EPA. Local authorities have struggled to provide an adequate infrastructure for waste management in their areas. Under pressure from the EU, central government in the 1990s clarified the responsibilities of local authorities and made them subject to licensing from the EPA. Even then, local authorities, particularly councillors, found it very difficult to agree to waste management plans that were highly unpopular among their constituents. Their response was to prevent agreement on waste management plans in many instances. This exacerbated conflict within many councils between the elected tier and the permanent local authority officials.

Since the decision to make the charging of waste levies mandatory from 2005, and the consequent delegation by many local authorities of waste disposal services to private companies, the role of local authorities in waste management continues to be problematic as local authorities juggle the conflicting functions of regulators as outlined above and as service providers. The coverage of waste management services in Ireland is by no means uniform, as current legislation allows households to opt out of collection services. Significant differences also exist in terms of the number of services local authorities and private operators provide with regard to waste disposal as local authorities have increasingly relinquished the operation of the waste collection market to the private sector (OECD 2008).

Central government, the regulatory agencies and local government form the core of the formal policy-making, regulatory and policy-delivery system. The formal system has delivered a better system of regulation and a higher level of recycling than previously, exceeding national and EU targets. Household collections have greatly increased the level of recycling and a significant proportion of the population have been induced to change their behaviour. This was achieved by carrots and sticks; carrots in terms of household recycling and sticks in terms of local charges by weight for local collection. However, other waste problems remain. For example, less than nine per cent of organic waste, largely food and some garden waste, was saved from landfill in 2007 and the quantity of biodegradable waste dumped in landfill increased by more than 5 per cent in the same year. According to the EPA, this has led to the distinct possibility of EU fines if the amount of biodegradable waste going to landfill is not reduced by 35 per cent in 2010 (Environmental Protection Agency 2009). Without the full implementation of the 'polluter pays' principle, the incentives available to alter behaviour will not be adequate.

The location of waste infrastructure also remains deeply problematic: Box 7.3 summarizes some of the major conflicts that have arisen.

Box 7.3 Selection of incineration conflict flashpoints

Goddamendy, West Dublin 1997

Proposal to incinerate made by: Foster Wheeler Power Systems and ESB.

Opposed by: local resident groups and VOICE environmental group (Dublin based).

Methods of protest used: petitions, representations to local politicians.

Proposal withdrawn.

Kilcock, Co. Kildare 1999–2000

Proposal to incinerate made by: Thermal Waste Management Limited who appealed An Bord Pleanála decision not to grant planning permission (also refused by Kildare County Council).

Appeal action opposed by: North Kildare-South Meath Anti-Incineration Alliance. Members established a steering committee, scientific and legal committee and fundraising committee. The Alliance set up a full-time office in Kilcock, employed a PR company and set up its own website. 6,000 objections were made to the Appeal, a series of public meetings held, local representatives lobbied and 65 stud farms made a statement against the incinerator.

Planning permission for proposed Quat refused by An Bord Pleanála.

Roscommon 2000

Action taken against inclusion of incineration option in Connacht waste management plan and siting of incinerator and superdump in Roscommon.

Opposed by: Roscommon Environmental Alliance.

Waste management plan abandoned incineration option.

Duleek, Carranstown, Co. Meath 2001–03

Proposal to incinerate made by: Indaver Ireland.

Opposed by: Louth-Meath Anti-Incineration Alliance and Boyne Valley and Newgrange Environmental Protection League.

Methods of protest used: 4,000 individual objections made; 27,000 signatures collected.

Incinerator proposal approved by An Bord Pleanála, 5 March 2003. In November 2005, the EPA granted a licence for the incinerator. Decision appealed to High and Supreme Courts. Construction of incinerator began in August 2008 and was completed in June 2011. Due to be operational in September 2011.

Clarecastle, Co.Clare 1996–99

Proposal to incinerate made by: Syntex Ireland/Roche Ireland. Incinerator to operate in own plant only.

Opposed by: Care For Clare, Clare Alliance Against Incineration.

Methods of protest used: protests with vehicle cavalcade, petitions, 80 families threatened to move from the area, judicial proceedings taken against EPA decision to grant licence. High Court upheld EPA decision.

Ringaskiddy, Co. Cork 2001–08

Proposal to build commercial toxic waste incinerator made by: Indaver Ireland.

Opposed by: Ringaskiddy and District Residents Association, CHASE (Cork Harbour Alliance for a Safe Environment), Irish Doctors' Environment Assoociation, Actor Jeremy Irons. See CHASE website: www.chaseireland.org.

6,000 objections made to planning application. An Bord Pleanála hearing took place in Neptune Stadium, Cork due to large turnout of objectors. EPA granted licence for commercial incinerator in November 2005. Construction of incinerator delayed due to various legal actions taken by CHASE.

Wexford 2000–01

Opposition to incineration option in South East Region Management Plan (in area known as SKEWW box – South Kilkenny, East Waterford, Wexford).

Opposed by: local councillors (waste plan rejected by Wexford County Council) and Research and Information Group (who proposed to put forward a candidate in the 2002 general election).

Incineration option dropped from Waste Management Plan.

'Coolmore Stud', Rosegreen, Cashel, Co. Tipperary 2002–03

Proposal to construct incinerator rendering plant by: National By-Products Ltd (CEO Jack Ronan) for the thermal treatment of meat and bone meal. Received planning permission from An Bord Pleanála and EPA.

Opposed by: a group led by racehorse trainer Aidan O'Brien and magnate John Magnier, who sought judicial review of the decision. They were supported by public figures such as Andrew Lloyd Webber, Alex Ferguson, local GPs (37 in all), An Taisce, Irish Farmers Association, Irish Creamery and Milk Suppliers Association, Sinn Fein, Dr Martin Mansergh, Special Advisor to Taoiseach Bertie Ahern and Fianna Fail candidate in 2002 general election. Public meetings were organized with attendance of up to 1,500 people. A 20,000 strong petition was gathered. In the High Court Aidan O'Brien threatened to leave Ireland. An MRBI poll was conducted on the issue (telephone poll of 500, 70 per cent opposed to incinerator). An Appeals Advice Centre was established in Fethard, Co. Tipperary and both sides employed Dublin-based PR firms.

In the end, Jack Ronan of National By-Products Ltd withdrew the application in April 2003. Earlier newspapers reported that Jack Ronan was subject to a vicious campaign of intimidation by those opposed to the incinerator (*Irish Times*, 4 October 2002).

Poolbeg, Ringsend, Co. Dublin 2003 – ongoing

Proposal to build incinerator originally made by: Treasury Holdings.

Opposed by: Combined Residents Against Incineration Group. EPA granted licence for a municipal waste incinerator in November 2008, contract awarded to US/Danish consortium Covanta Dong. Incinerator opposed by former Minister for the Environment John Gormley (incinerator will be in his own constituency) who has clashed publicly with Dublin City Manager John Tierney over Dublin City

Council moves to proceed with plant. Both Gormley and Tierney used independent reports on waste management by international consortium Eumonia and the Economic and Social Research Institute to back up their positions and Gormley has indicated that the waste management commitment to incineration would be scaled back.

Rathcoole Incinerator, Co. Dublin 2007–08

Plans for an incinerator in Rathcoole, Co.Dublin rejected by An Bord Pleanála in February 2009 due to the 'unacceptable risk' of polluting the environment. Incinerator had been opposed by South Dublin County Council, the National Roads Authority, local politicians, Rathcoole Against Incineration Dioxins (RAID) and more than 200 residents.

The planning application by Energy Answers International was made under the Strategic Infrastructure Bill 2006 which enables the fast-tracking of planning applications for projects deemed to be of a particular infrastructural significance, and thus bypasses any requirement to go through the local council's planning procedure (*Irish Times*, 22 July 2008).

In its ruling, An Bord Pleanála stated that, having regard to the approval already granted for an incinerator at Poolbeg, an additional incinerator would be in conflict with the waste management plan for the region.

Source: Taken from various issues of *Irish Times*: www.irishtimes.ie.

The deliberations on waste management within local authority council chambers act as a lightning rod for the tension between the need to tackle the waste problem, on the one hand, and the ability of local groups to resist and prevent the location of new waste treatment centres in their locality, on the other. The difficulty of mediating conflict about landfill and incinerators throughout the country guarantees that governance in this policy field is highly politicized and subject to veto players. Conflict manifests itself in localized flashpoints throughout the country and in the deep-rooted opposition to charges for waste collection. From the adoption of the 1996 Waste Management Act, flashpoints have erupted regularly between private waste facility developers, local authorities, the EPA and local environmental action groups over proposed incineration and landfill projects. Tovey and Share draw attention to the growth of 'populist' environmentalism in Ireland (Tovey and Share 2000). According to Tovey, this represents a 'relatively independent movement of dissent, by ordinary people working at the local level. Populist environmentalists may not necessarily see themselves as environmentalists' (Tovey 1992). The rise of such groups is well documented in newspapers. Frank McDonald, Environment Correspondent of the *Irish Times*, writing in 1997 said:

Any mention of plans for a new landfill dump leads to the formation of an instant action group to fight it all the way. But this is nothing compared to the whiff of an incinerator, which is guaranteed to generate much higher levels of public hysteria. (*Irish Times*, 28 February 1997)

The proliferation of such groups and their success in preventing the introduction of energy recovery operations in Ireland has acted as a major factor in ensuring that waste remains a problem for public policy. Whether such groups should be termed 'populist' environmental groups or simply representative of the pervasive NIMBY syndrome is a normative question.

Conclusion

This paper traced the evolution of efforts to modernize and update the regulatory framework, institutional capacity and policy paradigm on waste management in Ireland. A temporal perspective is necessary to capture the interaction between the expansion of waste on the one hand, and governmental efforts to come to terms with the nature of the problem and find solutions on the other. Throughout the 1990s, successive governments attempted to deal with the problem in a multi-dimensional manner, through legislation, new institutions and policy changes. Central government had to rely on the institutional capacity of other public authorities, notably the EPA and the local authorities, to carry out the new policy and institutional prescriptions. It is well established in implementation research that policy implementation in a multi-level system is far more problematic than at one level of government (Hill and Hupe 2002). Local authorities throughout the country have struggled to devise waste management plans and to implement them. Some progress has been made with recycling but it has had a marginal impact on tackling the growing problem.

Localism and populism together make it difficult for the formal governmental system to tackle the problem. The Irish electoral system creates a political opportunity structure in which it is very easy for local opposition to be mobilized and effective. Within local authorities, there is a clash between the elected councillors easily pressurized by their electorates and the managerial staff who are faced with the disposal of waste. The localism generated by the electoral system is not confined, however, to local politics. It impacts on the attitudes of national parliamentarians and members of the Cabinet. The incinerator issue presented a particular challenge to the Green Party once in government with Fianna Fáil, following the election of 2007. The Green Minister for the Environment, John Gormley, was obliged to manage competing positions: on the one hand his own party's total opposition to incineration and the particularly strong resistance within his own constituency base, and on the other a commitment by the previous administration to building several incinerators. The minister's actions in questioning the Poolbeg incinerator project, along with his proposed alternative plan to build no more than two incinerators in the country, placed him at variance with existing waste management policy.

The Irish political class appears unwilling to stand up to local protest given multi-member constituencies and party competition. There is little evidence that courageous political leadership would generate political returns. There is a poor capacity for risk assessment at the national and local levels and politicians and experts have failed to convey just what the risks are. Experts and officials have not managed to develop communication strategies to educate the public on the costs of waste disposal and the need to make choices.

Is there a way out of the institutional weaknesses identified in this chapter as the present system is clearly unsustainable? The EU will continue to exert pressure for change and over time European legislation bites. However, a consensus on Ireland's waste management strategy remains elusive and the political and institutional system seems incapable of overcoming and outflanking opposition. There is a considerable gap between the waste strategy and implementation (OECD 2008). There is also a considerable gap between policy-makers and between policy-makers and the public on this issue. The successful development of one municipal waste incinerator could perhaps act as a demonstration project that would overcome the fears that have led to such deep-rooted opposition to a technology that is part of the waste management strategies of most countries in Europe. The deliberative processes at national, county and local levels need to be developed so that individuals, families and businesses can explore how their waste can be minimized and dealt with. The provisions of incentives for those areas that host what is now regarded as undesirable may have an important role, as has the discussion of risk and choice.

Appendix

Table 7A. Irish EU waste infringements, 1997–2007

Date	Infringement response	Details of infringement
19 December 1997	Reasoned Opinion	Failure to adopt and send necessary implementing legislation for Hazardous Waste Directive.
30 June 1998	Application to ECJ	Failure to adopt and send all necessary national legislation to implement Packaging Waste Directive.
15 December 1998	Application to ECJ Case C-461/99 '7 December 2001 – Following the recent welcome finalization and notification of waste management plans by Ireland, a resolution to this case appears imminent.'	Failure to adopt and communicate waste management plans complying with Framework Waste, Hazardous Waste and Packaging Waste Directives.
28 January 2000	Reasoned Opinion	Failure to send a report required under Waste Shipment Regulation.
7 April 2000	Letter of Formal Notice	Possible incorrect application of: Environmental Impact Assessment Directive, Dangerous Substances Directive, EIA Directive, Framework Waste Directive and Groundwater Directive (operation of waste facility without a waste permit).
26 October 2000	Letter of Formal Notice	Failure to provide information on compliance with regard to four cases under Waste Framework Directive (non-respect of Article 10 of EC Treaty).
14 November 2000	Letter of Formal Notice	Non-respect of Sewage Sludge Directive (failure to submit adequate information for 1995-97).
10 April 2001	Letter of Formal Notice	Failure to correctly transpose and apply Waste Oils Directive.
26 July 2001	Reasoned Opinion	Failure to comply with Framework Waste Directive – failure to properly control unauthorized private and local authority waste storage and disposal operations and to properly regulate waste collection (Greenore, Co. Louth, Poolbeg, Dublin, wetlands in Co. Waterford and Fermoy, Co. Cork). Local landfills operating without licences.
30 July 2001	Letter of Formal Notice	Failure to comply with Waste Oils Directive
7 December 2001	Application to ECJ	Failure to respect Waste Framework Directive with regard to the controlled disposal and recovery of waste. (Uncontrolled private waste operations, Greenore, Poolbeg, Waterford, Fermoy)

Table 7A (continued)

Date	Infringement response	Details of infringement
1 October 2002	Reasoned Opinion	Failure to completely transpose and correctly apply Landfill Directive.
21 October 2002	Reasoned Opinion	Failure to transpose End-of-Life Vehicles Directive.
19 December 2002	Reasoned Opinion	Failure to apply certain provisions of Packaging Waste Directive and shortcomings in Irish legislation on implementing Packaging Waste Directive.
15 April 2003	Letter of Formal Notice	Failure to provide information about possible breaches of Groundwater Directive, Framework Waste Directive, Hazardous Waste Directive, Trans-frontier Waste Shipment Regulation, Dangerous Substances Directive and the Habitats Directive.
24 July 2003	Reasoned Opinion	Failing to bring national legislation into line with requirements of Framework Waste Directive in relation to urban waste water treatment plants (no system of permits in operation).
13 July 2004	Reasoned Opinion	Failure to clean up over five illegal waste sites; evidence of effective sanctions imposed on illegal waste operators also lacking.
28 October 2004	Negative judgement in ECJ (Case C-460/03)	Ireland condemned for failure to adopt and transmit legislation for failing to give effect to the End-of-Life Vehicles Directive.
26 April 2005	Negative judgement in ECJ (Case C-494-01)	ECJ condemned Ireland for general and persistent failure to comply with provisions of Waste Framework Directive concerning safe disposal of waste, an adequate network of disposal installations and permits for waste disposal operations.
2006	Case closed (Case C-460-03)	Commission decided to close a case concerning non-compliance with End-of-Life Vehicles Directive: October 2004 ECJ judgement.
17 October 2007	Illegal Waste Exports	Commission welcomes a cooperation document agreed between Ireland and the UK on combating illegal waste exports from Ireland to Northern Ireland.
17 October 2007	Letter of Formal Notice	Commission begins legal action against Ireland for inadequately transposing the Landfill Directive.

Bibliography

Börzel, Tanja A. and Thomas Risse. 2003. Conceptualizing the Domestic Impact of Europe. In *The Politics of Europeanization*, edited by Kevin Featherstone and Claudio Radaelli, 57–77. Oxford: Oxford University Press.

Coyle, Carmel. 1994. Administrative Capacity and the Implementation of EU Environmental Policy in Ireland. In *Protecting the Periphery: Environmental Policy in Peripheral Regions of the European Union*, edited by Susan Baker, Kay Milton and Steven Yearly, 62–79. Ilford: Frank Cass.

Department of Environment and Local Government. 1998. *Changing Our Ways: Policy Statement on Waste Management*. Dublin: Government Publications Office. Available at www.epa.ie/downloads/pubs/waste/plans/EPA_changing_our_ways_1998.pdf.

Department of the Environment and Local Government. 2002. Environmental Milestones 1992-1997. In *Making Ireland Development Sustainable*, 21–36. Dublin: Government Publications Office. Available at www.environ.ie/en/Environment/SustainableDevelopment/PublicationsDocuments/FileDownLoad,1845,en.pdf.

Department of the Environment, Heritage and Local Government. 2004. *Waste Management: Taking Stock and Moving Forward*. Dublin: Government Publications Office.

Environmental Protection Agency. 2001. *Ireland's Environment: A Millennium Report*. Wexford: Environmental Protection Agency.

Environmental Protection Agency. 2003. *National Waste Database Report 2001*. Wexford: Environmental Protection Agency.

Environmental Protection Agency. 2005. *The Nature and Extent of Unauthorised Waste Activity in Ireland*. Wexford: Environmental Protection Agency.

Environmental Protection Agency. 2009. *National Waste Report 2007*. Wexford: Environmental Protection Agency.

Flynn, Brendan. 2003. Much Talk But Little Action? 'New' Environmental Policy Instruments in Ireland. In *'New' Instruments of Environmental Governance? National Experiences and Prospects*, edited by Andrew Jordan, Rüdiger K.W. Wurzel and Anthony R. Zito, 137–56. London: Frank Cass.

Flynn, Brendan. 2006. *The Blame Game: Rethinking Ireland's Sustainable Development and Environmental Performance*. Dublin: Irish Academic Press.

Héritier, Adrienne, D. Kerwer, Christoph Knill, D. Lehmkuhl, M. Teutsch and A. Douillet. 2001. *Differential Europe: The European Union Impact on National Policymaking*. Boulder, CO: Rowman and Littlefield.

Hill, Michael and Peter L. Hupe. 2002. *Implementing Public Policy: Governance in Theory and Practice*. London: Sage.

Kelly, Mary, Hilary Tovey and Pauline Faughnan. 2007. *Environmental Attitudes, Values and Behaviour in Ireland*. Wexford: Environmental Protection Agency.

Laffan, Brigid and Jane O'Mahony. 2008. 'Bringing Politics Back In': Domestic Conflict and the Negotiated Implementation of EU Nature Conservation Legislation in Ireland. *Journal of Environmental Policy and Planning* 10 (2): 157–97.

O'Sullivan, Jack. 2001. An Approach to Resolving the Current Waste Management Crisis. *Irish Planning and Environmental Law Journal* 8 (1): 20–6.

OECD. 2008. Local Waste Management in the Local Government Sector. In *OECD Public Management Review: Ireland. Towards an Integrated Public Service*, 316–35. Paris: OECD.

Tovey, Hilary. 1992. Environmentalism in Ireland: Modernisation and Identity. In *Ireland and Poland: Comparative Perspectives*, edited by Pat Clancy, Mary Kelly, Jerzy Wiatr and R. Zoltaniecki. Dublin: Department of Sociology, University College Dublin.

Tovey, Hilary and Perry Share. 2000. *A Sociology of Ireland*. Dublin: Gill and Macmillan.

Tsebelis, George. 1995. Decision Making in Political Systems: Veto Players in Presidentialism, Parliamentarism, Multicameralism, and Multipartyism. *British Journal of Political Science* 25 (3): 289–325.

Tsebelis, George. 2002. *Veto Players: How Political Institutions Work*. Princeton, NJ: Princeton University Press.

8

Governing the city: institutional innovation and its consequences

Diane Payne and Peter Stafford

Introduction

An exploration of issues of governance through the changing process of urban renewal allows us to chart the changing patterns of cooperation and dialogue between different actor groups over time. Regeneration allows distinct and specific issues of urban governance to come to the fore, which would otherwise be lost if looking at a city as if it were 'stopped'. Indeed, some have argued that the study of regeneration projects allow the viewer to see the development of urban governance speeded up as if through time lag technology (Kubler 2004). The process from incubation to regeneration through to completion can take only ten to fifteen years, providing the observer with a short time period and a defined area to explore. Likewise, a regeneration project facilitates close examination of the make-up of and the interaction between actor groups such as metropolitan elites, community organizations and national organizations in a sometimes fast-moving and complex environment. This chapter is a study of the regeneration of the Temple Bar area of Dublin. Through this case study, the chapter explores innovative patterns of governance in Ireland's principal city, through the process of the regeneration of one of its most distinct areas.

This changing pattern of governance is highlighted through a period of urban regeneration in the 1990s in Dublin. During this period, the capital city of Ireland witnessed a huge expansion in the level of infrastructure, including office complexes, tourism and leisure facilities, and residential areas. Some of Dublin's most derelict and crime-ridden inner-city areas have been rejuvenated and regenerated as flourishing focal points for tourism, housing and business activities. This chapter seeks to explore the political dimension – and issues of democratic governance, or lack thereof – surrounding this process.

This chapter highlights a number of key findings from our research on the regeneration of the Temple Bar area of Dublin. Our analysis shows the unwillingness in Irish central public administration to transfer any major responsibility to the sub-national level, even for political decisions and policy initiatives in the area of local development and urban regeneration. While there has been some expansion in the role and responsibilities of local government and its elected and appointed officials, there is a much stronger tendency toward agency proliferation and ad hoc institution-building. This type of policy response, while flexible and responsive, has tended to enhance the influence of Irish central administration rather than strengthen local democratic capacity and responsibility.

Any inner-city urban regeneration project requires strong policy coordination across different administrative domains. In the nineties, the tendency was for Irish government departments to regard their work as autonomous of each other and take a sector-oriented view towards to policy-making. All the more remarkable, then, is our research finding that the Department of the Taoiseach played a central role in pulling together the various interests from across the relevant government departments in order to push the Temple Bar regeneration project forward.

The research demonstrates well how quickly and astutely political 'grassroots' actors, the local residents, can learn which actors are likely to be most powerful and perhaps more importantly, which actors are likely to be ineffective in the political process. In this research we also see the importance of informal network ties between actors in the political process. Network ties such as those based on collegiality and friendships, can provide the opportunity for efficient access to political influence through more informal channels, rather than taking the tardier route to political influence through formal institutional representation.

Regenerating Temple Bar

This research examines metropolitan governance, Irish style, through the lens of urban renewal policy in inner-city Dublin. In particular, this chapter explores the regeneration of Temple Bar, Dublin's much vaunted 'cultural quarter'. Regeneration projects have been undertaken in other Irish cities, but a Dublin-based regeneration project can provide interesting factors not seen elsewhere. Like many European countries, Ireland's capital city is its largest and most complex. As some Scandinavian case studies have shown, capital cities often provide especially interesting examples of innovative forms of urban governance, especially in smaller states which are dominated by their capital, or where that capital city has experienced large-scale speedy economic growth and immigration (Hansen 2004). Like many fast-growing European cities, Dublin has experienced changes in its local government, not least in matters of planning and regeneration, where many actors are forced to play 'catch-up' regarding their role in such matters.

Many actors involved in planning and local government in the city have looked to Temple Bar as one of Dublin's most significant and interesting renewal projects. Previously completed regeneration projects, such as the Dublin Corporation buildings on Wood Quay, had usually involved the large-scale destruction of the existing architecture and the building of completely new buildings – but as well as being important in terms of regeneration, Temple Bar was arguably one of Dublin's most important restoration projects. It was also on a scale much larger than previous renewal projects – 28 acres of dense buildings in the heart of the city centre including sites of Viking archaeology as well as other sites of historical importance.

More importantly, the Temple Bar project has been hailed as a turning point in the city government's attitude towards regeneration. Rather than retrospective repairs of buildings as they become derelict, the process of Temple Bar's regeneration saw the Council become more proactive and planning for future regeneration. There was also a cultural aspect to regeneration. Temple Bar became Dublin's cultural quarter, with pedestrianized streets, street theatre and pavement cafes. One senior architect involved in the plans believed that Temple Bar began the process of 're-Europeanization' of the city centre after the decline of its Georgian heyday.

A body of literature is emerging on Irish urban planning, driven not least by discussions on Ireland's recent economic boom, the so-called Celtic Tiger period which took off in the late 1990s, as well as the publication of details of various scandals regarding matters of corruption which occurred in some planning issues. The *Irish Times* newspaper journalist Frank McDonald has written a number of books on issues of local area and urban regeneration as well as environmental protection (McDonald 1985, 1989, 2000; McDonald and Nix 2005). A common theme across these books is specifically the destruction and the rebuilding of Dublin, from an architectural and environmental aspect. *The Destruction of Dublin* (1985) was written in the 'bleak period of the mid- to late-1980s' while the second book, *The Construction of Dublin* (2000) 'was written in the midst of a maelstrom of activity generated by Ireland's booming economy' (McDonald 2000). For the most part, existing research findings have *described* or mapped out the types of involvement that different types of political actors have in the policy process around the urban renewal of the Dublin area (Marshall 2002). In our research, the emphasis is on understanding *how and why* these particular mechanisms of governance have evolved over time and how they operate so as to successfully coordinate the actions of a range of very different policy actors in the urban renewal policy process.

Analytical framework

In seeking to understand the process of regeneration of Temple Bar and to fully explore the issues of metropolitan governance contained therein, the different successive phases of development will be explored in turn. Our research, like that of others, which have charted movements in urban governance, has split the regeneration process into three periods: the first is the initial start-up period where actors are gathered and motivated (Kuhlmann 2004). Secondly, the formalization period where legislation or public policy sets out the aims and the scope of regeneration. Thirdly, the implementation phase where responsibilities are given and a longer-term post-regeneration outlooks are taken (Blatter 2004). In this research, we identify and explain the evolution of the governance structure for the regeneration of Temple Bar within the broader changing political and social context. As this chapter shows, the governmental context within which the Temple Bar project began its first phase of regeneration was different from the post-Celtic Tiger city in which the restored Temple Bar began to flourish.

By the time this research was being conducted, Temple Bar was very well established and flourishing as a major commercial and cultural area of Dublin city. Examining the Temple Bar project at this stage allowed us to raise some conclusions about the innovative form of urban governance, which it has experienced through the process of its renewal. In 2003, Temple Bar Properties commissioned a study to examine the regeneration of the area in the dozen years since the formal legislation (i.e. Temple Bar Area Renewal and Development Act, 1991) was passed. In doing so, it noted that Temple Bar now needed to reflect on which aspects of its regeneration had been successful, which had not and how different bodies could work to rectify failures and continue success. It also called for stakeholders to be identified and the responsibilities they should have to be listed. In doing so, Howley Harrington, a team of Dublin-based architects, undertook a large-scale consultation process, finding out from various actors as well as citizen groups what they thought of the governance of Temple Bar and how it could be improved. Thus, by 2004 and the publication of the report, Temple Bar had been regenerated and the patterns of its governance for the next decade had been outlined (Howley Harrington Architects 2004).

Institutions and networks in policy-making

Public policy-making in Ireland and particularly that concerned with local development initiatives, involves a range of different interested actors in a multi-levelled network. Finding a way to coordinate and build collaboration across these different policy interests poses a real challenge, the so-called collective action problem. An institutionalist perspective provides a useful middle-range theory that highlights the importance of institutions in framing and structuring processes of public policy-making (Akkerman and Torenvlied 2001; Hall and Taylor 1996; March and Olsen 1996). Sociolological theory suggests that institutions can reduce the uncertainty attached with public policy-making, particularly where new policy actions are being initiated and where the future benefits are uncertain (Millar 2003; Mule 1999). These institutions are best viewed as multi-dimensional – consisting of formal and informal attributes (Raub 1997). The dimensions of institutions of relevance to this study are formal organizational structures, contractual based agreements and established rules for managing the urban renewal measures implemented in Ireland. The informal dimensions encompass social norms, values and customs that influence the way things are done and how the policy process is handled. Also of relevance to this study is how embedded actors are in their policy network as previous work suggests that networks have effects on cooperation through mechanisms such as the dispersion of information about the credibility of actors and informal sanctioning mechanisms (Raub 1997).

Throughout the nineties in Ireland, there were a proliferation of public/ private, partnership-based local development initiatives, often funded under the EU Structural Funds, which have led some authors to suggest that 'these developments in Irish sub-national governance might be construed as evidence of a move away from *governance as hierarchies* to new forms of *network governance*' (Adshead and Millar 2003). This new 'network governance' in Ireland is often described as 'bottom-up', flexible, consensus-based with an ad hoc and open membership involving multiple agencies and multi-levelled. In this study it is argued that while the flexibility allowed by network governance often might lead to very productive arrangements, network governance can also lead to conservatism as well as to openness to innovations. Therefore this research identifies the type of network characteristics of the relationships between the actors involved in the policy process. This network analysis is useful as it can help us understand how the position of the actor in the network may act as a resource or a constraint on the actor reaching his or her goals in the policy process (Dowding 1995).

The Irish institutional framework

Ireland's highly centralized and sector-oriented system of policy-making is closely modelled on the British structure of public administration, under which key decisions affecting the type of urban regeneration projects are adopted and the financial and policy implementation are all taken at the central government level. Local government in Ireland consists of a number of local and regional authorities at three levels. At county/city level: thirty-four local authorities are the mainline providers of local government services – twenty-nine county councils and five cities; at sub-county level: eighty town authorities carry out a representational role for the town with a varying range of local government functions; at regional level: eight regional authorities coordinate some of the county/ city and sub-county activities – they play a monitoring role in relation to the use of EU structural funds; two regional authorities, known as Regional Assemblies, were established in July 1999 under new structures for regional development. Executive decision-making and day-to-day management of local government is the responsibility of the city or county manager, who is directly appointed by the Minister for Environment and Local Government. The City and County Councils, comprising publicly elected representatives or 'county councillors' as they are generally referred to, have very limited decision-making powers. They have 'reserve powers' which implies that under some exceptions they may act to amend the county or city development plan.

The most striking characteristic of the Irish public policy system is the persistent tendency to establish a single-function state body that is first answerable to the central state authorities and often to a particular government department (Marshall 2002). In the absence of functioning sub-national local and regional authorities, many semi-state bodies and public bodies had regional levels of organization. At this level of organization, one finds the ad hoc growth of single function agencies and offices – quangos – arising mainly from decentralization of government departments and state agencies and operating as autonomous actors and independent of each other. Coyle and Sinnott point to 'a proliferation of regional bodies operating in differently constituted sets of regions' (Coyle and Sinnott 1992). More often than not, the boundaries of the territorial areas for which these different statutory bodies have responsibility, do not coincide with one another. Over the nineties, very substantial funding and impetus was given by the European Commission for local development and urban renewal initiatives in Ireland, including the Temple Bar project (Payne 1999; Payne, Mokken and Stokman 2000). Whilst bypassing local and regional authorities in Ireland, working partnerships have been formed instead between Ireland's central government 'lead' departments, these arm's-length agencies or quangos, the social partners, including business interests, trade unions and farmers, and micro-level groups at the community level, thereby satisfying the Commission's demand for broad participation and consultation.

This study was conducted using an extensive and in-depth analysis of relevant public documents and existing research on urban renewal, including spatial planning, and with particular reference to the urban area of interest. Semi-structured interviews were undertaken with a wide range of senior officials from public and private organizations, who were involved in the regeneration of Temple Bar. As outlined earlier, in examining this regeneration case study, we identified a number of phases of development, ranging from a start-up phase through to an implementation phase. The policy network of actors involved in each of the phases and for each case study was identified and measured (Akkerman and Torenvlied 2001). A non-technical overview of these network findings for each of the case studies is presented in this paper. We also sought to identify the types of formal institutional arrangements in place and emergent during each of these phases of development.

The Temple Bar case study

The Temple Bar case study is the story of the renovation and development of a mostly derelict twenty-eight acre site, situated in the inner city of Dublin on the south bank of the River Liffey. Composed of Georgian brick building and

Table 8.1 Phases and key events for Temple Bar

Phase	Phases of development and key events
Phase 1: Start-up (1965-89)	1965: *Transportation in Dublin* document
	1976: Skidmore, Owens and Merrill Report proposes Temple Bar as CIE depot
	1986: *Temple Bar – A Policy for the Future*, published by An Taisce
	1989: Temple Bar Development Council is established; Dublin City Council prepares an Area Action Plan for Temple Bar
Phase 2: Decisions and legislation (1990-91)	1990: Department of the Taoiseach and the Temple Bar Development Council prepares a proposal for EU funding of Urban Pilot Projects.
	1991: Dublin City Council's Temple Bar Area Action Plan included in Dublin City Development Plan, 1991 The Finance Act, 1991 The Temple Bar Area Renewal and Development Act, 1991
Phase 3: Implementation (1992-2003)	1992: Temple Bar Properties Ltd. publish Development Programme for Temple Bar
	1994: EU Structural Funds Operational Programme for Local Urban and Rural Development – Sub Programme 3, Measure 5
	2000: Development of Cultural Centres completed with the opening of the Project
	2003: Harrington Report recommendations.

cobbled streets, Temple Bar is one of the oldest parts of the city. Originally it was earmarked for demolition to be the site of Dublin's proposed central bus depot. Buildings were rented out on short-term leases at low rent, attracting independent clothes and music shops and over time, Temple Bar became known as Dublin's bohemian quarter. By the mid-1980s the proposal for a bus depot had become more unlikely and tentative steps were taken by the tenants of the area to preserve the unique nature of Temple Bar as Dublin's cultural quarter. From that point, regeneration gathered more actor groups and both the fabric and the purpose of the buildings were changed and improved.

Network and institutionalist embeddedness

The chapter traces the development of Temple Bar through the three phases sketched in Table 8.1. In doing so, it notes the critical junctures, or the points at which the patterns of cooperation in the governance of regeneration shifted. The table shows the timeline of major developments.

The following sections do not aim to tell the story of Temple Bar in full, but rather they outline the network and institutionalist embeddedness of the regeneration project, as described earlier. Ireland's heavily centralized political system and administration identifies the central government departments responsible for the proper auditing and management of programmes and policy. In the absence of either trusted informal, network-type mechanisms or formal mechanisms of coordination, there is always a chance that 'other actors' will strongly deviate from the policy recommendation of the central departments. These central government departments must have the guarantee that other actors with whom they collaborate at the implementation phase and will stick to the agreed programme of policy measures. Central government actors will overtly regard credibility as an extremely important attribute, in determining trustworthy partners in the networks for policy decision-making and subsequent policy implementation. Given the lack of real involvement afforded to the Irish local authorities by central government at the planning and decision-making phases (Phases 1 and 2), it is perhaps unsurprising that difficulties arise at the implementation phase regarding compliance in planning and execution (Torenvlied 2000).

Phase 1 (1965-89)
By 1976, the national Bus and Rail Company, *Córas Iompair Éireann* (CIE) had moved squarely behind the proposal to locate the central depot in the Temple Bar area. CIE began acquiring property in the area and leasing buildings at low rent to tenants such as artists and retailers. CIE were unwilling to invest in the upkeep of the fabric of the buildings so it was the tenants and residents of Temple Bar themselves who initiated the process of redevelopment in the late 1970s. The most important development during the start-up phase (i.e. Phase 1) was the establishment of the Temple Bar Development Council (TBDC), which represented the local, small-scale business and cultural interests and residents living in the area. In terms of the structure of the relationships between the various interests, the TBDC actor became the focal point (i.e. high centrality) of communication and influence in the policy network, particularly during this first phase of the regeneration of the Temple Bar area. Many of the initial actors knew each other because of their involvement with local art projects, but as one participant noted, it was unusual to work as allies rather than competitors for funding. Managers of art projects were unused to sharing their time and staff with other bodies, and the culture of cooperation was difficult to create outside the inner circle of enthusiasts. Great effort was made to draw in local residents and businesses, and maintain internal unity when producing public statements.

The effect of the highly centralized Irish political system is seen in the way in which the local actors such as Temple Bar Development Council and Dublin City Council interacted with each other in the first phase of the Temple Bar project. The Temple Bar Development Council produced a document with

several proposals for the regeneration of the area. These proposals were deliberately submitted to various bodies ranging from national to city level. This
was because the TBDC quickly recognized that it was important to engage key
actors at the national central level of government, in the hope that this would
apply downward pressure from national government onto the City Council. The
TBDC had also approached the Dublin City Council for assistance, financial
and other, for their proposal for the regeneration of the Temple Bar area. In the
research interviews, which were conducted with the senior officials from Dublin
City Council (then known as Dublin Corporation), it was indicated that at this
early stage the City Council had no cohesive over-arching development plan for
Dublin, nor did it have the finances to undertake one. For example, the sugges-
tion that the TBDC approach the central government Department of Finance
came from Dublin City Council itself, which was neither able to make financial
provisions on that scale itself, nor able to raise the public profile of the whole
proposal on its own initiative.

During the first phase of the Temple Bar regeneration project, the active policy
network comprised mainly local sub-national actors including relevant departments of Dublin City Council, with the EU Commission and the Department
of the Taoiseach involved only at the periphery of the network. However during
the later part of 1988, the policy network began to change as personal contacts
and friendships facilitated informal contact between the TBDC and Paddy
Teahon, the dynamic and influential General Secretary of the Department of the
Taoiseach, Charles Haughey. His access to the Taoiseach allowed the Temple
Bar residents to bypass the normal formal and time-consuming political ladder
and instead to have access to the heart of government.

Phase 2 (1990 – 91)
In the second phase of the project, there was a remarkable change in the composition and structure of the policy network. A number of new actors joined
the network, which primarily included several central government departments
and semi-state agencies such as the national Tourism Board, Bord Fáilte. These
were vital actors as they were able to give professional advice and credibility to
the voluntary and self-confessed amateurs within the TBDC. Moreover the
most central actor in the network became the Department of the Taoiseach. The
Taoiseach was in a position to pluck 'pet projects' from the pool of schemes for
his own attention. One actor involved in the plans believed that the Taoiseach,
Charles Haughey, saw Temple Bar as a visible cultural initiative in which he
could promote himself as a statesman in the dying days of his premiership.

In a conference on the future of Dublin's infrastructure and fabric in April
1987, Haughey noted: 'Temple Bar is one of the most important, traditional,
attractive and noteworthy parts of the city, and it has to be refurbished and
kept, and I won't let CIÉ near it' (Temple Bar Development Council 1988). In

order to motivate other residents, and to demonstrate the commitment of the Taoiseach, Temple Bar activists repeated Haughey's words, almost as a mantra.

Once the Temple Bar project was taken on board as a key area of responsibility of the Department of the Taoiseach, the administrative, financial and political resources effectively became available to the TBDC. The Taoiseach's Department worked directly with the TBDC and Dublin City Council to submit a proposal for funding under the EU Urban Pilot Project programme and this proposal was ultimately successful. More notable perhaps, was the speed and relative ease with which the subsequent legislation was passed in 1991 to establish the new institutional structure or quango to manage the development of the Temple Bar area into the future. Temple Bar Renewal Ltd. was set up with the remit to approve development proposals to enable them to avail of the incentives provided for in Chapter VII of the Finance Act, 1991. Temple Bar Properties Ltd. was (and still is) the Development Company for the Temple Bar Area, so designated under the Temple Bar Area Renewal and Development Act, 1991. The establishment of these two new companies provided the organizational and management framework to give form and focus to the renewal process (Montgomery 1995). In order to keep the momentum of progress, legislation was introduced on the last day of the sitting of Dáil Eireann, rather than waiting until after the summer recess. In such moments, the support of the national government came into its own. It is also useful to note that some of the key individuals involved in the original TBDC also subsequently took management responsibilities within Temple Bar Properties, and over a decade after the legislation was passed, continued to do so.

In the second phase of this project's development, again we see the impact of the centralized political system in Ireland and in this case, the major role of the Department of the Taoiseach. Over the course of the first (1989-93) and second (1994-99) rounds of Structural Funds for Ireland, Temple Bar attracted some IR£40.6m (€51.55m) in EU and state funding, of which IR£22.1m (€28.06m) came directly from the European Regional Development Fund. Despite the European Commission's strong desire for subsidiarity – policy-making and implementation at the lowest possible level – the Temple Bar project was managed in a way wholly consistent with the centralized Irish approach to governance (Marshall 2002). A key principle of the Reform of the Structural Funds legislation was the call for multi-level partnerships involving the public and private actors, at the relevant local, regional and central levels of administration within the member state. However, the lead department, in the case of Temple Bar, was that of the Department of the Taoiseach which implemented partnership and subsidiarity on its own terms, creating a brand-new state body, Temple Bar Properties Ltd., to serve as an implementing authority with the participation of local-level actors and the social partners. The development of Temple Bar remained a project under the auspices of the Department of the Taoiseach up until 1993, when there was a general re-organization of government departments. Responsibility for the Temple Bar project was then shifted to the Department of the Environment, a body better suited to overseeing the implementation of the project, following its incubation period in the Department of the Taoiseach. Throughout this time, the partnership between the local community in Temple Bar and central and sectoral-oriented government departments, particularly the Department of the Taoiseach, remained strong.

Whatever way we judge the Temple Bar project, the impact of the legislation introduced in 1991 is clear: it gave a new dynamic to the regeneration project and created new working patterns amongst the key partners to the process. However one key actor who remained unsatisfied with the process was the Dublin City Council, formally known as Dublin Corporation. During the 1990s there was a deep sense of grievance within Dublin City Council that it had been effectively sidelined in terms of the executive decision-making regarding the development of the Temple Bar area. Marshall has suggested that while

> Dublin Corporation was included on both of Temple Bar's management committees . . . 'day-to-day executive decisions remained the province of Temple Bar Properties [and] the city's elected government played a comparatively minor role in the formulation of redevelopment policy. The Corporation's only leverage over the Temple Bar project was in planning approvals; unlike the Docklands, Temple Bar was not designated an independent planning area. (Marshall 2002)

Our research interviews with senior officials within the Dublin City Council indicated that during the nineties, considerable organizational change took place within Dublin City Council and that it increased its internal capacity for strategic planning and development as well as its ability to take on large-scale regeneration projects. However, in the late eighties and early nineties, this level of capacity and perhaps organizational confidence was lacking within the Dublin Corporation.

In 1991, an architectural competition was launched to restore many of the Georgian buildings which give Temple Bar its character, and which were now crumbling. During the 1980s a group of former architecture students in Dublin began undertaking small commissions on a partnership basis. By 1991, these architects, despite working in different practices around the city, came together to put in a joint bid for the contract of restoring Temple Bar architecturally, under the name Group 91. Thus within the teams of architects involved in the restoration of Temple Bar, we can see a smaller network taking place. By awarding the contract to a group of like-minded architects, both they and Temple Bar Properties felt comfortable that every group would produce plans basically similar in outlook. Working with friends and colleagues whom they had known for nearly twenty years, the architects believed that they had a supportive environment in which to create, with the added benefit of small rivalries, which they knew would not escalate and threaten the projects. Once again, the relative smallness of the city had a direct impact on the look of the fabric of the buildings, and the absence of Dublin City Council's own architects is striking.

Phase 3 (1992–2014)

The speed at which the second phase moved into the third, largely post-regeneration, phase has been seen by some as testimony to the involvement of the Taoiseach and the success in attracting European funding. Indeed, there can be seen something of a virtuous circle – public support by the Taoiseach leading to successful funding bids, which in turn raise the profile of the project, thus attracting further governmental support. Of all the ministerial support that Temple Bar Development Council could have hoped for, that of the Taoiseach was the most welcome. His support for the project shaved years off the project, revealed hitherto hidden pools of financial support and facilitated access to experts. Having the architectural framework in place following Group 91's winning of the competition meant that planning applications could then be made. This put the regeneration of Temple Bar firmly in the sight of the city's residents. Full-page newspaper advertisements were taken out describing the buildings which would be restored. The architectural framework devised by Group 91 has subsequently been described as 'brilliant' (Howley Harrington Architects 2004) and the manner in which it was presented to the public – as a realistic but large-scale restoration project, not creating office blocks, but creating something for them – meant that the feedback from the public was largely supportive.

In 1992, the regeneration of Temple Bar turned its second corner. Legislation had been passed and the second part of Temple Bar – the West End – was earmarked for further regeneration into a mixed-use development of accommodation and housing. The cultural programmes, meanwhile, were secured with further European and domestic exchequer funding. The improved economy, coupled with the first cheap flights from the United Kingdom and Europe, brought tourists and money into the area, making it an attractive location in which to open a business, and raised its profile as a holiday destination.

In 1993, the support of the regeneration project moved from the Department of the Taoiseach to the Department of Environment, and the Minister for the Environment became the sole shareholder of Temple Bar Properties. In 2001, once the fabric of regeneration had been completed, the shareholder again moved, this time to Dublin City Council. In each move, many feared that the project would be lost within the sea of departmental responsibilities as it competed with other projects and responsibilities for ministerial attention, but the steady networking between grassroots activists and the government bodies ensured that this was not the case, and that Temple Bar received full attention.

Grassroots actors became formalized in this period, forming Traders in the Area Supporting the Cultural Quarter Limited (TASCQ Ltd.). TASCQ members include the pubs, restaurants and shops in the area. In return for a financial contribution, these businesses are promoted by Temple Bar Properties.

This changed with the advent of the third period of regeneration in Temple Bar. In 2003, TASCQ and Temple Bar Properties commissioned a future framework plan for the area. The last large-scale development plan for the area had been in 1993, with Temple Bar's Development Plan. Since then, Temple Bar had changed, and it was felt that a consultation exercise amongst actor groups and the production of a definitive and detailed plan for the next decade of the area was needed, to put the development back on track. In the completed report issued in 2004, the architectural firm commissioned with the report noted: 'It is about ten years since the "new" Temple Bar was born and is now about time to assess a way forward for the next decade. Every city centre is in a constant state of change and flux, not least Temple Bar' (Howley Harrington Architects 2004). By 2003, the regeneration of the main part of Temple Bar was complete, the buildings were all occupied and the West End development had recently been completed. A decade after legislation was introduced, its most major flaw was clearly discernable – the large number of 'super pubs' which had been listed as a cultural service in the 1991 legislation and to whom it was difficult to refuse planning permission. Indeed, the excessive amounts of alcohol available in Temple Bar has meant that 'Temple Bar has become more renowned for its drinking than anything else' rather than for the cultural events (Howley Harrington Architects 2004). The 2004 Plan aimed to redress the balance away from Temple Bar ('the temple of bars') to the cultural quarter, which would open up the area to more people than those on stag weekends or an extended pub-crawl. A responsibility for the cleanliness and the character of the area was given to the traders, through the auspices of TASCQ, but there was clearly a role for the City Council, not just in street lighting and street cleaning, but also in the training and supervision of door staff and the investigation of breaches of planning laws in the area.

More importantly, by 2003, the role of the City Council had changed, as well as the attitude of the Temple Bar authorities towards it. The 2004 Urban Framework Plan listed the City Council as a major stakeholder in Temple Bar, having a strong role to play in the further development of the area. There had traditionally been an ambiguous relationship between Temple Bar and the City Council, characterized by an unwillingness to get involved, and then a readiness to undertake some small actions when pressurized from the national government or from Temple Bar activists. In the 2004 Framework Plan, the City Council had become a needed and welcome stakeholder in the continued development of the plan, and many within the Council were pleased, at last, to be so.

Conclusion

Our empirical research has spanned a critical time period in the urban regeneration of Dublin's inner city. From the case study presented, it is clear that the formal and informal institutions of Ireland's centralized government remain deeply rooted and powerful. While recognizing the innovative character of partnership-based policy coordination, this research also points to the important underlying governance mechanisms at work which primarily depend on central government departments initiating or directly engaging with micro-level community actors and social partners in the early stages of a local development initiative. Moreover in the 1990s there was a significant increase in the capacity of central government departments to effectively engage directly with local-level actors and social partners more generally, often for the purposes of managing EU funds (Payne 1999). With regard to the EU Structural-funded urban projects, such as Temple Bar, the central government sectoral department established a separate body to manage the structural-funded urban projects, rather than go through the existing local authority structures and the elected base of local representatives.

For some commentators, the new institutional structures created, such as Temple Bar Properties, are seen in a negative light. Marshall argues that 'the creation of a special regime for Temple Bar further eroded the power of existing local authorities' (Marshall 2002). For others, such as Montgomery, 'the government was careful and very sure to keep Dublin City Council at arm's length from the whole initiative . . . the effect has been to free the area from the dead hand of bureaucracy', thereby ensuring efficient implementation and progress (Montgomery 1995). Russell suggests that 'local authorities acted as facilitators and enablers of private sector development, rather than as the key drivers or implementing agencies of urban renewal' (Russell 2001). Certainly these contrasting critiques go to the heart of the debate about the principle of local democratic participation and representation in this emergent Irish urban governance model. Moreover, this issue becomes more relevant when it is noted that the Temple Bar governance structure was later replicated throughout the Dublin area as additional European funds were directed to urban initiatives.

The story of evolving governance patterns in Dublin is also one of growing and persistent calls for greater representation in the policy process. While this call has been echoed across the Irish political system, in particular, public and private actors at sub-national level have become more aware and confident in their own potential contribution to the policy process. Moreover the impact of the various EU-financed initiatives directly targeting local communities has allowed new actors to enter the policy networks, which have traditionally been centralist and hierarchical. Marshall suggests that 'grass-roots actors, accustomed to a place at the table following a decade of EU-mandated partnership arrangements, show no intention of withdrawing from the urban policy process despite the progressive wind-down of EU funding for Dublin city-region' (Marshall 2002). The ad hoc approach to partnership governance in Ireland has led to a kind of confusion about the distinction between participative and representative democracy. Often this has resulted in the pursuit of partnership-led governance for its own sake, with little attention paid to who is representing who, on what basis and with what capacity to do so. This research points to the general lack of trust, which characterizes local-level relationships between the local public elected representatives and the local private sector and community interests. Local urban development initiatives are seen to be successful often in spite of local government, which has usually felt threatened and sidelined by these activities.

The introduction of the various local government reforms from the mid-1990s onwards promises a stronger coordinating role for democratically elected local government in Ireland. Moreover, these reforms also attempt to incorporate into their model of local government the widespread demand and popularity of a participatory form of local governance. However the research findings presented here show that, by themselves, these reforms are quite limited and do not adequately facilitate city and county councils to engage constructively with local partners and establish a clear advisory role or voice for the local community and social partners in local government policy. While this move towards a more formalized approach to partnership at the local level and within local government is welcomed by many of those involved, the really difficult and thorny issues of enhancing the financial and other resources, management capacity and policy remit of democratically elected local government in Ireland remains essentially untouched. In the absence of real progress on this front, Ireland's favourite response, innovative but ad hoc, effective but of dubious democratic credentials, the ubiquitous quango seems likely to remain the only game in town.

Bibliography

Adshead, Maura and Michelle Millar, eds. 2003. *Public Administration and Public Policy in Ireland*. London: Routledge.

Akkerman, A. and Rene Torenvlied. 2001. A Tentative Explanation for Coordination in Dutch Social Partnership. Paper presented at workshop 'The Celtic Tiger and the Dutch Miracle: Social Partnership and Collective Bargaining in Ireland and the Netherlands', 4 December. Dublin: University College Dublin, Department of Sociology.

Blatter, J. 2004. Metropolis Unbound, Rebound or Unbundled? New Forms of Regional Governance in German Metropolitan Areas. ECPR Joint Sessions Workshop Paper. Uppsala, Sweden.

Coyle, Carmel, and Richard Sinnott. 1992. Europe and the Regions in Ireland: A View From Below. Centre for European Economic and Public Affairs (CEEPA) Working Paper. Dublin: University College Dublin.

Dowding, Keith. 1995. Model or Metaphor? A Critical Review of the Policy Network Approach. *Political Studies* 43: 136–58.

Hall, Peter A. and Rosemary Taylor. 1996. Political Science and the Three New Institutionalisms. *Political Studies* 44 (4): 936–57.

Hansen, K. 2004. Modern Citizenship and Participation in a Metropolis. ECPR Joint Sessions Workshop Paper. Uppsala, Sweden.

Howley Harrington Architects. 2004. *A Future for Temple Bar: Urban Framework Plan 2004.* Dublin: Howley Harrington Architects.

Kubler, K. 2004. Impacts of New Regionalism on the Relationship between the Citizens and the State: Evidence from Switzerland. ECPR Joint Sessions Workshop Paper. Uppsala, Sweden.

Kuhlmann, S. 2004. From 'Napoleonic Centralism' to 'Democratie de Proximité': The Metropolis of Paris Between Global and Local Challenges. ECPR Joint Sessions Workshop Paper. Uppsala, Sweden.

March, James G. and Johan P. Olsen. 1996. Institutional Perspectives on Political Institutions. *Governance* 9 (3): 247–64.

Marshall, A.J. 2002. European Regional Policy and Urban Governance: Assessing Dublin's Experience. ECPR Joint Sessions Workshop Paper. Turin, Italy.

McDonald, Frank. 1985. *The Destruction of Dublin.* Dublin: Gill and Macmillan.

McDonald, Frank. 1989. *Saving the City: How to Halt the Destruction of Dublin.* Dublin: Tomar.

McDonald, Frank. 2000. *The Construction of Dublin.* Cork: Gandon.

McDonald, Frank, and M. Nix. 2005. *Chaos at the Crossroads.* Cork: Gandon Books.

Millar, Michelle. 2003. Institutionalism 'Old' and 'New': Exploring the Mother and Child Scheme. In *Public Administration and Public Policy in Ireland: Theory and Methods*, edited by Maura Adshead and Michelle Millar, 129-46. London: Routledge.

Montgomery, J. 1995. The Story of Temple Bar: Creating Dublin's Cultural Quarter. *Planning Practice and Research* 10 (2): 135-72.

Mule, R. 1999. New Institutionalism: Distilling Some 'Hard Core' Propositions in the Works of Williamson and March and Olsen. *Politics* 19: 145-51.

Payne, Diane. 1999. Policy-Making in the European Union: An Analysis of the Impact of the Reform of the Structural Funds in Ireland. PhD Thesis, Interuniversity Centre for Social Science Theory and Methodology (ICS). University of Groningen. Groningen, Netherlands.

Payne, Diane, Robert J. Mokken and Frans Stokman. 2000. European Union Power and Regional Involvement: A Case Study of the Political Implications of the Reform of the Structural Funds for Ireland. In *Decision Rules in the European Union: A Rational Choice Perspective*, edited by P. Moser, G. Schneider and G. Kirchgassner, 103–40. London: Macmillan.

Raub, Werner. 1997. *Samenwerking in duurzame relaties en sociale cohesie.* Amsterdam: Thesis Publishers.

Russell, Paula. 2001. Integrated Urban Renewal in Ireland: Constraints to Achieving Integration in the HARP Project Dublin. European Urban Reserch Association Conference Paper Copenhagen, Denmark.

Temple Bar Development Council. 1988. *Submission to Dublin Corporation Planning Department*. Dublin: Temple Bar Development Council.

Torenvlied, Rene. 2000. *Political Decisions and Agency Performance*. Dordrecht: Kluwer Academic.

9

Exceptional or local? The governance of crime and security

Aogán Mulcahy

Introduction

One of the most striking recent developments within the field of criminology has been the growth of interest in issues of governance and regulation. This literature has examined the diversification of security provision, particularly through an expansion of private or commercial security as well as the emergence of new hybrid public–private forms of policing (Johnston and Shearing 2003; Wood and Dupont 2006; Wood and Shearing 2006). These various transformations raise important concerns in light of traditional definitions of the state as the monopoly provider of policing (and 'legitimate coercion' generally). Moreover, some authors argue that shifts evident within the US in particular are emerging as a global template providing the intellectual and policy framework for other countries to follow as they seek to engage with issues of crime and justice in their own local contexts (Garland 2001; Jones and Newburn 2007; Wacquant 1999). In this chapter, I examine the governance of crime and security in Ireland in light of the issues raised by this literature. First, I elaborate the key features of criminology's engagement with governance. Second, I outline the historical context of the governance of crime and security in Ireland, both in terms of the stability that for decades characterized this field, and a series of changes from the 1970s and 1980s onwards that radically altered it. In the third section, I examine some of the most significant recent Irish developments in this area, before concluding with some observations on the challenges that these developments pose for the democratic governance of security in Ireland.

Criminological shifts and the rise of the governance paradigm

For decades, the mainstays of criminological writing were the development of robust theoretical models to explain the nature and dynamics of particular forms of crime, and research into the operation of the criminal justice system. In recent years, however, criminology has witnessed the emergence of a sustained focus on issues of governance and regulation. Of course governance always was at the heart of the discipline, but this generally had been cast within a state-centred framework, as 'government' rather than a more pluralistic 'governance', as the work of state institutions, rather than practice *per se*. This was particularly evident in the manner in which policing was invariably associated with the public state police, and social control more generally was narrowly equated with the formal criminal justice system. The recent criminological shift towards 'governance' arises from several factors. In addition to the influential work of specific theorists such as Michel Foucault, Nikolas Rose, and Burchell and his colleagues (Burchell, Gordon and Miller 1991; Foucault 1977; Rose 1989), it reflects in particular the reconfiguration of the state in light of ongoing global processes of social change, and the diversification of the market of security provision.

One of the key imperatives of the neo-liberal political regimes that came to power in several Western countries in the 1970s and 1980s (most commonly associated with the Conservative Party under Margaret Thatcher in the United Kingdom, and the Republican Party under Ronald Reagan in the USA) was to promote the market over the state. This position held that the state, especially in light of the economic restructuring arising from the 1970s fiscal crisis, had over-extended its reach. By comparison with the market, it was depicted as an ineffective and inefficient service provider that restricted individual choice and undermined individual responsibility. As such, the proper role of the state was recast in the metaphorical shift from 'rowing' the boat to 'steering' it (Osborne and Gaebler 1992). This minimalist role was in turn associated with other factors.

First, it reflected the changing political order under conditions of globalization, whereby the mobility of capital and information (and, much less so, people), the emergence of various forms of political and economic transnational governance, and the increasing interconnectedness and interdependency of the global political sphere repeatedly called into question the state's capacity to govern (Beck 1992; Castells 2000; Ericson and Stehr 2000). Second, the state's ability to offer a decisive solution to crime seemed to be contradicted by the apparent worldwide and dramatic increase in crime levels since the 1960s, to the extent that high crime levels became a 'normal social fact' (Garland 1996: 446). Although the police role as 'crime-fighters' was firmly embedded in popular culture, research suggested that the 'limits of the sovereign state' (Garland 1996) were all too apparent insofar as crime levels were concerned. Political, economic, demographic and cultural factors were seen as exerting far greater influences on levels of crime than anything the police could do; as such, it was important that the public develop realistic (and by definition, more limited) expectations of what the police could accomplish in isolation. Accordingly, the quest for decisive 'solutions' to crime was gradually displaced by an 'actuarial justice' perspective (Feeley and Simon 1994) that instead focused on identifying 'high-risk' populations and managing the behaviour of such 'unruly' individuals. Accordingly, the focus of criminal justice agencies moved towards issues of prevention, surveillance, management and regulation, rather than the eradication of criminal behaviour as such.

Related to this, one of the key factors explaining criminology's focus on governance is the recognition that the state is only one player among many in terms of security provision, albeit one that holds a pivotal role not least in terms of the regulation of this expanded security market. Whereas the public or state police were generally considered the primary (and perhaps even the only) authority in terms of crime prevention, the state's monopoly on security provision is no more. 'Private' security staff now outnumber the 'public' (or 'state') police in many – if not most – industrialized countries.[1] This proliferation of private security agencies, and public–private partnerships and hybrids extends to international governance, and there is now a significant transnational private security sector that undertakes many of the functions previously associated with government, including providing security to heads of state, guarding defence installations and playing significant roles in various military operations (Gill 2006; Johnston 2006; Newburn 2007; O'Reilly and Ellison 2006).

This diversification of security provision does not necessarily conform to a hierarchical structure in which the state holds the dominant role while the private sector is relegated to the role of 'junior partner'; instead this new landscape of security provision is 'multilateral' in nature (Bayley and Shearing 2001), involving an extensive network of actors and agencies. It making this point, it is important to bear in mind the diverse range of activities that private security officers undertake: while some play an active role in crime prevention, others play a more surveillance-oriented and back-stage role. Moreover, the growth of the private security industry also coincides with a huge reduction in the number of individuals working in 'secondary social control' occupations (such as park wardens). Jones and Newburn suggest that the expansion of private security is therefore not the decisive break with the past it may at first glance appear to be, and instead reflects more the 'formalization' of social control mechanisms (Jones and Newburn 2002).

Nevertheless, this blurring of the public–private boundary and the emergence – in place of a single state-centred response – of networks of agencies and actors to address crime and security raises significant issues related to equity and democracy (Loader and Walker 2006). In 1983, Shearing and Stenning warned of the 'new feudalism' that could emerge from conditions in which the vast tracts of property that were controlled by private interests – what they termed 'mass private property' – were 'policed' by private security to impose corporately sanctioned visions of social order (Shearing and Stenning 1983). While Shearing and Stenning highlighted shopping malls as a prosaic example of this trend, increases in the number and size of residential 'gated communities' (Davis 1992) also served as a potent reminder of the social divisions and segregation that might increasingly be manifested through a contraction of the public sphere, and differential access to safety and security on the basis of individuals' purchasing power. Johnston and Shearing outline this apocalyptic vision of the future (and, in some places, the present):

> public space is privatised, the urban landscape is militarised, video-surveillance is endemic, city life is 'feral', vigilantism is rife and those who can afford to do so retreat behind 'gated' enclaves, protected by private guards. (Johnston and Shearing 2003: 141)

These concerns are evident in Garland's argument that contemporary crime control policies in the Western world are shaped by a tendency on the one hand towards 'partnership and prevention' and, on the other, towards 'punishment and expressiveness' in which evidence-based policy and rational debate play a secondary role to a more emotive and visceral demand for a punitive policy response (Garland 2001). Garland associates this combination of 'volatile and contradictory punishments' (O'Malley 1999) with the gradual emergence of a 'culture of control' whereby societies are effectively consumed by crime-related fears and anxieties, leading to a massive expansion of the public and private security sector and a vast increase in the number of people in prison or under the supervision of the justice system (Simon 2007).

Against this dystopian vision of the broad trajectory of social control, admittedly largely based on the discrete experiences of the USA and the UK, a number of other authors offer a decidedly more optimistic account of the potential of these various transitions (Bayley and Shearing 2001; Johnston and Shearing 2003; Shearing 2005; Wood and Dupont 2006; Wood and Shearing 2006). This approach seeks to overcome the defensive criminological response to the expansion of private security – 'How can we re-impose state police control over policing?' (Johnston and Shearing 2003: 11) – with a more empirically based assessment, and appreciation, of the potential of the diversification of security provision. This focus upon the potential of 'nodes' (or key hubs) within security networks views them as an innovative means of overcoming the exclusionary practices of the state *and* the market, by harnessing local expertise to maximize local capacity and promote local democracy. This involves securing the participation of relevant local actors and organizations to address the complexity of crime-related problems in their local environment (such as schools, the voluntary sector, transport organizations, and so on). Models of nodal governance have also been advocated as a means of addressing more serious security problems. For example, Dupont, Grabosky and Shearing argue that nodel governance can have an important role to play in dealing with problems of police legitimacy and effectiveness in 'weak and failing states' (Dupont, Grabosky and Shearing 2003), and the nodal logic of 'policing as everybody's business' underpinned the report of the Patten Commission on policing in Northern Ireland and has been applied in South Africa and elsewhere (Fleming and Wood 2007; Johnston and Shearing

2003). This nodal-based framework for the governance of security has been criticized, however, for appearing to downplay or neglect the role of the state, which Loader and Walker argue 'remains indispensable to any project concerned with optimizing the human good of security' (Loader and Walker 2006: 183).

Therefore, while the growth of criminological interest in governance and regulation is one of the defining features of recent criminological writing on security, its full impact on the governance of security is less apparent. This work does, however, offer insights into recent developments in Ireland. Before turning to this, I first outline the historical context of crime and policing in Irish society, highlighting the various factors which lent this field of activity such stability.

The historical context

The context of crime and policing in Ireland for much of the twentieth century was one of remarkable continuity and stasis. In the years immediately following independence, political instability in various parts of the state caused predictable problems for the police and the political establishment generally (Brady 2000; O'Halpin 1999). This was particularly evident in western and border areas where republican sentiments were strong, and conflict related to this continued up till the Second World War. Nevertheless, by the 1930s most parts of Ireland were characterized by high levels of political stability, and the upheaval surrounding the formation of the state and the subsequent civil war appeared to be largely resolved.

This political stability, however, did not simply arise from the 'bedding down' of the state as its birthing pains subsided and its institutions took root. It also arose from the conjunction of various factors that gave post-independence Ireland its distinctive social character. First, the dominant cultural nationalism of the day privileged specific conceptions of community and identity. Independence had, of course, provided access to new routes of social mobility through the various positions to be filled within the state infrastructure, but for the most part Irish nationalism was underpinned by visions of a rural idyll, characterized by asceticism and innocence.

Second, this privileging of rural innocence largely consisted of making a virtue out of a necessity, for in the years following independence, Ireland's economy was precarious (Garvin 2004). The government's policies of economic protectionism as a means of fostering indigenous industries were a disaster, and little investment was made to stimulate the economy. A trade war with Britain in the 1930s also proved costly, and it was not until the 1960s in particular that coherent policies of economic development were pursued. This in turn involved a decisive shift towards industrialization and foreign investment, and away from any lingering notions of rural self-sufficiency, yielding a severe contraction of the agricultural sector.

Third, the limited economic prospects in Ireland ensured a constant stream of emigrants from its shores. Ireland's population was in continual decline from the 1840s through to the 1960s, by which time the 1961 census recorded a population of 2,828,341 people. The emigration of such a significant proportion of the population – at one point more people born in Ireland were living abroad than in Ireland – ensured that any criminal behaviour they engaged in featured in the statistics of their host country rather than their country of origin (O'Donnell 2005a: 118–9).

Fourth, Irish society was dominated by social conservatism. Much of this emerged from the prominent role played by the Catholic Church in the spheres of education, sexuality and public morality generally (Ferriter 2009; Inglis 1998, 2003). This was bolstered by other factors, including the high level of ethnic homogeneity and monocultularism, and the profound localism that was reflected in the development of a strongly clientellist brand of politics. Within this context, much social control was exercised in spheres other than the formal criminal justice system, and involved a blurring of the line between morality and criminality. Thus, unmarried mothers, alcoholics and the mentally ill were subjected to regimes of social control that often were more extensive and open-ended than those applied to convicted criminals. As Kilcommins *et al.* note, in 1956 'one in every hundred Irish persons was detained within a closed institution' (Kilcommins, O'Donnell, O'Sullivan and Vaughan 2004: 76). Of these, though, only a small number (574 people in total) were detained in prisons and other criminal justice institutions, while the vast majority (a further 29,308 people) were confined in a variety of other institutions, including industrial schools, hospitals and homes for unmarried mothers. In effect, for every person confined within the criminal justice system, a further 51 people were confined in various 'welfare' institutions (O'Sullivan and O'Donnell 2007).

Collectively, these various factors provided a socio-political stability that militated against demands for far-reaching changes to particular spheres of government. In addition, however, two factors internal to the field of crime and crime control also ensured that it largely escaped scrutiny: the low crime levels that prevailed, and the model of policing that developed following independence.

In comparison with other European states, crime levels in Ireland were strikingly low. In 1958 the Minister for Justice reassured the public that Ireland was 'freer of crime than almost any other country' (Allen 1999: 153), and Rottman described crime levels prior to 1964 as 'negligible' (Rottman 1980). The level of public anxiety aroused by crime also appeared minor. Between 1980 and 1994, even following a large and sustained increase in crime levels from the mid-1960s onwards, a series of public attitude surveys repeatedly saw crime feature at or near the bottom of a list of issues that respondents identified as the most important problems facing the country (Kilcommins *et al.* 2004, 132–41). Such was this apparent lack of concern that Adler (1983) characterized Ireland as one of a small number of countries 'not obsessed by crime' (Adler 1983). As a consequence, police numbers were allowed to fall and a significant number of barracks were closed. The general lack of political debate on issues of crime and justice led Rolston and Tomlinson to describe criminology as 'Ireland's absentee discipline' (Rolston and Tomlinson 1982).

In addition to this, two key factors in the development of policing proved consequential. First, pragmatism demanded that the policing void that developed in many parts of Ireland during the war of independence and the civil war be filled as quickly as possible. As such, the organisational structure of the police force – An Garda Síochána – was closely based on that of its predecessor force, the Royal Irish Constabulary (RIC). Although the RIC had been a central part of the British administration in Ireland and played a military as well as a policing role, its efficiency and effectiveness were widely admired (it had been the template for many of Britain's imperial police forces). Moreover, the fact that several senior RIC officers were involved in designing the new force ensured predictable similarities between the RIC and the Garda Síochána. As a consequence, the heavily centralized structure of the RIC became the heavily centralized structure of the Garda Síochána.

This centralization, however, co-existed with a keen determination that the legitimacy of this new police force would be firmly established through a consensually based relationship with the public, expressed in the oft-quoted edict by Michael Staines (the first Garda commissioner) that: 'The Civic Guard will succeed not by force, or numbers, but on their moral authority as servants of the people.' While this vision of policing was apparent in a number of highly symbolic measures that sought to distinguish the 'civic'-oriented Garda Síochána from the heavily militarized RIC – not least through the choice of name (meaning 'guardians of the peace') and the policy that it would be an unarmed force – it was also manifested in a number of further measures that crafted close links between policing and the cultural nationalism of the day (McNiffe 1997; Mulcahy 2008). These included the prominence given to the Irish language (at one stage, training was initially provided through English and then repeated through Irish), and to links between the Catholic Church and the police (McNiffe 1997: 135–9). For instance, 250 officers (out of a force of approximately 7,000 members at the time) went on a pilgrimage to Rome in 1928,[2] while 340 travelled to Lourdes in 1930; and up until the 1980s, Garda recruits were marched to a Catholic church for Mass every Sunday. Police involvement in Gaelic sports was another important dimension of this. As Brady put it, 'with their sporting prowess, they were to "play their ways into the hearts of the people"'(Brady 2000: 117). The involvement of Garda officers in amateur and vociferously 'Gaelic' sports, organized on a geographic basis in which affiliation with and loyalty to a specific community (the 'parish', the 'country') was preeminent, provided a ready means of identifying the police with 'the people'; to this day it remains a prominent feature of police culture in Ireland.

These various factors reflected particular notions of nation and community that privileged the role of the Garda Síochána and limited the scrutiny applied to it. The manner in which the police came to embody particular characteristics of the imagined community at the heart of Irish cultural nationalism was especially significant in this regard, for it constituted this institution as self-evidently 'natural' and appropriate to the challenges and demands of policing Irish society. The governance of security in this context was structured through almost implicit understandings of the proper nature of Irish society, the role of the police, and the empathetic manner in which the police would regulate the boundaries of community (Mulcahy 2008). This situation, however, would not last.

Crime and crisis in a changing Ireland

From the mid-1960s onwards, the field of crime and crime control increasingly featured on the public agenda. Against the broad backdrop of social change in Irish society, particularly through increased urbanization, mobility and secularization, this period witnessed dramatic pressures being exerted on the police and the overall framework of crime prevention and community safety. Crime levels rose dramatically from the mid-1960s onwards; the number of indictable crimes nearly doubled during the second half of the 1960s, and increased six-fold in the twenty-year period between 1964 and 1983, when for the first time the threshold of 100,000 recorded offences was crossed. Although surveys indicate that the population at large may have been more concerned with economic and employment issues (Kilcommins *et al.* 2004), increased governmental concern with crime and the police response was fully apparent (Association of Garda Sergeants and Inspectors 1982; Vaughan 2004).

One key dimension of this was the emergence in the late 1970s of a serious heroin problem concentrated in particular parts of Dublin. Prior to then, problems associated with illegal drugs in Ireland were minuscule by international standards, and attracted little attention from the Gardaí. As such, the rapid upsurge in heroin use found the Gardaí ill-prepared for this development. The rapid increase in heroin use in the early 1980s and a subsequent peak in the mid-1990s was evident not merely in the health issues involved, but also in the wider social consequences of a large number of addicts concentrated in particular areas of Dublin. One survey in a north inner-city area in 1982–83 found that '10 per cent of the fifteen to twenty-four age group had used heroin in the year prior to the survey, with 93 per cent of that group admitting that they had taken heroin at least once a day' (Kilcommins *et al.* 2004: 226). The ripple effects of drug use were immense, and one Dublin City Council official[3] described it as the 'biggest problem' associated with local authority housing estates generally, while Keogh estimated that over the course of a single year known drug-users committed two-thirds of all crime in the Dublin metropolitan area (Keogh

1997). Senior Gardaí interviewed by Brewer *et al.* noted that drugs had been 'the biggest single influence on the crime profile during their time of service' (Brewer, Lockhart and Rodgers 1997: 46–7), its impact exceeding that of the Northern Ireland conflict, while government officials were 'shaken' by the scale of heroin-related problems in Dublin. The situation was further complicated by the fact that communities in which heroin use was concentrated repeatedly claimed that state indifference had greatly contributed to the escalation of the problem, and that direct community action was necessary against suspected drug dealers. Cumulatively, this volatile mixture of drugs and drug-related crime, marginalization and vigilante activity had an immensely negative impact on police–community relations in many quarters (Bennett 1988; Mulcahy and O'Mahony 2005; Punch 2005).

The outbreak of widespread violence in Northern Ireland in the late 1960s and the subsequent development there of a sustained armed conflict also brought very specific pressures to bear on the police. Enormous amounts of resources were absorbed by the conflict, and it was directly implicated in fundamental changes in security policies generally. Some crimes, such as armed robberies, increased dramatically in number, as these were often undertaken by paramilitaries as a key source of funds. The dangers facing the police also increased. Prior to the conflict, 1942 was the last year in which a Garda was murdered. Since 1970, 14 officers have been murdered, 12 of them by republican paramilitaries (Mulcahy 2005).

Developments in the governance of crime and security

While the various developments outlined above posed considerable challenges for the criminal justice system, arguably the most significant drivers of the state's response arose from changes in other spheres of the political arena. From the mid-1990s onwards, political reactions to crime and policing shifted from a context in which issues of law and order had been reasonably muted factors in party politics, to one in which they took a pre-eminent role. Historically, Fine Gael had been most closely associated with the mantle of 'law and order party', but that changed dramatically in the run-up to the 1997 General Election. John O'Donoghue, the Fianna Fáil justice spokesperson at the time, promoted an uncompromising 'law and order' agenda, and the party went on to form a coalition government with the Progressive Democrats on the basis of an explicit 'tough on crime' stance (O'Donnell and O'Sullivan 2003).

This new agenda encompassed various means to expand the scope and scale of the criminal justice system, including an extensive prison-building programme, an increase in police numbers, and new measures to target crime and disorder, including a constitutional amendment to limit access to bail, lengthy sentences for drug offenders, and other explicitly populist measures such as 'zero-tolerance' policing. This echoed the development of 'popular punitiveness' (Bottoms 1995) in other settings, whereby stringent responses to crime had been implemented largely on the basis of politically vocal and emotive sentiment (Garland 2001). The prison population duly increased, from a daily average of 2,141 individuals in custody in 1994, to a total of 4,380 inmates by July 2010 (figures from Irish Prison Service), while the number of police personnel rose from 10,816 in 1995 to 14,603 by December 2009 (as well as a further 232 trainee Gardaí). These changes, however, occurred against a backdrop of an overall decline in crime levels. The level of homicides and violent crimes generally rose significantly in the late 1990s (O'Donnell 2005b), but these do not account for the vast expansion of the prison population. The new era of law and order was, first and foremost, a political creation. Yet although demonic depictions of criminals underpinned much of the policy agenda advanced during the late 1990s, the nature of specific developments within the field of crime and policing was often more nuanced. This was especially evident in relation to drug dealers and organized criminal gangs. While they had increasingly featured as modern-day folk devils, one of the most significant measures used against them emerged from the sphere of civil justice.

Between punitiveness and civil justice: the Criminal Assets Bureau

The Criminal Assets Bureau (CAB) was established in 1996 (Walsh and McCutcheon 1999). The Criminal Justice Act, 1994 had introduced measures to prevent money-laundering (largely through tighter regulation of the banking industry), and the Proceeds of Crime Act, 1996 allowed for the proceeds of crime to be frozen and forfeited, but the emergence of the CAB signalled a more focused approach on targeting the financial proceeds of crime. In particular, the 1996 murder of crime reporter Veronica Guerin apparently due to her ongoing coverage of organized criminal gangs gave this measure far greater impetus. Its political salience was firmly established through the perception that a new type of 'super-criminal' had emerged against whom new and innovative measures were required (Vaughan 2004).

The CAB was significant in several respects. First, it specifically targeted the proceeds of crime, rather than crime itself. Second, it operated under civil law and its associated burden of proof ('the balance of probabilities') rather than the higher level ('beyond a reasonable doubt') required for criminal cases. The judge in one case involving CAB (Gilligan v. Criminal Assets Bureau) justified the agency's existence on the basis of the advent of:

> an entirely new type of professional criminal who . . . renders himself virtually entirely immune to the ordinary procedures of criminal investigation and prosecution . . . [necessitating use of the] lower probative requirements of the civil law . . . not to achieve penal sanctions but to effectively deprive such persons of such illicit financial fruits of their labours. (Quoted in Vaughan 2004: 65)

Third, although headed by a Garda Superintendent, the CAB was staffed by personnel drawn from various backgrounds, and it also worked in close cooperation with other agencies in Ireland and beyond, factors which it claimed were central to its success:

> The unique multi-agency aspect of the Bureau provides a synergy that would not otherwise be possible in a single agency operation . . . The assistance provided by the broader international law enforcement community cannot be underestimated and was once again a significant factor in the work of the Bureau. (CAB 2000: 25)

In terms of its impact, the CAB became 'probably the most highly praised development in Irish policing in the last ten years' (Kilcommins *et al.* 2004: 228). It was involved in a number of high profile asset seizures, while it also claimed responsibility for 'the displacement of major criminal figures, many of whom have left the jurisdiction since coming to the attention of CAB'.[4] The CAB stated that its structure and modus-operandi 'have been identified as models for other countries which are in the process of targeting the proceeds of crime' (CAB Annual Report for 1999: 5, para 3.2), resulting in a regular flow of international delegations anxious to learn from its success. Subsequently, an international network was established of agencies targeting the proceeds of crime, the Camden Assets Recovery Interagency Network (CARIN), of which Ireland was nominated to hold the first presidency given its prominent role in this field.

Local authorities, communities and partnership

While the CAB remained a prominent measure in targeting organized crime, simultaneously a series of further developments were under way which, arguably, are at least as significant in shaping the contours of social control in contemporary Ireland. These, however, rested more on logics of *prevention and partnership* rather than *punishment and expressiveness* (Garland 1996) and, as such, are more modulated and nuanced in their tone and content than their more strident policy counterparts. These measures represent part of a gradual change in government thinking and policy formation that, in relation to specifically policing matters at least, can be traced back to the influential reports from the Committee of Inquiry into the Penal System (Whitaker 1985) and the Interdepartmental Group on Urban Crime and Disorder (Interdepartmental Group on Urban Crime and Disorder 1992). Recognizing the limits of the 'fire brigade' model of policing, these reports highlighted the clear links between crime, deprivation, and antagonistic relationships with the police, and emphasized the need for sustained multi-agency partnership approaches to crime prevention issues. This theme of partnership was further promoted in a number of interventions in these debates (National Crime Council 2003).

Local authorities have taken on a far greater role in this respect, and have become one of the key pillars of this putative partnership.[5] The impetus for this arose from persistent problems with crime, disorder and anti-social behaviour in local authority estates, much of which was drug-related (McAuliffe and Fahey 1999). As a consequence, local authorities became more involved in estate management through such measures as the establishment of area housing offices to provide local on-the-ground services in specific estates. One local authority official described how: 'we really adopted the whole concept of consultation with residents . . . I think the results of that or the outcome of that are probably not measurable in financial terms, but certainly we have much less problems in our estates than we had years ago'. The most significant development in the process of extending the council's role was the 1997 Housing (Miscellaneous Provisions) Act which provided for 'exclusion orders' to be made against 'illegal occupiers' and tenants engaged in illegal or anti-social behaviour. This gave local authorities enhanced powers to sanction their tenants and ultimately evict them. One council official described this as 'the year that we took our role seriously in relation to getting rid of drug dealers out of our flat complexes'.

Since the 1997 Act was introduced, the number of evictions for anti-social behaviour has dropped steadily: from 44 in 1998 to 30 in 1999, 12 in 2000, 10 in 2001, 8 in 2002 and 15 in 2003 (figures supplied by Dublin City Council). The Council carried out a higher number of evictions of 'illegal occupiers' allegedly involved in anti-social behaviour, although this figure too has dropped since the introduction of the Act (from 97 in 1998, to 23 in 2003). While these powers can become an important resource for the police, one senior Garda officer nevertheless spoke of his concern at the 'massive powers' involved, wondering whether they were 'draconian'. As one housing official stated, 'About five years ago we were very inactive in relation to dealing with these problems. Five years on, we're very proactive and that brings its own problems.'[6]

This proactive approach also has implications for the nature of the consultation that occurs with local authority tenants. Because of the impact that drug-related issues have had on local authority housing estates generally, residents identified policies surrounding the allocation of tenants as particularly significant. Moreover, it is an issue over which the boundaries of 'consultation' and community involvement in official decision-making are tested and negotiated (see also McAuliffe and Fahey 1999). One official explained the process of consulting with representatives of residents' groups and the complex issues involved:

> We would ask them do you have any information that we don't know about why
> this person shouldn't get an allocation. Now they've no veto on it . . . but they do
> have an input . . . Now in some estates, there's no doubt that the residents would
> have felt that they should have total say in who comes into their flat scheme or
> flats complex . . . It could just be very politically motivated. They could feel that
> the corporation has let them down so often before that they would like control
> for themselves . . . But it's always a difficult battle for us if we meet a Residents'

Association where there might be two or three extremely strong people . . . Because they're very active and very strong doesn't [mean] that they're actually doing better for their community. They could have personal agendas, they could have political agendas. So we do have to be very careful about who we deal with and make sure that they do have some kind of representation or some kind of mandate. But there's no doubt at times there's people that have become the spokesperson for a community and mightn't be acting in their best interests. It's just something that we have to deal with. We have to dance around because you have to keep people on board at the same time.

The greater involvement of local authorities in estate management and with it the greater availability of the sanction of eviction gave added weight to allocation decisions. Away from the glare of publicity and the procedural requirements of the formal criminal justice process, these hugely consequential decisions become a quasi-policing environment in which the resource of accommodation (and its potential removal) is dependent first and foremost on a contract with a landlord, with the potential input of residents' representatives (Crawford 2003). Moreover, the fact that police have been in attendance at some meetings adds a further dimension to this process. As one resident noted: 'If, you know, the guards need to be involved in, you know, in assessing somebody's right to live in a particular area, it's like, there's a worrying aspect about it as well.'

The Garda Síochána Act, 2005 significantly extended the mandate of local authorities in relation to the governance of crime and security, specifying that: 'A local authority shall, in performing its functions, have regard to the importance of taking steps to prevent crime, disorder and anti-social behaviour within its area of responsibility' (37.1). The Act also provided for various mechanisms of police–public consultation (discussed further below). Lest these measures be dismissed out of hand for their modesty, it is necessary to recognize that they represent a considerable departure from established practices. There is, quite simply, no tradition of formal police–community consultation in Ireland. The Act's stipulation that the force now has a statutory requirement to obtain the views of the public, provides for the first time a legislative footing for police–public consultation in the country. Moreover, the Act also provided for the establishment of a Garda Reserve, a voluntary part-time force who would work in support of attested members of the force.[7]

The Act outlines a number of specific ways in which local authority involvement in crime prevention may occur, such as the provision of closed circuit television schemes, but the most prominent mechanism of local authority involvement is in relation to the establishment of 'joint policing committees' (JPCs) in each local authority area (with the cooperation of the Garda Commissioner). The stated function of JPCs is 'to serve as a forum for consultations, discussions and recommendations on matters affecting the policing of the local authority's administrative area' (36.2). The Act specifies that JPCs are obliged to keep under review the 'levels and patterns of crime, disorder and anti-social behaviour in the area' and 'the factors underlying and contributing to' these; and to 'advise the local authority concerned and the Garda Síochána on how they might best perform their functions having regard to the need to do everything feasible to improve the safety and quality of life and to prevent crime, disorder and anti-social behaviour within the area'. The Act also notes that JPCs may, in consultation with the local Garda Superintendent, establish local policing fora within specific neighbourhoods in the area, and coordinate the activities of such fora.

Accountability and oversight mechanisms

A further significant development in the governance of security relates to the scrutiny applied to the police. This has occurred through two main approaches, comprising on the one hand a greater focus upon issues of organizational efficiency, and on the other, significant changes in the system of police accountability.

In relation to organizational efficiency, a broad programme of reform was instituted throughout the public sector in the 1990s as a key plank of the modernizing agenda promoted by the Fianna Fáil/Progressive Democrat coalition government. Under the auspices of the Strategic Management Initiative, this prioritized issues of institutional effectiveness and efficiency, but it also involved a thorough review of the entire organizational structure of An Garda Síochána (Garda SMI Implementation Steering Group 2004). The 2005 Act added some further measures to the managerial toolkit. It provided for performance measures to be introduced within the force and for the establishment of a 'Professional Standards Unit', and it designated the Garda Commissioner as the Accounting Officer of the force. Importantly, the Act also provided for the establishment of a Garda Inspectorate with the goal of ensuring that 'the resources available to the Garda Síochána are used so as to achieve and maintain the highest levels of efficiency and effectiveness in its operation and administration, as measured by reference to the best standards of comparable police services' (117.1).

In terms of the police complaints system, up until the 1980s police accountability in Ireland was based on an 'internal' model in which investigations into allegations of police misconduct were investigated by other officers. Following the scandal surrounding the police investigation into the 1984-85 Kerry Babies case – in which the police secured confessions from a woman and other members of her family in rural Kerry to the effect that she had killed her baby and then disposed of the body by having it thrown from a cliff some forty miles away, despite forensic evidence indicating that this could not have occurred (Inglis 2003) – the Garda Síochána Complaints Board (GCSB) was established in 1987. The GSCB was an independent body, but its remit was largely restricted to overseeing police investigations of complaints. Its impact, however, was negligible, and the GCSB itself repeatedly criticized the government for failing to provide it with the resources necessary for it to execute its role effectively. A series of high-profile scandals into allegations of police corruption in Donegal and of police assault against 'May Day' protesters in Dublin city centre in 2002 gave further enormous impetus for the development of a more robust mechanism to secure police accountability (Conway 2010).

Reflecting these various events and concerns, the Garda Síochána Act, 2005 provided for the establishment of a Garda Síochána Ombudsman Commission. Although the function of the Ombudsman Commission was the familiar one of recording and investigating complaints against police officers, the significance of the Commission was that it constituted a fully independent system, and had the added objective of promoting public confidence in the complaints system. The Commission was also given the power to make reports to the Minister for Justice on matters concerning grave or exceptional circumstances (80.5), and to 'examine' a 'practice, policy or procedure' of An Garda Síochána with a view to preventing or reducing the incidence of complaints associated with them (106.1).

Conclusion

Many of the measures that now form key pillars of structure and thought within the changing landscape of the governance of security in Ireland are novel creations. Their emergence in the aftermath of a sustained period of stability and stasis stands as one dimension of wider social change unfolding across Irish society. Given the short period of time in which they have been in operation, their consequences are not yet fully apparent, and this nascent process requires close attention from researchers to determine the full nature and contours of this process. Nevertheless, on the basis of this admittedly brief and selective review of developments in the governance of crime and security in Ireland, some conclusions may be drawn.

First, there is no doubt that democratic governance and accountability of the police was significantly enhanced by the Act through its introduction of the Ombudsman Commission. Legislative provision for Joint Policing Committees and Community Policing Fora also constitutes a significant and welcome departure from established practices in Irish policing, whereby public consent to policing was often assumed rather than demonstrated. However, this democratic impulse has proceeded hand in hand with a centralizing tendency that casts a question mark over the potential of these measures (Mulcahy 2008).

For instance, one of the main concerns with the Act is the extent to which the implementation of its provisions are dependent on guidelines issued by the Minister of Justice. Moreover, while the Act specifies that the Minister may 'revise' the guidelines or withdraw them and issue new ones, it does not specify any grounds on which this might occur, nor does it impose any requirement to consult with the Joint Policing Committees themselves. The democratic thrust of the Act was also undermined by the requirement that the Ombudsman Commission's ability to 'examine' a 'policy, practice or procedure' could only be undertaken at the request of the Minister for Justice, and by the further stipulation that the Minister for Justice may issue directives to the Garda Commissioner 'concerning any matter relating to the Garda Síochána', with which the Commissioner must comply.

Given that the Office of the Police Ombudsman for Northern Ireland (OPONI) had been such a core feature of policing reforms in Northern Ireland, which in turn had been widely acclaimed as an authoritative statement of best practice in policing (Ellison 2007; Mulcahy 2006), it is rather ironic that the most significant overhaul of policing in the history of the Irish state should be so ambivalent towards these developments. For example, although modelled in principle on the OPONI, the scope and powers of the Ombudsman Commission fell short of what had been introduced in Northern Ireland, perhaps in an effort to prevent the emergence of an overly robust Ombudsman.[8] Moreover, in 2004 the Minister for Justice rejected calls for an oversight body equivalent to the Northern Ireland Policing Board, stating that such a structure 'would diminish if not remove the supervisory role of Dáil Éireann', despite the fact that the Dáil's traditional and ill-defined role in performing this function is ineffective (Walsh 1998). As he stated in evidence to a Dáil committee: 'What is good for Northern Ireland is not necessarily good for a sovereign state' (Joint Committee on Justice 2005: 28). Thus while some specific components of the 'new managerialism' agenda may be seamlessly applied in one jurisdiction following their introduction in another – such as the Garda Inspectorate, which closely mirrors the role and functions of Her Majesty's Inspectorate of Constabulary in Britain – others, which are more closely focused on issues of democratic accountability and thus more central to core issues of state, may not. In this respect, the local trumped the global.[9]

This raises the related question of Ireland's location within broader frameworks of change. Here, Garland's theory of the development of a 'culture of control' offers a troubling vision of the trajectory of crime control under conditions of late modernity (Garland 2001). Yet as discussed earlier in this chapter, welfare institutions in Ireland historically were responsible for a very extensive system of social control, in which the scale of confinement dwarfed the numbers committed to the state's formal criminal justice system (Kilcommins et al. 2004; O'Sullivan and O'Donnell 2007). Moreover, the great expansion of the formal system of social control in Ireland from the mid-1990s onwards arose largely from the convergence of specifically local factors, rather than general punitive pressures that Garland associates with late modernity per se. These include: public outrage surrounding the 1996 murder of crime journalist Veronica Guerin; the 1997 Fianna Fáil/Progressive Democrat government's 'law and order' agenda (itself a considerable departure from Irish tradition, within which issues of crime and justice were never as overtly politicized as was the case in the USA and the UK); and greatly increased economic capacity to finance this expansion (also a historical novelty). Furthermore, risk logics are conspicuous for their absence within the Irish policy context, itself reflecting the poor connections between empirical evidence and criminal justice policy development in Ireland.

The implosion of Ireland's economy in 2008 – partly as a result of the collapse of the international banking sector, but largely driven by Ireland's disastrous dependence on an unsustainable property bubble – adds a further dimension to these debates. On the one hand, it led to a huge reduction in government spending and with it, a much curtailed ambition as far as the further expansion of the criminal justice system was concerned (notwithstanding the government's decision to proceed with some projects, most notably the construction of a large prison complex – Thornton Hall – on the outskirts of Dublin). One the other, it led to a more vocal preoccupation with the relationship between deprivation and crime, particularly lethal violence associated with the drugs market, an issue which had been simmering in Irish society for several years. The number of murders and manslaughters increased from 45 in 2004 to 84 in 2007, falling to 55 and 57 in 2008 and 2009 respectively. A series of policy and legislative measures were introduced in an effort to curb 'gangland' violence (Campbell 2010; Conway and Mulqueen 2009), but this criminal activity very much bore the stamp of local factors, through the development of, and competition between, criminal gangs seeking control over the lucrative drugs market and in localized contexts of deprivation and marginalization.

On the basis of these various factors, analysis of the governance of crime and security in Ireland adds a note of caution in regard to grand theories, raising the question of whether processes apparently unfolding in the USA and the UK – and which Garland uses to underpin his discussion of the crime complex as a globalizing phenomenon – are, in fact, the exception rather than the rule. In this respect, the challenge for researchers is to disentangle the various factors involved in the ideas and practices that define and embody the criminal justice system, and to identify and understand the weight and tenor of specifically local factors, and their complex, uneven, and sometimes contradictory interaction with wider processes.[10] The cause of democratic governance requires, then, a balancing act to be managed, one that nurtures local initiatives while being receptive to developments in other jurisdictions. This entails promoting those recent initiatives that carry the promise of equity and accountability, and of enhancing local capacity to address and solve pressing problems of crime and insecurity. In this regard, local police–community consultative mechanisms and the Ombudsman Commission have enormous promise. Ensuring that their potential is fully realized will, however, require public awareness, political commitment, and resources – ingredients that were not always present in the formulation and implementation of criminal justice policy in the past.

Notes

1 Johnston suggests that this is by a factor of almost 2:1 in Britain, and perhaps as much as 7:1 in South Africa (Johnston 2006). Estimates of the size of the private security sector in Ireland vary considerably, but in scale it probably does not exceed that of the public police (Vaughan 2004).

2 The commitment involved in undertaking such pilgrimages was significant. McNiffe notes that the Garda officers 'sacrificed half of their annual leave and the equivalent of nine weeks' pay' to do so (McNiffe 1997).

3 This and subsequent quotations are taken from research on policing and crime prevention in marginalized communities (Mulcahy and O'Mahony 2005).

4 See. www.garda.ie/angarda/cab.html.

5 Discourses of partnership were already a key pillar of the multi-agency task forces' approach which was developed to address problems associated with the use of illegal drugs, and also was a prominent feature of economic policy underpinning the 'Celtic Tiger'.

6 Some of the difficulties associated with the application of these enhanced powers were crystallized by the case of Noel Cahill. He died in January 2003 after developing hypothermia while sleeping rough outside the local authority flat from which he had been evicted in October 2002, following allegations that some of his acquaintances had been engaged in anti-social behaviour in his flat (*Irish Times* 2 and 3 February 2003). Other concerns about local authority powers of eviction were expressed in 2008 by the Irish Human Rights Commission.

7 In December 2009, the Garda Reserve comprised 478 operational officers, with a further 167 in training.

8 Nuala O'Loan, the Northern Ireland Police Ombudsman, had been politically unpopular in some quarters for her apparent willingness to pursue allegations of police misconduct irrespective of any political embarrassment this caused.

9 In relation to developments across Europe to target organized crime, Den Boer suggests that while greater European integration 'has increased the transparency and knowledge of one another's systems', it has not produced a convergence of criminal justice system responses – a process she characterises as 'horizontal cross-pollination' rather than the centralized imposition of specific initiatives (Den Boer 2001).

10 For an analysis of the local–global nexus in an Irish context, see Inglis (2010).

Bibliography

Adler, F. 1983. *Nations Not Obsessed With Crime*. Littleton, CO: Rothman.

Allen, G. 1999. *The Garda Síochána: Policing Independent Ireland, 1922–1982*. Dublin: Gill and Macmillan.

Association of Garda Sergeants and Inspectors. 1982. *A Discussion Paper Concerning Proposals for a Scheme of Community Policing*. Dublin: AGSI.

Bayley, D. and D. Shearing. 2001. *The New Structure of Policing*. Washington DC: National Institute of Justice.

Beck, U. 1992. *The Risk Society: Towards a New Modernity*. London: Sage.

Bennett, D. 1988. Are They Always Right? Investigation and Proof in a Citizen Anti-Heroin Movement. In *Whose Law and Order?*, edited by M. Tomlinson, T. Varley, and C. McCullagh, 21–40. Belfast: Sociological Association of Ireland.

Bottoms, A. 1995. The Philosophy and Politics of Punishment and Sentencing. In *The Politics of Sentencing Reform*, edited by C. Clark and R. Morgan, 17–49. Oxford: Clarendon.

Brady, C. 2000. *Guardians of the Peace*. London: Prendeville.

Brewer, J., B. Lockhart and P. Rodgers. 1997. *Crime in Ireland: 'Here Be Dragons'*. Oxford: Clarendon.

Burchell, G., C. Gordon and P. Miller, eds. 1991. *The Foucault Effect: Studies in Governmentality*. Chicago: University of Chicago Press.

Campbell, L. 2010. Responding to Gun Crime in Ireland. *British Journal of Criminology* 50 (3): 414–34.

Castells, M. 2000. *The Rise of the Network Society*. Oxford: Blackwell.

Conway, V. 2010. *The Blue Wall of Silence: The Morris Tribunal and Police Accountability in the Republic of Ireland*. Dublin: Irish Academic Press.

Conway, V. and M. Mulqueen. 2009. The 2009 Anti-Gangland Package: Ireland's New Security Blanket? *Irish Criminal Law Journal* 19 (4): 106–13.

Crawford, A. 2003. Contractual Governance of Deviant Behaviour. *Journal of Law and Society* 30: 479–505.

Criminal Assets Bureau (CAB). 2000. *Annual Report for 1999*. Dublin: Stationery Office.

Davis, M. 1992. *City of Quartz*. London: Vintage.

Den Boer, M. 2001. The Fight Against Organised Crime in Europe: A Comparative Perspective. *European Journal of Criminal Policy and Research* 9 (3): 259–72.

Dupont, B., P. Grabosky and C. Shearing. 2003. The Governance of Security in Weak and Failing States. *Criminal Justice* 3 (4): 331–49.

Ellison, G. 2007. A Blueprint for Democratic Policing Anywhere in the World? Police Reform, Political Transition, and Conflict Resolution in Northern Ireland. *Police Quarterly* 10 (3): 243–69.

Ericson, R. and N. Stehr, eds. 2000. *Governing Modern Societies*. Toronto: University of Toronto Press.

Feeley, M. and J. Simon. 1994. Actuarial Justice: The Emerging New Criminal Law. In *The Futures of Criminology*, edited by D. Nelken, 173–201. London: Sage.

Ferriter, D. 2009. *Occasions of Sin: Sex and Society in Modern Ireland*. London: Profile Books.

Fleming, J. and J. Wood, eds. 2007. *Fighting Crime Together: The Challenges of Policing and Security Networks*. Sydney: University of New South Wales Press.

Foucault, M. 1977. *Discipline and Punish: The Birth of the Prison*. London: Allen Lane.

Garda SMI Implementation Steering Group. 2004. *Garda SMI Implementation Steering Group-Final Report*. Dublin: Stationery Office.

Garland, D. 1996. The Limits of the Sovereign State: Strategies of Crime Control in Contemporary Society. *British Journal of Criminology* 36 (4): 445–71.

Garland, D. 2001. *The Culture of Control: Crime and Social Order in Contemporary Society*. Oxford: Oxford University Press.

Garvin, T. 2004. *Preventing the Future: Why Was Ireland So Poor For So Long?* Dublin: Gill and Macmillan.

Gill, P. 2006. Not Just Joining the Dots But Crossing the Borders and Bridging the Voids: Constructing Security Networks After 11 September 2001. *Policing and Society* 16 (1): 27–49.

Inglis, T. 1998. *Moral Monopoly: The Rise and Fall of the Catholic Church in Ireland.* Dublin: University College Dublin Press.

Inglis, T. 2003. *Truth, Power and Lies: Irish Society and the Case of the Kerry Babies.* Dublin: University College Dublin Press.

Inglis, T. 2010. Sociological Forensics: Illuminating the Whole from the Particular. *Sociology* 44 (3): 507–22.

Interdepartmental Group on Urban Crime and Disorder. 1992. *Urban Crime and Disorder: Report of the Interdepartmental Group.* Dublin: Stationery Office.

Johnston, L. 2006. Transnational Security Governance. In *Democracy, Society and the Governance of Security*, edited by J. Wood and B. Dupont, 33–51. Cambridge: Cambridge University Press.

Johnston, L. and C. Shearing. 2003. *Governing Security: Explorations in Policing and Justice.* London: Routledge.

Joint Committee on Justice, Equality, Defence and Women's Rights. 2005. *Report on Community Policing.* Dublin: Government Publications Office.

Jones, T. and T. Newburn. 2002. The Transformation of Policing? Understanding Current Trends in Policing Systems. *British Journal of Criminology* 42 (1): 129–46.

Jones, T. and T. Newburn. 2007. *Criminal Justice and Policy Transfer.* Maidenhead: Open University Press.

Keogh, E. 1997. *Illegal Drug Use and Related Criminal Activity in the Dublin Metropolitan Area.* Templemore: Garda Research Unit.

Kilcommins, S., I. O'Donnell, E. O'Sullivan and B. Vaughan. 2004. *Crime, Punishment and the Search for Order in Ireland.* Dublin: Institute of Public Administration.

Loader, I. and N. Walker. 2006. Necessary Virtues: The Legitimate Place of the State in the Production of Security. In *Democracy, Society and the Governance of Security*, edited by J. Wood and B. Dupont, 165–95. Cambridge: Cambridge University Press.

McAuliffe, R. and T. Fahey. 1999. Responses to Social Order Problems. In *Social Housing in Ireland*, edited by T. Fahey, 173–90. Dublin: Oak Tree Press.

McNiffe, L. 1997. *A History of The Garda Síochána.* Dublin: Wolfhound.

Mulcahy, A. 2005. The 'Other' Lessons from Ireland? Policing, Political Violence and Policy Transfer. *European Journal of Criminology* 2 (2): 185–209.

Mulcahy, A. 2006. *Policing Northern Ireland.* Cullompton, Devon: Willan.

Mulcahy, A. 2008. Policing, 'Community' and Social Change in Ireland. In *Justice, Community and Civil Society: A Contested Terrain*, edited by J. Shapland, 190–208. Cullompton, Devon: Willan.

Mulcahy, A. and E. O'Mahony. 2005. *Policing and Social Marginalisation in Ireland.* Dublin: Combat Poverty Agency.

National Crime Council. 2003. *A Crime Prevention Strategy for Ireland: Tackling the Concerns of Local Communities.* Dublin: National Crime Council.

Newburn, T. 2007. Governing Security: The Rise of the Privatized Military. In *Crime,*

Social Control and Human Rights, edited by D. Downes, P. Rock, C. Chinkin and C. Gearty, 195–210. Cullompton, Devon: Willan.

O'Donnell, I. 2005a. Crime and Justice in the Republic of Ireland. *European Journal of Criminology* 2 (1): 99–131.

O'Donnell, I. 2005b. Lethal Violence in Ireland, 1841–2003: Famine, Celibacy and Parental Pacification. *British Journal of Criminology* 45 (5): 671–95.

O'Donnell, I. and E. O'Sullivan. 2003. The Politics of Intolerance – Irish Style. *British Journal of Criminology* 43 (1): 41–62.

O'Halpin, E. 1999. *Defending Ireland*. Oxford: Oxford University Press.

O'Malley, P. 1999. Volatile and Contradictory Punishment. *Theoretical Criminology* 3 (2): 175–96.

O'Reilly, C. and G. Ellison. 2006. Eye Spy Private High: Reconceptualizing High Policing Theory. *British Journal of Criminology* 46 (4): 641–60.

O'Sullivan, E. and I. O'Donnell. 2007. Coercive Confinement in the Republic of Ireland: The Waning of a Culture of Control. *Punishment and Society* 9 (1): 27–48.

Osborne, D. and T. Gaebler. 1992. *Reinventing Government: How the Entrepreneurial Spirit is Transforming the Public Sector*. Reading, MA: Addison-Wesley Publishing.

Punch, M. 2005. Problem Drug Use and the Political Economy of Urban Restructuring: Heroin, Class and Governance in Ireland. *Antipode* 37 (4): 754–74.

Rolston, B. and M. Tomlinson. 1982. Spectators at the 'Carnival of Reaction'? In *Power, Conflict and Inequality*, edited by M. Kelly, L. O'Dowd and J. Wickham, 21–40. Dublin: Turoe Press.

Rose, N. 1989. *Governing the Soul: The Shaping of the Private Self*. London: Routledge.

Rottman, D. 1980. *Crime in the Republic of Ireland*. Dublin: Economic and Social Research Institute.

Shearing, C. 2005. Nodal Security. *Police Quarterly* 8 (1): 57–63.

Shearing, C. and P. Stenning. 1983. Private Security. *Social Problems* 30: 125–38.

Simon, J. 2007. *Governing Through Crime*. Oxford: Oxford University Press.

Vaughan, B. 2004. Accounting for the Diversity of Policing in Ireland. *Irish Journal of Sociology* 13 (1): 49–70.

Wacquant, L. 1999. How Penal Common Sense Comes to Europeans: Notes on the Transatlantic Diffusion of Neoliberal Doxa. *European Societies* 1 (3): 319–52.

Walsh, D. 1998. *The Irish Police*. Dublin: Round Hall/ Sweet and Maxwell.

Walsh, D. and P. McCutcheon. 1999. *The Confiscation of Criminal Assets*. Dublin: Roundhall Press.

Whitaker, T.K. 1985. *Report of the Committee of Inquiry into the Penal System*. Dublin: Stationery Office.

Wood, J. and B. Dupont, eds. 2006. *Democracy, Society and the Governance of Security*. Cambridge: Cambridge University Press.

Wood, J. and C. Shearing. 2006. *Imagining Society*. Cullompton, Devon: Willan.

10

E-governance: new technologies, local government and civic participation

Lee Komito

Introduction

Civic participation, glossed as individuals identifying themselves as citizens with a duty to act for the 'public good', seems to be in decline. This decline, particularly when expressed as decreased political participation, and evidenced by reduced voter turnouts and a general alienation from government (Blondel and Sinnott 1998; van der Eijk and Franklin 1996), form part of the 'democratic deficit' that has been on the agenda of many governments in recent years. It has often also been linked with a decline in stocks of social trust, norms and networks which people can draw on to solve common problems, commonly known as 'social capital' (Putnam 1993, 2000).

Many governments have addressed this decline by attempting to increase public involvement in the formulation of government policy and the provision of services. This policy shift has been described as an increased focus on 'governance' rather than government (Pierre 2000). Participation in policy formation by non-government interests has often involved varying kinds of organizations: economic interest groups (e.g. trade unions, employers, agricultural groups), social interest groups (minority ethnic or religious groups, disabled, homeless, elderly) or local community groups. These organizations now find their involvement in the policy process has been legitimized. Such organizations often describe themselves as part of the political process but not party political: they articulate broad political issues while remaining outside the formal electoral system.

In Ireland, this enhanced involvment has often been formalized as 'social partnership' [for discussion of this, see Chapter 5 in this book]. Initially, partnership in Ireland focused on economic policies and involved trade unions and employers. More recently, social partnership has involved community and voluntary groups and has extended to social as well as economic policy formation.

In any representative democracy, citizens elect others to articulate their concerns. In partnership, the range of groups and organizations increases and the range of concerns articulated widens. The number and range of citizens whose interests are represented should also increase. However, despite the widening of representation, there remain individuals whose concerns remain unrepresented in this expanded arena of policy discussion. Many reasons may explain lack of participation. There may be a lack of information about the policy decisions being made or a lack of information about how to have an input into such decisions. Citizens may distrust the impartiality and fairness of those making decisions, so that citizens do not believe their interventions would be effective.

A common explanation is that people are content with the existing system, and they see no reason for greater participation. They are happy, as citizens, to hold the elected representatives accountable at election time, and do not want to directly participate in policy formation. This is the 'free rider syndrome' (Olson 1965): citizens know that, even without their intervention or participation, appropriate decisions will be made and so they choose not to 'waste' their precious resources of time and effort. Civil apathy may be cost-effective for individuals; while outcomes could be better, citizens get 'good enough' governance.

This latter explanation, however, can only be partially accurate. Grassroots protest groups often develop and, in Ireland, the rise of single-issue political candidates who campaign on community issues (e.g. hospitals, aid for disabled children, waste management, local employment, refuse charges) indicate that, for many people, policy outcomes are sometimes not 'good enough'. However, while single-issue flashpoints (such as bin charges) mobilize citizens to organize into ad hoc groups which campaign and protest, these groups tend to disband once the issues is resolved or postponed. This is clear evidence of an interest in policy participation, even if there are inadequate structures to facilitate that participation.

New technologies have often been expected to provide a means for greater participation. Many governments, including European Union member states and the EU itself, have sought to use new information and communication technologies to increase public participation in dialogue, discussion and consultation. These projects have been described as 'eparticipation' or 'einclusion', and have included online forums, virtual discussion rooms, electronic polls and electronic voting. Reviews of these projects have indicated some success, but they remain pilot projects (OECD 2003). There has been little evidence of new technologies emerging that encourage significant numbers of citizens to participate in policy formation. For example, while EU policies have been clear and detailed about improving governmental efficiency and service delivery through technology, the same can not be said of electronic governance or addressing the democratic deficit by improving public participation in the making of policy. A European Union policy document, *The Role of eGovernment for Europe's Future*, could only propose that all eGovernment strategies should 'promote . . . online democratic participation' (Commission of the European Communities 2003).

Ireland and electoral clientelism

New technologies can have an impact on public participation and the wider political system, and Ireland provides an interesting example of this. Irish politics has been shaped by a lack of administrative information and accountability, linked with a strong tradition of informal social and political action, that has been characteristic of Ireland since its independence. Ever since Chubb described politicians as local men who looked after their constituents' interests by 'going about persecuting civil servants', Irish politics has been understood in terms of electoral clientelism (Chubb 1963). Chubb suggested that the Irish politician's primary task was to mediate between his local constituents and the state's administrative apparatus. Voters wanted state services, and politicians helped or appeared to help people obtain those services. Irish citizens have believed that, in order to obtain a government benefit or service, politicians had to intercede on the citizens' behalf. Citizens, it was thought, did not receive state benefits as their right; they received benefits as personal favours granted by powerful and beneficent politicians as a reward for political support. The tacit exchange of political support for special personal preference has been a cornerstone of Irish politics since independence (Gallagher and Komito 2010).

Various factors which have promoted and maintained political clientelism have been suggested, but lack of administrative information and accountability, distrust of the impartiality of the civil service, lack of confidence in the efficacy of interventions, and a monopoly by politicians on knowledge of the bureaucratic process are all central to clientelism (Komito 1984, 1989a, 1992).[1] The informal networks of clientelism are exclusionary and foster the private use of public resources for personal gain (Clapham 1982). Such clientelist networks would now be seen as examples of negative 'bonding' social capital (Putnam 2000), and government policies would encourage more open public participation.

For many years, state structures helped maintain the market for electoral clientelism. Bureaucratic procedures were slow and inefficient, so it was difficult for citizens to obtain information about their entitlements, redress in the event of incorrect decisions, or proof that their case was being fairly decided. In the 1960s and 1970s, the degree of state intervention in Ireland increased, and citizens' dependence on state assistance grew. Growth in demand led to delays in providing assistance, but, while civil servants responded slowly, if at all, to voters, they responded quickly to politicians who intervened on behalf of voters. This increased the demand for clientelist exchanges. Civil servants also provided little public information about the services or entitlements that were increasingly important for citizens, which increased the value of the information which politicians were able to dispense (Komito 1984).

These are primarily information issues, and were altered by the introduction of information systems in the civil service in the 1990s. The justification for IT investment was to improve the efficiency of service provision (Pye 1992), and indeed the speed of processing cases increased.

Although information and communication technologies (ICTs) often do not alter organizational practices (Kling 1996), in this case, new information systems altered the market conditions for clientelist exchanges. Administrative delays had previously sustained the market for politicians to 'sell' their ability to provide information about the status of applications (Komito 1989a). The introduction of office information systems speeded the processing of cases and made it easier for citizens to directly enquire about cases, so the 'market value' of political interventions lessened. Furthermore, direct queries by citizens previously produced either no answer or an answer only very slowly, because it was so costly to assemble the information; office information systems now enabled easier monitoring of cases by citizens (Komito 1998). Finally, Freedom of Information legislation has required that procedures and criteria for decisions be recorded, and available to the general public (Government of Ireland 1997); often, this has been done by making such information available via the Internet.

With increased accountability and access, citizens found they could monitor and influence the administrative processes of the state to a greater extent than previously possible. This has altered the clientelist 'market' – that is, the demand for politicians' special access, and thus the 'charge' which politicians can demand for their service and the 'price' which citizens are willing to pay for the service. Because citizens have alternative means of accessing information, the need for politicians' access to information about services and processes has diminished considerably. A survey in the 1970s showed that 17 per cent of Dublin respondents had contacted a politician at some point. Another survey in 1991 showed that 24 per cent of all citizens and 21 per cent of Dublin residents had contacted politicians in the previous year (Komito 1989b, 1992). In contrast, a 2003 study of social values and social capital found that the figure had dropped to 14 per cent of all respondents and 13 per cent of Dublin respondents (National Economic and Social Forum 2003).

A survey of 'political culture' in the late 1960s showed a strong preference for contacting politicians rather than officials or local community figures (Raven and Whelan 1976). In contrast, the number who had contacted an official or community representative was 10.7 per cent for all respondents and 13 per cent for Dublin respondents (National Economic and Social Forum 2003). Thus, not only has the level of contact with politicians decreased, but the relative importance of politicians as compared with other figures has also decreased. This marks a significant shift away from clientelist political exchanges in Ireland.

With a decrease in the electoral value of clientelist exchanges, politicians are finding other means of attracting marginal voters. The 1990s saw the growth of policy-oriented political parties (left-wing, right-wing, nationalist and environmental), and, more recently, the growth of community candidates who articulate the concern of citizens in a particular locality, including issues such as increased development investment in rural areas of Ireland, investment in local medical services, and so on (Murphy 2010). The growth of 'policy' politics and single-issue community candidates is not solely the result of new technologies decreasing politicians' monopoly over information, but the success of these parties and candidates is an indication that the political market has changed, and politicians can now 'sell' themselves to the electorate through policy actions.

This does not mean that individual clientelist networks are irrelevant; politicians report that voters still expect politicians to be available, but that such activities are now one of many resources in the politician's portfolio, and by no means the most important. While politicians would still report that electoral success requires maintaining a local presence, the abolition of the dual mandate in 2003 has meant that TDs can no longer sit on County and City Councils. They must, increasingly rely on local councillors to look after individual citizens, and are more likely to involve themselves only when local interest groups (e.g. residents' associations, school committees) are active.[2]

This move from individual constituents' queries has also been linked to an increased number and activity of Dáil committees that exercise oversight over government departments. These committees provide national politicians with a greater role as mediator between interest groups and the state rather than individuals and the state (Gallagher 2010). Whether on local or national issues, national politicians are now more likely to mediate between groups and the state, rather than individuals and the state.

It is difficult to prove that new technologies have been the major reason for this shift towards a system of more open public policy decisions and resource allocation (in contrast to the use of public resources for individual personal gain), but they have clearly been significant.[3] The clientelist exchange of individual political support for state benefit is far less central as a basis for the structure of Irish politics, and so new technologies have contributed to a significant transformation in Irish politics.

New technologies and policy networks

Unfortunately, the evidence that new technologies encourage greater political participation in policy, in Ireland or elsewhere, is less apparent. One of the earliest experiments in the use of technologies to enhance public participation at local level was in Santa Monica in 1989 (Docter and Dutton 1998), and it was one of a number of experiments in community building using new technologies (Tsagarousianou and Tambini 1998). In many of these studies only a small percentage of the local population used the technology, so it has been difficult to make extrapolations about technology, community and participation. Since then, however, there have been studies of communities in which a majority of residents use new technologies (Huysman and Wenger 2003; Wellman and Haythornthwaite 2002).

A community of special relevance for this discussion is Blacksburg, Virginia in the United States. This community was the recipient of significant technology investment in the mid-1990s, and by 2001 it was a 'wired community': over 75 per cent of local businesses had their own web sites, over 80 per cent of residents had internet access (which included discussion lists), and over 120 non-profit organizations subscribed to a bundle of Internet services that included information-sharing software (Kavanaugh and Patterson 2002). Did the prevalence of these technologies encourage greater community participation as well as political participation? While new technologies increased the levels of participation amongst those who were already active, and made their actions more effective, the evidence is less clear that new technologies led to new people becoming involved (Kavanaugh and Patterson 2002). Increased technology usage over three years did not lead to increased community involvement, as measured by memberships in formal voluntary organizations or by amount of activity in these organizations.[4] On the contrary, research suggests that the people who use new technologies for policy issues tend to be people who are already activists – those who already 'network' (or, in social capital parlance, have bridging links based on weak or thin network ties) use new technologies to network more effectively (Agre 2002; Kavanaugh and Reese 2003).

The effective use of new technologies by voluntary groups is evident throughout the world; social movements use new technologies to organize internally and challenge existing government policies and even government structures (Della Porta and Diani 2006; Melucci 1996). Anti-globalization protests, usually timed to coincide with meetings of either the World Trade Organization or the G8 group of nations, are obvious examples of such movements (Johnson and Bimber 2004; Kahn and Kellner 2004). These groups, however ephemeral, have 'real space' manifestations in concrete political actions, which disrupt activities and claim headlines, and mobilize people across nations (Surman and Reilly 2003). However, the aim in a participative process is to engage citizens in an ongoing process of dialogue, rather than a series of protests which tend not to involve either protest groups or governments in dialogue. It has been suggested that three general modes of civic participation in policy formation can be identified: information, consultation, participation (Macintosh 2004; OECD 2003). At the most minimal level, technology can be used by governments to enable one-way information flows. In this mode, new technologies may be used as a mass media communication channel, similar to newspapers, pamphlets, radio or television, or narrowly directed at particular individuals or groups, but there is no scope for interaction. For example, local authorities and national government departments make information available, via web pages, electronic newsletters or even electronic mail, on a range of government activities. Information is made available, as governments choose, on issues that governments choose, in the format that governments choose.

A more interactive mode would be consultation, in which governments engage citizens, seeking their opinions on specific issues. This consultation can take place via electronic discussion lists, often web-based. These forums, organized around policy issues, encourage citizens to indicate the extent to which participants agree with the proposals and why, perhaps enabling citizens to suggest alternatives. In the consultation processes, the issues are formulated by policy-makers, and citizens are restricted to responding to pre-selected issues, often in a predetermined manner. This is the electronic equivalent of a survey, and mechanisms include e-petitions and e-referenda, as well as developing online 'communities of interest' in which interested or selected citizens participate in structured discussions. Governments still determine the issues and the rules. An example of popular, rather than official, consultation is the increasing number of telephone polls, in which radio or television listeners respond to a simple yes/no question by phoning or texting the appropriate number. This can provide a large number of responses in a very short time; in Ireland, some have had participation rates of over ten thousand phone calls.[5]

At the most inclusive level would be participation, in which citizens actively engage in defining issues, structuring the consultation process, and having a clear impact on final policy outcomes. This tripartite distinction is sometimes 'fuzzy' at the edges, as is any distinction between 'top-down' and 'bottom-up' structures for policy participation.

There are now many examples of one-way information flows in Ireland. Some information has to be available so that services can be delivered online (e.g. tax rules are made available to encourage people and companies to file tax returns online), while other information has resulted from the Irish government's desire for Open Government and its need to conform to Freedom of Information legislation. Information made available this way can be used by local groups to mobilize citizens and become the basis for political action. In a recent case, government attempts to nominate a retired judge to the European Investment Bank had to be withdrawn. The Irish government acted as though the nomination had already gone through but, when activists discovered that, according to European documentation, the nomination still had to be approved, public opinion forced the government to rescind its nomination (O'Toole 2000). At the community level, residents' groups will scan web lists of planning applications and then make submissions to influence planning decisions and, if necessary, organize protests and neighbourhood meetings. Official information dissemination can be the basis for extra-governmental participation by social movements and interest groups.

Sometimes, individuals and interest groups combine a number of different technologies in ways that become vehicles for consultation, whether local authorities or national governments intend this or not. Politicians receive queries from citizens via email, which they often act on and then inform citizens, either individually or collectively via an electronic newsletter, of the policy response. More significantly, residents and community groups use technology to organize their own activities and coordinate representations to politicians and officials. Officials now receive 'round robin' emails – a message will have been distributed to members of a residents' group or sports club and each will then send the message to local officials. It is clear to officials that the message has simply been reproduced, but, for officials, it is a straw poll of those who feel strongly enough about an issue to engage in some level of policy discussion, and is taken seriously as an indication of community opinion.

In 2003, there was a controversy regarding a large residential plan for Adamstown in South County Dublin which attracted significant local and national media attention.[6] The controversy led to a substantial number of email messages to the County Council, as well as more traditional protests (individual letters, representations from residents' groups, politicians being lobbied, and so on). Although there was no electronic bulletin board to facilitate discussion of the issue, the concerns raised by these interventions were addressed and responded to in the form of a series of Frequently Asked Questions (FAQs) which were available on the Council web site. Politicians and other interested parties consulted the information and conveyed that information back to residents via public meetings. One result was a dedicated web site on these issues.[7] This ad hoc interaction was 'consultation' in a limited fashion; the web site served only as a mechanism to explain and persuade. The council responded to questions that were raised and decided if the issue required action, but the local authority determined the issues about which it would seek citizen input, determined the scope of consultation, and reserved for itself the right to a final determination.

A similar strategy was followed by Meath County Council in 2005-6, with regard to a contentious plan for a motorway near an archaeological site. In response to concerns about the motorway, Meath County Council launched a dedicated web site in 2005.[8] The aim of the site was to persuade as well as inform, but any impact on policy was limited to the traditional avenues of politicians and interest groups. There was no mechanism by which citizens could contribute their opinions, or engage in an electronic dialogue with the local authority.

The Mobhaile project

Attempts to facilitate electronic discussions on local issues tend to have very low participation rates; participation in Dublin city's site, for instance, is minimal (Arnold and Gibbs 2003). However, there is no technological impediment to providing greater policy participation, even if community network experiments have not been encouraging. An obvious precondition of participation is that citizens need evidence that their participation can change policy outcomes, and evidence suggests that low participation rates are linked to a perception that participation has little impact (The Power Inquiry 2006). Rothstein points out that trust is rarely given unconditionally, especially to governments composed of unknown and unaccountable individuals (Rothstein 2003).

The first step to earning that trust is to demonstrate that citizen input will have an impact on government. One solution is online consultation on specific projects which demonstrate that input on these issues has had an impact on policy deliberations. For instance, an e-consultation research project, funded as part of North–South government initiatives in 2004, has encouraged participation and discussion of issues and agendas by citizens in organizations such as Waterways Ireland.[9] Eventually, this may create the necessary sense of trust, but it will be a long-term process, especially when the impact of citizen input on policy outputs may be very minor. The most significant problem with such an initiative, as with other similar initiatives (OECD 2003) is that citizens need to be sufficiently engaged in policy processes to find and use the site. As with the Blacksburg project, the question remains, how to involve those who are not already involved?

A strategy by which such involvement could be engineered would be to use the improvements in administration and service provision resulting from e-government investments as a lever to encourage public participation. Trust could be earned, based on actual interactions that citizens have with particular agencies of the state. That trust, once gained, could be extended to other agencies of the state and transmuted into a social capital that leads to greater commitment to civil society. An increasing number of local authority services are available online (paying for refuse collection is one example), and there has been a consistent increase in the number of people availing of online services (Central Statistics Office 2003, 2006). Continual interactions with local authorities on the provision of services such as road maintenance, lighting repair, public amenities such as parks and so on could provide evidence that local authorities listen and respond to citizens. This lesson that citizens can exercise influence could be transposed to the policy arena, encouraging citizens to believe that they can also influence policy decisions.

Mobhaile is a project initiated in 2004 which provides an example of an information system that combines e-government and e-participation functions. As citizens use the system to access government services and benefits, they could also use the system to participate in policy formulation. It was developed by the Local Government Computer Services Board in conjunction with a number of local authorities in Ireland including South County Dublin, Westmeath, Tipperary North and South, Meath and Mayo. The project name derives from an Irish term which roughly translates as 'my community' and provides a community interface for both government and community information.[10]

The system can use information that exists on local authority information systems (e.g. planning applications, bin charges, availability of sports grounds) and make it available to the general public in an interactive format. That information can be combined with links to other government service providers (e.g. Department of Health, Revenue Commission), as well as information about social and economic activities in a community.

Information about local services is accessed through a geographical interface, so that individuals access the information of relevance to their locality. It will be possible to connect to the site and obtain information only about those portions of services (e.g. waste collection, bus routes, planning submissions) relevant to a local neighbourhood. Since only those services that are relevant to the local area are presented, this has obvious benefits in fostering a sense of geographical community. Residents will be able to exchange information about the services and issues of relevance to that locality, whether it is to tell each other when the street light will be fixed or whether the planning permission for a nearby development was approved.

The information system enables two-way information flow, so that a service fault can be reported (e.g. faulty street light or abandoned car) by locating it on a map. Such a service is obviously beneficial to the local authority, since it enables rapid notification of problems that need attention. More significant, though, is the enhanced accountability and participation it provides for citizens. The geographical input/output format is linked with an open-ended web form so that individuals can pinpoint a location on a digital map and then write a text that indicates a problem – whether that problem is a broken street light, abandoned car, blocked drain, or any other issue which requires attention. Citizens can receive evidence that their participation is effective because they receive feedback on the particular issues raised. Such a responsive system improves citizens' trust in, and increases citizens' power over, the local authority system.

The web interface extends to 'community building' because it can also display local social and economic services as well as government services. Some information is picked up automatically from the local authority own information systems (e.g. business premises from local taxation lists), but business or voluntary groups can also register with the local authority. There are many benefits of being registered; in addition to location information, businesses and groups can contribute announcements or descriptions about their activities. A business can register the service it sells and provide information about that service; a church can provide information about church services; or a sports club can provide information about matches to be played. Once registered, groups have access to a targeted local audience, and can also be notified by the local authority of issues that affect their particular locality. They can also use the service for internal organizational tasks (discussion board for members, email notifications about meetings, shared documents, and so on). All of this creates a local information portal in which the range of local community activities can be accessed. The portal functions as a local notice board combined with local town hall, encouraging the easy diffusion of salient information that is relevant to local residents. Crucially, the definition of 'salient' is only partially defined by outsiders; it is also defined by the local residents who contribute information.

Individuals will access the local Mobhaile site for specific service requests, but, once habituated to using the site, they can also use it for community participation and policy input. The project contains elements that encourage individual participation and the extension of that participation into ad hoc community activity. For instance, members can write personal 'blogs' (online diaries); blogs are one of the easiest means of making personal opinions available to a wide audience currently available on the Internet. Community groups can use the system to enhance membership participation, but can also encourage participation by previously non-involved citizens.

The project moved from design to pilot stage throughout 2005-6, and many of the functions were slow to become available for citizens who wished to use Mobhaile. The political benefits will also be dependent, to some extent, on a parallel Irish government project for citizen electronic authentication, which will enable citizens to carry out a range of confidential transactions with government departments via the site.[11] As with Mobhaile, progress on authentication systems for citizens has also been slow. For the moment, Mobhaile remains an encouraging, but not yet realized, vision of citizen participation.

Conclusion

The Mobhaile project provides an intriguing example of how individuals could be encouraged to become involved in policy formation. The operative word, however, is 'could'. Previous examples of local policy debates suggest that local authorities are not always willing to cede policy-making to local residents. In interviews, officials in local authorities described themselves as being the guardians of the 'public interest', and believed that local activists were often not always representative of general community opinion.[12] Local activists may have vested interests, and decisions could be determined by those individuals who are most vociferous and best organized: decisions based on those who shouted loudest, as one local official commented (Komito 1985). Additionally, such activists come and go; it is the local authority who will be held accountable for the consequences of policy outcomes.

Even if the community, as a whole, votes on an issue, there may still be a balance to be struck between the 'common good' versus the 'not in my back yard' approaches to policy. When an issue mobilizes a large number of citizens, new technologies enable ad hoc groups to organize effectively and quickly in order to exert pressure on local authorities. This 'swarming' effect is often very effective, and local authorities have to respond. The problem, from the local authority's perspective, is that, once the issue has been resolved, the mobilized citizens often fade into the background as the ad hoc groups lose coherence. For many officials, retaining the right to decide their response to community input is a legal, as well as a moral, necessity. It is a means of ensuring that the wider community is not excluded from participation by unrepresentative activists, and that the public good is safeguarded.[13] However, the correct balance on these issues is not obvious, as continual problems with residential planning in Ireland shows (Komito 1983); officials are not always correct in their decisions; policy must involve balanced contributions from citizens and politicians as well as officials.

The issues of legal accountability and democratic representation must be addressed, but there are means by which information systems can facilitate such problems. If local government will not (or can not) cede decision-making responsibility to ad hoc individual and group inputs by local citizens, there are alternative solutions. Local authorities could formalize the procedures for policy input. For instance, when a local housing estate wishes to change its name, the authority conducts a plebiscite and will abide by the decision of a sufficient number of authenticated voters. The same can be done on a wider range of policy issues; citizens could authenticate their identity, via Mobhaile, and then the local authority could use the outcome as a valid expression of democratic decision making.

Even on those issues where the local authority feels they must retain final legal responsibility, the consultation process could at least be documented in a transparent manner. Policy input could be recorded, and the process by which that input is considered could be documented and available for inspection. If citizens had evidence that their views were seriously considered, and could see evidence that their views sometimes altered policy outcomes, then the demonstrable benefits of participation might provide sufficient incentive for further participation.

Technological solutions to the problems of accountability, representation and participation can be found, if there is sufficient commitment by local authorities. The Mobhaile project provides an example of information systems that can facilitate policy input from citizens normally excluded from policy input processes. It capitalizes on the demonstrated affordances of new technologies, levering the use of new technologies to obtain government services to encourage initial participation. Such interaction demonstrates that the system is trustworthy and that citizens' interventions can be effective in service delivery, for a very low 'cost' for the citizen in either time or effort. If governments demonstrate responsiveness, then the effectiveness of interventions encourages further participation, thus creating a virtuous circle of ever greater participation.

Fundamental to this process is local authorities listening to citizens and responding to issues that they raise in a meaningful way. If this happens, then in every interaction with the local authority, citizens learn that they can influence policy outcomes at local level. The current use of new technologies to present information, as with the Adamstown and motorway developments previously mentioned, will not be sufficient to persuade citizens that electronic participation has a meaningful or measurable impact. If government policy seeks to encourage the formation of policy communities, then governments must be responsive to interventions and engage in a dialogue with individuals. The evidence remains to be provided that governments are willing to cede participation, or even meaningful consultation, to citizens. Without that evidence, the transformative potential of new technologies on governance will remain unrealized.

Notes

1 Other factors include strong party loyalty on the part of voters, the electoral system of single transferable votes and multi-seat constituencies, and cultural traditions developed during colonial domination (sometimes described as a 'dependency culture').

2 The exclusion of TDs from local authorities has not been without its problems. TDs recently complained that 'city and county managers no longer respond to them, access to files has been curbed, while constituency representations are being ignored' (*Irish Times*, 29 July 2006: 7). This emphasizes the need for TDs to access new sources of power and publicity.

3 New technologies have had indirect, as well as direct, consequences. For instance, Freedom of Information legislation has provided for more open and transparent government decisions, but the move from paper to electronic documents has reduced the cost of Freedom of Information transactions and so enabled more information to come into the public domain.

4 This assumes, of course, that social capital is measurable by memberships in voluntary associations or the level of participation in voluntary associations, which is debatable. The main advantage of memberships in voluntary associations is that they can be relatively easily measured by surveys (Newton 1999).

5 The participants may be unrepresentative due to self-selection and are still only a small percentage of the total population of over three and a half million people, but a sample size of ten thousand is still likely to have predictive value. For instance, in April 2002, 72 per cent of the 8,430 participants were dissatisfied with the bishops' statement on clerical child sex abuse (*Irish Times*, 10 April 2002). In October 2003, three out of four of 16,000 particpants agreed that residents should pay to have rubbish collected, which was during a high visibility protest over such charges (*Sunday Independent*, 19 October 2003).

6 See www.sdublincoco.ie.

7 See www.adamstown.ie.

8 See www.m3motorway.ie.

9 See www.e-consultation.org; www.waterwaysiteland.org

10 See www.mobhaile.ie.

11 See www.reach.ie.

12 This information comes from interviews conducted in 2004, and research conducted from 1978-1980 (Komito1985).

13 It should be noted the local officials (especially in the late 1970s and the 1980s) were often concerned with safeguarding the public good as much from politicians as from citizens.

Bibliography

Agre, Philip E. 2002. Real-Time Politics: The Internet and the Political Process. *The Information Society* 18: 311-31.

Arnold, Michael and Martin R. Gibbs. 2003. Intranets and Local Community: 'Yes, an Internet Is All Very Well, But Do We Still Get Free Beer and Barbeque?' In *Communities and Technologies*, edited by Marleen Huysmans, Etiene Wenger and Volker Wulf, 185-204. Boston: Kluwer Academic Publishers.

Blondel, Jean and Richard Sinnott. 1998. *People and Parliament in the European Union: Participation, Democracy and Legitimacy*. Oxford: Oxford University Press.

Central Statistics Office. 2003. *Information Society Statistics – Ireland 2003*. Dublin: Government Publications Office.

Central Statistics Office. 2006. *Information Society and Telecommunications 2005*. Dublin: Government Publications Office.

Chubb, Basil. 1963. 'Going About Persecuting Civil Servants': The Role of the Irish Parliamentary Representative. *Political Studies* 11 (3): 272-86.

Clapham, Christopher, ed. 1982. *Private Patronage and Public Power*. London: Frances Pinter.

Commission of the European Communities. 2003. *The Role of E-Government for Europe's Future*. Brussels: Commission of the European Communities.

Della Porta, Donatella and Mario Diani, eds. 2006. *Social Movements: An Introduction*. Oxford: Blackwell.

Docter, Sharon and William H. Dutton. 1998. The First Amendment Online: Santa Monica's Public Electronic Network. In *Cyberdemocracy: Technology, Cities and Civic Networks*, edited by Roza Tsagarousianou, Damian Tambini and Cathy Bryan, 125-51. London: Routledge.

Gallagher, Michael. 2010. The Oireachtas: President and Parliament. In *Politics in the Republic of Ireland*, edited by John Coakley and Michael Gallagher, 198-239. London: Routledge.

Gallagher, Michael and Lee Komito. 2010. The Constituency Role of Dáil Deputies. In *Politics in the Republic of Ireland*, edited by John Coakley and Michael Gallagher, 230-62. London: Routledge/ PSAI Press.

Government of Ireland. 1997. *Freedom of Information Act, 1997*. Dublin: Government Publications Office.

Huysman, Marleen and Etiene Wenger, eds. 2003. *Communities and Technologies*. Boston: Kluwer Academic Publishers.

Johnson, Diane and Bruce Bimber. 2004. The Internet and Political Transformation Revisited. In *Community in the Digital Age: Philosophy and Practice*, edited by Andrew Feenberg and Darin Barney, 239-61. Lanham: Rowman and Littlefield Publishers.

Kahn, Richard and Douglas Kellner. 2004. Virtually Democratic: Online Communities and Internet Activism. In *Community in the Digital Age: Philosophy and Practice*, edited by Andrew Feenberg and Darin D. Barney, 183-200. Lanham: Rowman and Littlefield Publishers.

Kavanaugh, Andrea L. and Scott J. Patterson. 2002. The Impact of Community Computer Networks on Social Capital and Community Involvement in Blacksburg. In *The Internet in Everyday Life*, edited by Barry Wellman and Caroline A. Haythornthwaite, 325-44. Oxford: Blackwell.

Kavanaugh, Andrea L. and D. Reese. 2003. Weak Ties in Networked Communities. In *Communities and Technologies*, edited by Marleen Huysman, Etienne Wenger and Volker Wulf, 265–86. Boston: Kluwer Academic Publishers.

Kling, Rob, ed. 1996. *Computerization and Controversy: Value Conflicts and Social Choices.* London: Academic Press.

Komito, Lee. 1983. Development Plan Rezonings: The Political Pressures. In *Promise and Performance: Irish Environmental Policies Analysed*, edited by John Blackwell and Frank Convery, 293-302. Dublin: Resource and Environmental Policy Centre, UCD.

Komito, Lee. 1984. Irish Clientelism: A Reappraisal. *Economic and Social Review* 15 (3): 173–94.

Komito, Lee. 1985. *Politics and Clientelism in Urban Ireland: Information, Reputation, and Brokerage.* Ann Arbor, Michigan: University of Michigan.

Komito, Lee. 1989a. Dublin Politics: Symbolic Dimensions of Clientelism. In *Ireland From Below: Social Change and Local Communities*, edited by Chris Curtin and T. Wilson, 240-59. Galway: Galway University Press.

Komito, Lee. 1989b. Politicians, Voters and Officials: A Survey. *Administration* 37 (2): 171–96.

Komito, Lee. 1992. Brokerage or Friendship? Politics and Networks in Ireland. *Economic and Social Review* 23 (2): 129–45.

Komito, Lee. 1998. Paper 'Work' and Electronic Files: Defending Professional Practice. *Journal of Information Technology* 13: 235–46.

Macintosh, Ann. 2004. Characterizing E-Participation in Policy-Making. In *Proceedings of the 37th Hawaii International Conference on System Sciences*. Available at http://doi. ieeecomputersociety.org/10.1109/HICSS.2004.1265300.

Melucci, Alberto. 1996. *Challenging Codes: Collective Action in the Information Age.* Cambridge: Cambridge University Press.

Murphy, Gary. 2010. Interest Groups in the Policy-Making Process. In *Politics in the Republic of Ireland*, edited by John Coakley and Michael Gallagher, 327-58. London: Routledge.

National Economic and Social Forum. 2003. *The Policy Implications of Social Capital.* Dublin: National Economic and Social Forum.

Newton, Kenneth. 1999. Social Capital and Democracy in Modern Europe. In *Social Capital and European Democracy*, edited by Jan Van Deth, Marco Maraffi and Kenneth Newton, 3–24. London: Routledge.

O'Toole, Fintan. 2000. Historic Defeat for Cronyism as Hugh O'Flaherty Bows Out. In *Irish Times*, 2 September.

OECD. 2003. *Promise and Problems of E-Democracy: Challenges of Online Citizen Engagement*. Paris: OECD.

Olson, Mancur. 1965. *The Logic of Collective Action: Public Goods and the Theory of Groups*. Cambridge, MA: Harvard University Press.

Pierre, Jon, ed. 2000. *Debating Governance: Authority, Steering and Democracy*. Oxford: Oxford University Press.

Putnam, Robert D. 1993. *Making Democracy Work: Civic Traditions in Modern Italy*. Princeton, NJ: Princeton University Press.

Putnam, Robert D. 2000. *Bowling Alone: the Collapse and Revival of American Community*. New York: Simon and Schuster.

Pye, Robert. 1992. *An Overview of Civil Service Computerisation, 1960-1990*. Dublin: Economic and Social Research Institute.

Raven, John and Christopher T. Whelan. 1976. Irish Adults' Perceptions of Their Civic Institutions and Their Own Role in Relation to Them. In *Political Culture in Ireland: The Views of Two Generations*, edited by John Raven, Christopher T. Whelan and P.A. Pfretzschner, 7-84. Dublin: Institute of Public Administration.

Rothstein, Bo. 2003. Social Capital, Economic Growth and Quality of Government: The Causal Mechanism. *New Political Economy* 8 (1): 49-72.

Surman, Mark and Katherine Reilly. 2003. *Appropriating the Internet for Social Change: Towards the Strategic Use of Networked Technologies by Transnational Civil Society Organizations*. New York: Social Science Research Council.

The Power Inquiry. 2006. *Power to the People: The Report of Power. An Independent Inquiry into Britain's Democracy*. York: York Publishing Distribution. Available at www.powerinquiry.org/report/index.php.

Tsagarousianou, Roza and Damian Tambini, eds. 1998. *Cyberdemocracy: Technology, Cities and Civic Networks*. London: Routledge.

van der Eijk, Cees and Mark N. Franklin. 1996. *Choosing Europe? The European Electorate and National Politics in the Face of Union*. Ann Arbor: University of Michigan Press.

Wellman, Barry and Caroline A. Haythornthwaite, eds. 2002. *The Internet in Everyday Life*. Oxford: Blackwell.

11

Conclusion: changing Irish governance

Niamh Hardiman

The chapters contained in this volume prompt two questions. Firstly, how and why have governance patterns developed as they have? And secondly, what are the priorities for political reform to address the shortcomings in Irish governance identified in these chapters?

Institutional change

Understanding how state power is exercised requires us to look not just at individual institutions, but at how 'institutional fields' are structured (Pierson and Skocpol 2002: 695–6). Elected politicians, employees in various branches of the public service, organized economic and social interests, and citizens as voters, may interact with one another in different ways, depending on the issues we choose to focus on. The institutional context within which they engage with one another and through which policy is made and implemented also change over time, as the chapters in this book have shown. Drawing together the various elements of these stories, we might attempt an account of how gradual institutional change takes place (Mahoney and Thelen 2010; Streeck and Thelen 2005; Thelen 2003).

The initiative for change might be deliberate and might come either from political entrepreneurs or innovators on the one hand, or from those at the receiving end of the policy. If there is an active process of reform, we might expect those involved to have a clear sense of who the winners and losers are likely to be. Those who hope to gain from change are most likely to support it, and those who will lose out from any alteration to the status quo may be expected to resist or oppose change. Alternatively, change might come about without deliberate or intentional action behind it, merely through different actors pursuing their own priorities within structures that facilitate or accommodate to what is going on. This may make it harder to discern who the winners or losers are likely to be, though the effects may be profound.

Mahoney and Thelen identify four 'modes' of institutional change, where the rules and expectations that shape the interactions between the different actors are modified in different ways (Mahoney and Thelen 2010: 15–18).

'Displacement' involves the cessation of old routines, and innovative rule-making that changes the framework of interactions. It implies intentionality and activism, and therefore perhaps a more overt process of institutional change than some of the others.

'Drift', on the other hand, is a mode of institutional change in which the old rules, designed for one purpose, become displaced in their effects through changes in the surrounding context, and end up encouraging or facilitating different kinds of behaviour and producing new kinds of outcomes that no-one might explicitly have intended.

'Conversion' is a mode of change in which the old rules stay in place but their interpretation is subject to change, and so they end up being enacted differently. This implies that some group finds it advantageous to reinterpret the rules and their application in a particular institutional field.

'Layering' occurs when new rules do not displace or convert older rules, but coexist with them. The new rules must presumably be intentionally introduced; they may be introduced to meet perceived defects in existing rules; but the interaction between old and new rules can have unintended consequences of their own.

Change through displacement

Change through displacement can be identified in several policy areas. New mechanisms for dealing with urban regeneration, as we have seen, involved institutional innovation that bypassed established structures of local government. A coalition of interests between the Department of the Taoiseach and local communities, supported by construction industry interests, bypassed local government entirely. From the government perspective, this removed a logjam in planning process; from the community perspective, this actually increased their voice and leverage. But the reasons for perceived institutional sclerosis remained unexamined and therefore unreformed.

A similar point may be made about e-governance experiments. These generate excitement among users at the potential for involvement and communication flows. But they quickly encounter resistance from established structures. The required engagement with political reform, if it is to be undertaken, must come from central government itself.

Other examples of institutional innovation can be identified too: social partnership, for example, displaced the earlier model of industrial relations. But distributive conflicts are played out between actors within institutions, as well as between actors across institutional fields, and when the distribution of benefits or of costs ceases to be acceptable to participants, the continuity of the institution is thrown into question. So it was that social partnership, having endured through economic crisis, through the boom years, and through the trials of the first years of EMU, was eventually ended by government itself in the context of fiscal crisis. The wage rigidities that now made its continuation difficult for government to accept were themselves the result of earlier compromises to achieve new agreements. The 'benchmarking' of public sector pay in 2004, and the failure to drive through reforms in public sector structures and practices, meant there was no further room for manoeuvre within existing structures. Executive fiat on pay rates displaced network governance; but its durability remains uncertain.

Change through drift

Institutional change through 'drift' may be identified in some of the elements contributing to economic crisis, particularly in the inadequacies of financial regulation. The separation of the powers of financial regulation away from the Central Bank in 2003 involved a degree of institutional innovation. But the rules were not new; the office of the financial regulator was not lacking in staff or resources; and there was strong continuity in the personnel staffing the new office. An already established preference for the financial sector to exercise self-governance was allowed to persist. But the surrounding economic environment was changing dramatically in the context of European Monetary Union. Lax regulation in an era of cheap credit created burgeoning opportunities for financial institutions to engage in increasingly risky lending behaviour. The financial regulator was accountable to parliament, and Oireachtas committees did hold periodic hearings with bank representatives and regulators. But the relevant committees were under-resourced and under-equipped to provide the technical grilling that would have been required to find out the truth about bank under-capitalization and exposure to risk. Banks had almost collapsed before – AIB, for example, had been the beneficiary of an expensive taxpayer bail-out during the 1980s – so none of this was new. But no institutional backstops had been put in place to prevent the same thing happening again. The financial sector 'drifted' into disaster.

A similar observation might be made about the conduct of fiscal policy. High levels of discretion are available to Irish Finance Ministers. When they are committed to fiscal probity, their discretionary powers are an asset to ensuring fiscal consolidation (Debrun, Moulin, Turrini, Ayuso-i-Casals and Kumar 2008; Hallerberg, Strauch and von Hagen 2007). But their freedom of action also means that there is little institutional friction to obstruct tendencies toward over-spending during an economic upturn.

The governance of healthcare also shows a tendency to change through 'drift'. The Irish healthcare system cannot be said to have been purposively designed to function as it does. Rather, the piecemeal accretion of partial accommodations, each intended to achieve different purposes, has given rise to a system of rules that incentivizes private insurance and that reinforces two-tier provision. Tax breaks were introduced to enable more people to buy private insurance at a time when this extended to a minority of the population, and when means-tested eligibility rules for access to public care were still restrictive. It amounted to a hidden subsidy to the private sector, as in the US (Hacker 2006). The slow but inexorable expansion of the numbers with private healthcare cover made further private provision more likely. The origins of the twin modes of provision made it plausible to characterize private cover as relieving pressure on the public sector. Economic crisis stalled the drift toward explicit two-tier hospital provision through tax-incentivized 'co-location' of private and public facilities. But three decades of 'drift' in the application of rules meant that any return to more equitable funding models was bound to be difficult.

Change through conversion

Institutional change may come about through 'conversion', whereby the rules governing behaviour do not change, but they are enacted differently. The Irish party system itself might be thought of as undergoing change in this way. Contextual change in society created a new set of demands on political parties over time. The electoral system remained the same. Parties adapted to new conditions by finding new means of mobilizing voter support, new ways of defusing conflicts, and new ways of absorbing challenges. The fluidity of the larger parties' ideological commitments facilitated these changes.

Among the concerns that have emerged in recent years about Irish politics is the pattern of funding for political parties. Several new sets of reporting requirements were introduced to try to ensure that politicians declared all their financial and other interests, were not open to improper influence through accepting political donations greater than a fixed amount, and otherwise adhered to standards of probity and good conduct. All these rules remain in place. But it has become clear that the application and enactment of the rules is open to some flexibility. Under- or non-reporting does not attract serious sanction. Verification of statements is problematic. Powers of effective enforcement are weak. But perhaps more fundamentally, there appears to be a disjuncture between the normative preferences of many active politicians and the rules to which they are obliged to adhere. The same rules stay in place, but the practice has shifted. Occasionally scandals erupt due to, for example, politicians' particularly egregious use of unvouched expenses, or travel allowances that fund long-distance primary residences more usually considered to be holiday homes. But the impetus for change, whether of party funding rules, or of remuneration of politicians, would have to emanate from the political executive itself, precisely the group that would stand to lose most from systematic reform. Hence the preference for letting well enough alone.

Change through layering

Institutional change brought about through 'layering' of rules on top of one another is the fourth category under consideration. When deficiencies become apparent in older rules, it may seem desirable to remedy these through the introduction of new rules. We can see this happening in the area of waste management, for example; also in security and policing policy. Changes in the surrounding society throw up new challenges for existing practices, but it is often an outside agency of some sort that requires the implementation of new rules. EU directives required compliance with new environmental quality standards. These were often adopted slowly and with a time lag; Ireland has not been an enthusiastic implementer of EU initiatives in this area, as they may potentially conflict with too many vested interests and established practices.

Conformity with new reporting and behavioural requirements often sits uneasily with unreformed underlying practices. It is still easy for local protest groups to mobilize veto-power protest movements, and even for their preferences to trump the considered views arrived at through evidence-based assessment. But protest groups still experience the need to mobilize as they may feel excluded from the experts' deliberative processes; the local authorities are still buffeted by competing pressures; and localist and clientelist pressures still get channelled directly through to the Minister of the Environment. More fundamental change in the design of the political system itself is left unexamined.

Policing practices have similarly seen new rules introduced alongside older established practices. Better accountability mechanisms and improved transparency arrangements can certainly be welcomed as an improvement. But they have been introduced on top of a system that still depends heavily on centralized political direction. The tension between the two sets of practices is ongoing.

Perhaps the most significant area in which the layering of institutional rules may be discerned from the studies in this book concerns the role of the legislature. It has long been recognized that the Irish legislature or Oireachtas is very weak, and that the powers of government come close to former British Lord Chancellor Lord Hailsham's acerbic 1976 comment about British government, that it amounted to 'elective dictatorship'. Holding the government accountable, and ensuring appropriate accountability from the public administration, has resulted in a range of institutional reforms over the last two decades. But introducing new levels of reporting and new accountability offices, in a context in which the balance of power still lies overwhelmingly with the political executive, might be expected to have a somewhat limited impact. And is it hardly surprising if the interactions between existing democratic accountability mechanisms in the legislature, limited as they are, and the new layers of rules, result in unexpected gaps in coverage, clashes of jurisdiction, and counter-productive implementation. What is really at issue is the weakness inherent in the legislature itself and the dominance of the executive. New layers of rules treat the symptoms of accountability deficit without addressing the causes.

Reform of Irish governance

The stability of a political system requires that it be capable both of exercising 'domination', in the sense of monopolizing the mechanisms of rule, including coercion, within the national territory, and also commanding 'allegiance', that is, securing legitimacy in the eyes of those subject to its rule (Gerth and Mills 1970; Migdal 2009). Both the policy effectiveness and the democratic legitimacy of the Irish state and governance practices are in question.

Four areas of Irish public life in which institutional reform is called for emerge from the studies in this book: firstly, the capacity of the legislature to hold the executive to account and to make substantive contributions to the process of legislation; secondly, practices of recruitment to the executive that would enhance its capacity to make coherent and effective policy choices; thirdly, the need for delegated governance to work in a genuinely independent way; and fourthly, reform of structures of accountability in public sector management itself.

Reform of the legislature

The degree to which the political executive in Ireland dominates the legislature is very marked, compared with other European countries, as Table 11.1 suggests. Ireland lies with Britain and Greece at one end of the European spectrum. The government can use party discipline to set the agenda and enact its legislative agenda through control over the party whip. But this is only possible because the rules governing the conduct of the legislature itself make this possible. In every area of parliamentary activity, from the order of business, to the practices within legislative committees, to the election of the Speaker or Ceann Comhairle, the current rules and practices favour the incumbent government. The true line of division is not between governing party and opposition, but between the Cabinet and everyone else in the legislature, for government party backbenchers have as little function as members of the opposition in the Irish legislature.

Opening out political debate and exposing issues to effective scrutiny would require a far-reaching reform of parliamentary practices, including an increase in the powers of committees to engage in real and informed policy debate (MacCarthaigh 2005; Strøm, Müller and Bergman 2006). These issues are a good example of change in which the only agent capable of bringing about change is the very one that stands to lose most from institutional reform. Yet without a radical shift in the balance of power between executive and legislature, the possibility of effective and democratic accountability for the exercise of power will never be realized.

Table 11.1 **Index of executive dominance over the legislature**

Executive strength	Country	Score
High	Greece	5
	Ireland	4
	UK	4
Medium	Germany	2
	France	1
	Netherlands	1
	Portugal	1
	Spain	0.5
Low	Belgium	−1
	Denmark	−1
	Finland	−1
	Italy	−1
	Norway	−1
	Iceland	−2
	Sweden	−4

Note: This index is derived from Döring 2001, Tables 1 and 2. Table 1 itemizes executive-enhancing legislative rules. These have been recoded as a sum of pluses and minuses to provide a single score. Table 2 itemizes committee-strengthening parliamentary rules; a single score was similarly derived from this. The total from Table 2 was subtracted from Table 1 to give an index of executive dominance (Döring 2001).

Constraining the powers of the executive also implies putting limits on the discretionary decisions of the Minister for Finance, and subjecting fiscal policy to more sustained scrutiny prior to its implementation. Economic crisis and discussions at the level of the European Commission have revitalized debate about the role of independent and impartial fiscal councils to give policy advice. In mid-2011 the Irish government appointed a new five-member fiscal council, consistent with the requirements of the EU-IMF loan programme agreed in November 2010 (Kinsella 2011). Table 11.2 summarizes their role in a number of western democracies.

The introduction of a fiscal council with powers to advise on budgetary strategy may have the merit of creating more active debate about govern-ment economic strategy. But comparative experience suggests that the role of economic advisers does not displace or even necessarily constrain the scope of political choice. Economic strategy involves many technical elements, but is ultimately a matter of political decision-making in which one of a number of potential trade-offs and distributive balances is chosen. The ideas and values underlying policy choices are not given – there are always political choices to be made. Ireland has 'chosen' a particular kind of low-tax and low-services

Table 11.2 Fiscal councils

Country	Name	Status	Role	Established
Austria	Public Debt Committee	Funded by the Central Bank	Recommendations on the direction of fiscal policy	2002
Belgium	High Council of Finance	Chaired by Minister of Finance; has external representatives	Medium-term objectives for budget deficits, basis for government negotiations	1989
Canada	Parliamentary Budget Office	Parliamentary advisory body	Independent analysis of government estimates and economic trends	2006
Denmark	Economic Council	Tripartite advisory body, with independent experts	Economic reports and forecasts	1962
Hungary	Fiscal Council of Hungary	Independent state institution	Macro-economic forecasts; fiscal planning advice	2009
Netherlands	Netherlands Bureau for Economic Policy Analysis	Independent research institute	Forecasts for the budgetary planning process, expertise, advice	1945
Slovenia	Fiscal Council	Independent advisory body	Assessments of the public finances	2009
Sweden	Fiscal Council	9 members, plus a secretariat	Independent evaluation of the government fiscal policy	2007
UK	Office for Budget Responsibility	Three members, and secretariat from HM Treasury	Independent assessments of public finances	2010
USA	Congressional Budget Office	Advisory body to the Congress	Impartial assessments ('scoring') of policy proposals	1974

Source: Simon Wren-Lewis, Fiscal Councils www.economics.ox.ac.uk/members/simon.wren-lewis.

model, but this was not inevitable (Nolan 2009). Even if the range of available choice under the extreme duress of fiscal crisis is constrained, decisions about the distributive consequences of adjustment still have to be made politically. Advisers may be influential once the policy goals have been chosen, but do not normally shape the objectives themselves (Lindvall 2009; Mandelkern and Shalev 2010). Thus the creation of a fiscal council would not by itself introduce any new counter-balance to the tendency of fiscal policy to be exercised in a pro-cyclical manner. What would be required as a counterweight to ministerial discretion is, once again, the capacity of informed political opinion to be aired in a deliberative context, with real powers to shape policy, within the national parliament.

Recruitment to government

The incentives to politicians to respond to localist concerns, to accommodate conflicting priorities, and to diffuse protest through absorption, all tend to weaken the capacity of governments to engage seriously with competing policy alternatives. The talents that are helpful to getting elected in Irish politics may not necessarily be most appropriate for holding ministerial office. Some commentators hold that the electoral system not only facilitates but also causes pressure on politicians to devote much attention to constituency politics and to be responsive to local lobby group concerns (Carty 1981). But others suggest that the situation is more complex, that the electoral system is just one contributory factor, and that changing the electoral system might make relatively little difference to party political behaviour (Gallagher and Komito 2010; Sinnott 2010). The mode of recruitment to government office therefore merits consideration in its own right. Here too we find that the Irish experience, along with the British, is at one extreme of comparative European practices, as Table 11.3 shows.

In Ireland, only members of the legislature, and normally only members of the Dáil itself, can ever hold ministerial office. There is no realistic possibility that governments would routinely use even their existing limited powers to appoint up to two Senators with relevant policy expertise directly to government. The promise of career advancement to ministerial office is an important tool for a Taoiseach in maintaining control over the parliamentary party, and one they would be slow to relinquish voluntarily. Yet even in Britain, on whose Westminster system the Irish political system is modelled, governments have to recruit more widely to ministerial office through appointments made to the House of Lords.

Delegated governance

In formal terms, Ireland has a full array of institutions of delegated governance. Bodies that function at 'arm's length' from government perform a vital role in demonstrating the credibility of government commitment to standard-setting

Table 11.3 Separation of the functions of members of the legislature and the executive

	Westminster-type systems	Complete separation of executive and legislature	Mixed models
Recruitment	Ministers must come from within parliament, including the upper house. Some key personnel have to come from the lower house.	No minister may also hold a seat in the legislature and must resign seat if appointed to government. Not necessarily appointed from the legislature.	Ministers may but need not be from parliament. They may keep their seats in the legislature. Mixed practices on appointing non-parliamentary or experts as ministers.
Examples	Ireland Britain	France Netherlands Norway	Most West European democracies

Source: Inter-Parliamentary Union, Parline database www.ipu.org/parline-e/mod-oversight.asp.

and good performance. Some are of long standing: indeed the centrally important Office of the Comptroller and Auditor-General is a constitutional function. Some are newer, such as the range of Ombudsman offices that have been created over time. Regulatory functions are among the fastest-growing areas in which new state agencies have been established since the 1980s (Hardiman and MacCarthaigh 2010). But the differentiation in practice between institutions of governance in Ireland is, at present, incomplete. This makes it more difficult to ensure that proper standards of conduct are being adhered to in many areas of public life.

There is no optimal design for institutions of delegated governance. Across Europe, the same functions may well be carried out by institutions that are constituted differently, depending on countries' specific experiences and the need to relate appropriately to other actors in public life (Thatcher and Stone Sweet 2004). What is vital is that the delegated powers are strong enough to discharge the oversight tasks which they have been set, and what this normally requires is that the institution responsible is insulated from political influence. This does not remove delegated powers themselves entirely from democratic accountability (although the judiciary is in a special category). Typically, powers that are given to non-majoritarian institutions are themselves kept under review by the legislature. The stronger and more effective the powers of a regulator or Ombudsman, the more important it is that there be strong powers of reporting, investigation and scrutiny vested in the relevant (all-party) committees of the legislature.

The institutional design of delegated governance in Ireland has proved to be deficient in a number of important areas, as the chapters in this volume have indicated. Most strikingly, the office of the Financial Regulator has 'a history of being a servant of the banks, not a master' (Ross 2009: 69). In the wake of the financial crisis, significant efforts have gone into strengthening its powers and making it much more visibly independent of government (Central Bank and Financial Services Authority of Ireland 2010). But reforms are still needed in other policy areas. Institutionalizing appropriate oversight of policing, for example, is still a work in progress.

Public sector reform

Reform of the public sector is a recurrent theme in Irish political discourse, but the debate has lacked substance and clear priorities are difficult to discern. The Strategic Management Initiative (SMI) which senior civil servants initiated in the 1990s adopted many of the objectives of New Public Management (NPM), such as improving service efficiency and responsiveness to end-users of services. But it was not accompanied by any real commitment to using market mechanisms to achieve measurable performance targets, and in the absence of strong political drivers, it lacked coherence (Hardiman and MacCarthaigh 2011; OECD 2008). Indeed, some areas of organizational reform, such as the creation of the Health Services Executive, which was intended to streamline and rationalize health service delivery, increased public scepticism over the capacity of the public sector to function effectively. This in turn increases public disillusionment with the capacity of politicians to make any real difference to people's quality of life. An unresponsive public service tends to reinforce people's sense that they need someone to mediate for them, to 'go about persecuting civil servants' on their behalf, and this further reinforces the clientelist and personalist role of politicians (Chubb 1963). It seems impossible to secure real accountability when things go wrong; time after time, it seems 'the system is to blame' (Hardiman 2010).

There is a paradox here: people have strong if inchoate views about what the state should be doing, but low expectations of what it can achieve. This helps explain phenomena such as the slow drift toward two-tier provision in healthcare and other areas of social services. And yet a well-functioning public service is an integral part of a strong democratic political culture. Reform of the structures of parliamentary decision-making and representation would be incomplete without parallel reform of the public administration.

The public service should not be seen as simply passively discharging the policies of the government of the day. The impartiality and political neutrality of the public service play a key role in building and maintaining widespread social trust (Rothstein and Teorell 2008). These traditional core ideals of bureaucracy fell out of fashion when the ideas of New Public Management took hold during the 1980s and 1990s. But just as the 'market fundamentalism' of neo-liberal economic theory came to be seen as deeply problematic, so also the deficiencies of New Public Management became clearer over time. Many practical difficulties became apparent in translating ideas about markets and competition into public service delivery, and calls for 'joined-up government' began to gather pace (Christensen, Lie and Laegreid 2007; Olsen 2006). But more than this, it became clearer that there are competing normative assumptions involved about what the state is for and how it should engage with its citizens (Flinders 2011; Pierre and Rothstein 2011).

Terms such as 'citizen' and 'rights' are freighted with quite a different moral significance than, for example, 'customer' and 'efficiency'. Yet debates about public values barely exist in Ireland, where more effort has been expended on the appearance of reform than on serious reflection about what we might want the state to do in different policy areas (O'Ferrall 2008).

Inter-related reform priorities: tackling crony capitalism

All four areas of institutional weaknesses are inter-related. The scale of the problems of public governance in Ireland is considerable. Public trust in the Irish government fell steadily as the crisis progressed. During 2009 and 2010 (prior to the general election and change of government in February 2011), as reported by Eurobarometer polls, (see Figure 11.1), it fell to a point lower than in any other European state.

Powers of independent parliamentary scrutiny are curtailed because of the dominance of the executive, and because party discipline curbs the independence of individual deputies. The policy capacity of the government is restricted, because it is embedded in the legislature, and subject to the same logic of electoral competition grounded in community service. The ability to establish some distance from special interests and lobby groups, to aggregate policy, to take account of public-interest considerations, and to work in a mode of 'embedded autonomy', is thereby limited. The functioning of state agencies is not subject to consistent oversight, because all too often the boards themselves are dominated by political appointees (Clancy, O'Connor and Dillon 2010). Impartial standard-setting and rigorous scrutiny is compromised if it is subject to direct or indirect political intervention.

What all of these issues share in common is the spillover effect of party domination of the political process. By this it is not meant that any single party prevails consistently. Ireland is a fully functioning democratic system with pluralist party competition, which respects freedom of association and

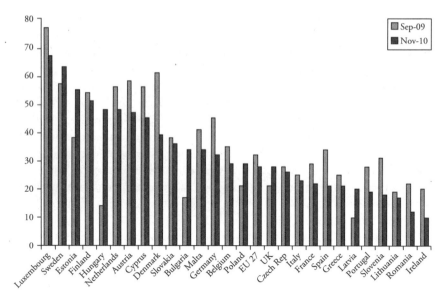

Source: Eurobarometer 71 (September 2009), 74(November 2010)

Figure 11.1 Public trust in national governments in Europe, 2009–10

political competition, and has regular changes in the composition of government. There are serious problems of white-collar crime, corruption and organized crime. Yet Ireland scores quite highly on conventional international indices of freedom and probity in public affairs such as the Freedom House Index and Transparency International Perceptions of Corruption (Department of Justice and Law Reform 2010; Freedom House 2010; Transparency International 2009: 48).

The issue is rather that the design of many state institutions is not strong enough to resist the encroachment of government parties' interests and preferences into other areas of public life. At its most severe during the 2000s, the interests of bankers, builders, developers and property-owners were permitted to undermine public interest considerations and even sustainable development priorities. But whistle-blowers in all walks of Irish life enjoy scant protection; independent critical analysis is too easy to marginalize; and institutional arrangements that suit powerful interests proved impossible to shift until the whole train had been comprehensively derailed.

Although many of these features of the Irish political system have long been recognized, reform requires an incumbent government to implement changes that directly limit its range of influence. Governments have tended to prefer a minimalist approach to self-binding in institutional design, rather than the robust and far-reaching changes proposed here.

Conclusion: governance challenges in hard times

This Conclusion has suggested, on the basis of the chapters gathered in this book, that the need for institutional reform in Ireland is concentrated in the areas of parliamentary politics and the functioning of the public sector. Political legitimacy depends both on formal electoral participation and representation, or 'input' legitimacy, and on perceptions of policy effectiveness, or 'output' legitimacy. If the former is defective, as Fritz Scharpf and others have suggested is the case in the European Union, the latter may be able to provide some substitute (Scharpf 1999, 2001). But legitimating government activity in the national context requires both responsive and efficient political institutions. On both fronts, we have seen that Irish governance structures are deficient.

The net effect is that Ireland's reflexive learning capacity is low – political actors display a weak ability not only to learn from past mistakes but also to anticipate future adaptive needs and to act on them in a timely manner. Douglass North has argued that while much attention has been paid to the need for allocative efficiency to support continued economic growth, what may be even more important is what he terms adaptive efficiency, that is, 'the set of institutions that readily adapt to the shocks, disturbances, and ubiquitous uncertainty that characterizes every society over time' (North 2005: 78). Irish political institutions display very poor adaptive efficiency. They have suffered from a dearth of critical analysis and from the veto power of those most opposed to change.

But the broader international challenges to political performance arising from the economic crisis that started in 2008 may be more intractable than any considered here so far. The politics of the Eurozone constrains nation-states' capacity to devise their own solutions. Firstly, internal deflation is the only option available to regain competitiveness, but on the scale that is required by the need to resolve both sovereign debt and financial system crisis, this is a strategy that entails its own legitimation challenges (Dellepiane and Hardiman 2010a, 2010b). The experience of the 1980s in Ireland suggests that beyond a certain point, tax compliance becomes more difficult to secure, as citizens come to resent the distortion of the 'fiscal bargain' whereby they consent to pay taxes in exchange for delivery of public services (Levi 1988). Secondly, the extent of reliance on external funders, and the conditions of the EU–IMF loan, limits sovereign policy choices quite severely. The massive transfer of wealth implied by the need to recapitalize the banks mainly through reliance on taxpayers may yet create a crisis of political sustainability in the countries of the European periphery. National economic stabilization prospects were now inseparable from wider questions about European economic governance (Gros 2010).

But in addition, processes of globalization present new challenges to all countries' domestic governance capabilities. The scope for national governments to make effective sovereign choices for their own citizens is constrained by growing economic interdependencies. Wolfgang Streeck poses the question as to whether it is not now more appropriate, instead of discussing 'markets within states', to think in terms of 'states within markets', that is, globalized markets over which nation-states have little control but to which they must nevertheless accommodate. The dimensions of the emerging international political economy are as yet unclear, but Streeck's monitory reflections might usefully be borne in mind:

> The consequences . . . for the options available to national policy-making are nothing short of dramatic, and so are the implications for the relationship between politics and the economy, and in particular for the extent to which states can hope to govern, or at least to moderate, the impact of economic forces on their citizens' living and working conditions. (Crouch, Streeck, Whitley and Campbell 2007: 540–1)

If this is indeed the shape of the challenges to come, the problems of designing policies that will be both effective and legitimate may well be considerable, as the capacity to fund and organize provision of infrastructural investments, job creation at an appropriate level of skill, educational provision, healthcare, social services and income protection, comes under even greater stress. But this is not to counsel passivity in the face of transnational trends. However curtailed the scope of policy choice may be, state structures remain the principal 'gateway' between national communities and world markets, even and perhaps especially when the effects of world markets are experienced 'within' the national economy rather than as an external phenomenon (Weiss 2003). National politics still matters for the terms on which its citizens are required to adjust. This makes it all the more important that the design of domestic political institutions should be kept under constant review, and that reforms deemed necessary are introduced as a matter of urgency.

Bibliography

Carty, R. Kenneth. 1981. *Party and Parish Pump: Electoral Politics in Ireland*. Waterloo, Ont.: Wilfrid Laurier University Press.

Central Bank and Financial Services Authority of Ireland. 2010. *Banking Supervision: Our New Approach*. Dublin: CBFSA. Available at www.financialregulator.ie/press-area/press-releases/Pages/CentralBankPublishesnewStrategicapproach.aspx.

Christensen, Tom, Amund Lie and Per Laegreid. 2007. Still Fragmented Government or Reassertion of the Centre? In *Transcending New Public Management: The Transformation of Public Sector Reform*, edited by Tom Christensen and Per Laegreid, 17–42. Aldershot: Ashgate.

Chubb, Basil. 1963. 'Going About Persecuting Civil Servants': The Role of the Irish Parliamentary Representative. *Political Studies* 11 (3): 272–86.

Clancy, Paula, Nat O'Connor and Kevin Dillon. 2010. *Mapping the Golden Circle*. Dublin: TASC. Available at www.tascnet.ie/upload/file/MtGC%20ISSU.pdf.

Crouch, Colin, Wolfgang Streeck, Richard Whitley and John L. Campbell. 2007. Institutional Change and Globalization: Colloquium. *Socioeconomic Review* 5 (3): 527–67.

Debrun, Xavier, Laurent Moulin, Alessandro Turrini, Joaquim Ayuso-i-Casals and Manmohan Kumar. 2008. Tied to the Mast? National Fiscal Rules in the European Union. *Economic Policy* 23 (54): 297–362.

Dellepiane, Sebastian and Niamh Hardiman. 2010a. The European Context of Ireland's Economic Crisis. *Economic and Social Review* 41 (4): 471–98.

Dellepiane, Sebastian and Niamh Hardiman. 2010b. *Fiscal Politics In Time: Pathways To Budget Consolidation 1980–2000*. Dublin: UCD Dublin European Institute. Available at www.ucd.ie/dei/wp/WP__10-02_Dellepiane_and_Hardiman.pdf.

Department of Justice and Law Reform. 2010. *Organised and White Collar Crime*. Dublin: Department of Justice and Law Reform. Available at www.justice.ie/en/ JELR/White%20Paper%20on%20Crime%20Discussion%20Document%20No. %203%20-%20Organised%20and%20White%20Collar%20Crime.pdf/Files/White %20Paper%20on%20Crime%20Discussion%20Document%20No.%203%20-%20 Organised%20and%20White%20Collar%20Crime.pdf.

Flinders, Matthew. 2011. Markets, Morality and Democratic Governance: Insights from the United Kingdom. In *Administrative Reforms and Democratic Governance*, edited by Jean-Michel Eymeri-Douzans and Jon Pierre, 132-48. London: Routledge.

Freedom House. 2010. *Freedom in the World 2010*. Washington DC: Freedom House. Available at www.freedomhouse.org/template.cfm?page=363&year=2010&country =7844.

Gallagher, Michael and Lee Komito. 2010. The Constituency Role of Dáil Deputies. In *Politics in the Republic of Ireland*, edited by John Coakley and Michael Gallagher, 230-62. London: Routledge/ PSAI Press.

Gerth, Hand H. and C. Wright Mills, eds. 1970. *From Max Weber: Essays in Sociology*. London: Routledge.

Gros, Daniel. 2010. All Together Now? Arguments for a Big-bang Solution to Eurozone Problems. *Vox*, 5 December Available at www.Voxeu.org/index.php?Q=Node/5892.

Hacker, Jacob S. 2006. *The Great Risk Shift: The Assault on American Jobs, Families, Health Care and Retirement and How*. Oxford: Oxford University Press.

Hallerberg, Mark, Rolf Strauch and Jürgen von Hagen. 2007. The Design of Fiscal Rules and Forms of Governance in European Union Countries. *European Journal of Political Economy* 23 (2): 338–59.

Hardiman, Niamh. 2010. Institutional Design and Irish Political Reform. *Journal of the Statistical and Social Inquiry Society of Ireland* XXXIX (November): 53–69.

Hardiman, Niamh and Muiris MacCarthaigh. 2010. Organizing for Growth: Irish State Administration 1958-2008. *Economic and Social Review* 43 (3): 367–93.

Hardiman, Niamh and Muiris MacCarthaigh. 2011. The Un-Politics of New Public Management in Ireland. In *Administrative Reforms and Democratic Governance*, edited by Jean-Michel Eymeri-Douzans and Jon Pierre, 55-67. London: Routledge.

Kinsella, Stephen. 2011. *Five Go Mad on Fiacal Rules*. Available at www.irish economy. ie/index.php/2011/07/08/five-go-made-on-fiscal-rules.

Levi, Margaret. 1988. *Of Rule and Revenue*. Berkeley, CA: University of California Press.

Lindvall, Johannes. 2009. The Real but Limited Influence of Expert Ideas. *World Politics* 61 (04): 703–30.

MacCarthaigh, Muiris. 2005. *Accountability in Irish Parliamentary Politics*. Dublin: Institute of Public Administration.

Mahoney, James and Kathleen Thelen. 2010. Introduction: A Theory of Gradual Institutional Change. In *Explaining Institutional Change: Ambiguity, Agency and Power*, edited by James Mahoney and Kathleen Thelen, 1-37. Cambridge: Cambridge University Press.

Mandelkern, Ronen and Michael Shalev. 2010. Power and the Ascendance of New Economic Policy Ideas: Lessons from the 1980s Crisis in Israel. *World Politics* 62 (03): 459–95.

Migdal, Joel S. 2009. Researching the State. In *Comparative Politics: Rationality, Culture, and Structure*, edited by Mark Irving Lichbach and Alan S. Zuckerman, 162–92. Cambridge: Cambridge University Press.

Nolan, Brian. 2009. Policy Paper – Income Inequality and Public Policy. *Economic and Social Review* 40 (4): 489–510.

North, Douglass. 2005. *Understanding the Process of Economic Change*. Princeton, NJ: Princeton University Press.

O'Ferrall, Fergus. 2008. The Erosion of Citizenship in the Irish Republic: The Case of Healthcare Reform. Seminar paper presented at the UCD Humanities Institute of Ireland (HII), 22 February.

OECD. 2008. *Review of the Irish Public Service*. Paris: OECD.

Olsen, Johan P. 2006. Maybe It Is Time to Rediscover Bureaucracy. *Journal of Public Administration Research and Theory* 16 (1): 1–24.

Pierre, Jon and Bo Rothstein. 2011. Contending Models of Administrative Reform: The New Public Management versus the New Weberianism. In *Administrative Reforms and Democratic Governance*, edited by Jean-Michel Eymeri-Douzans and Jon Pierre, 121-31. London: Routledge.

Pierson, Paul and Theda Skocpol. 2002. Historical Institutionalism in Contemporary Political Science. In *Political Science: State of the Discipline*, edited by Ira Katznelson and Helen Milner, 693–721. New York: Norton.

Ross, Shane. 2009. *The Bankers: How the Banks Brought Ireland to its Knees*. Dublin: Penguin Ireland.

Rothstein, Bo and Jan Teorell. 2008. What is Quality of Government? A Theory of Impartial Government Institutions. *Governance* 21 (2): 165–90.

Scharpf, Fritz W. 1999. *Governing in Europe: Effective and Democratic?* Oxford: Oxford University Press.

Scharpf, Fritz W. 2001. Notes Towards a Theory of Multilevel Governing in Europe. *Scandinavian Political Studies* 24 (1): 1–26.

Sinnott, Richard. 2010. The Electoral System. In *Politics in the Republic of Ireland*, edited by John Coakley and Michael Gallagher, 111-36. London: Routledge/ PSAI Press.

Streeck, Wolfgang and Kathleen Thelen. 2005. Introduction: Institutional Change in Advanced Political Economies. In *Beyond Continuity: Institutional Change in Advanced Political Economies*, edited by Wolfgang Streeck and Kathleen Thelen, 1-39. Oxford: Oxford University Press.

Strøm, Kaare, Wolfgang C. Müller and Torbjörn Bergman, eds. 2006. *Delegation and Accountability in Parliamentary Democracies*. Oxford: Oxford University Press.

Thatcher, Mark and Alec Stone Sweet, eds. 2004. *The Politics of Delegation*. London: Frank Cass.

Thelen, Kathleen. 2003. How Institutions Evolve: Insights from Comparative Historical Analysis. In *Comparative Historical Analysis in the Social Sciences*, edited by James Mahoney and Dietrich Rueschemeyer, 208-40. Cambridge: Cambridge University Press.

Transparency International. 2009. *Annual Report*. Available at www.transparency.org/publications/annual_report.

Weiss, Linda, ed. 2003. *States in the Global Economy: Bringing Domestic Institutions Back In*. Cambridge: Cambridge University Press.

Index